Lecture Notes
in Business Information Processing   **260**

More information about this series at http://www.springer.com/series/7911

Marcello La Rosa · Peter Loos
Oscar Pastor (Eds.)

Business Process Management Forum

BPM Forum 2016
Rio de Janeiro, Brazil, September 18–22, 2016
Proceedings

 Springer

Editors
Marcello La Rosa
Queensland University of Technology
Brisbane, QLD
Australia

Oscar Pastor
Universidad Politècnica de Valencia
Valencia
Spain

Peter Loos
DFKI
Universität des Saarlandes
Saarbrücken, Saarland
Germany

ISSN 1865-1348   ISSN 1865-1356 (electronic)
Lecture Notes in Business Information Processing
ISBN 978-3-319-45467-2 ISBN 978-3-319-45468-9 (eBook)
DOI 10.1007/978-3-319-45468-9

Library of Congress Control Number: 2016948606

Printed on acid-free paper

This Springer imprint is published by Springer Nature
The registered company is Springer International Publishing AG Switzerland

Preface

The International Conference on Business Process Management (BPM) is the premium forum for researchers, practitioners, and developers in the area of BPM. This year, the Steering Committee welcomed the idea of creating a new sub-track, called the "BPM Forum," with separate proceedings, in the spirit of the successful CAiSE Forum. The BPM Forum took place together with BPM 2016 during September 18–22 in Rio de Janeiro, Brazil, hosted by the Federal University of the State of Rio de Janeiro.

The forum aimed at gathering papers that showcase fresh ideas and emerging topics in the BPM discipline. The papers had to demonstrate potential for stimulating interesting discussions at the conference, even if they were not yet at the same level of maturity as the regular papers that are accepted at BPM. We selected these papers from those that were not accepted to BPM 2016, based on the recommendation of the senior Program Committee members, after discussing with the Program Committee (PC) members that were assigned to review the papers. Special care was taken to avoid overlap with the workshops associated with the BPM Conference.

As a result, we selected 13 papers out of 106 papers. The papers in this volume cover topics related to process modeling, process execution, and to management aspects of the BPM discipline. Each paper was reviewed by four PC members and by one senior PC member who moderated the discussion and wrote the meta-review. Overall, the review process involved 20 senior PC members and 89 PC members.

We would like to express our gratitude to the BPM Steering Committee for welcoming the idea of the BPM Forum, and to Flavia Maria Santoro, the organizing chair, and her team, for helping us with its implementation. We would also like to thank the PC and the broader reviewer community for their dedicated commitment, and in particular the senior PC members for moderating the review process and preparing the paper recommendations. Finally, we would like to congratulate the authors of all submitted and accepted papers for their high-quality work, and thank them for choosing the BPM Forum as their outlet for publication.

We hope you will find this volume an interesting reading to stimulate your BPM thinking.

September 2016

Marcello La Rosa
Peter Loos
Oscar Pastor

Organization

The BPM Forum was a sub-track of BPM 2016, which was organized by the Federal University of the State of Rio de Janeiro, and took place in Rio de Janeiro, Brazil.

Steering Committee

Wil van der Aalst (Chair)	Eindhoven University of Technology, The Netherlands
Boualem Benatallah	University of New South Wales, Australia
Jörg Desel	University of Hagen, Germany
Schahram Dustdar	Vienna University of Technology, Austria
Marlon Dumas	University of Tartu, Estonia
Manfred Reichert	University of Ulm, Germany
Stefanie Rinderle-Ma	University of Vienna, Austria
Barbara Weber	Technical University of Denmark, Denmark
Mathias Weske	HPI, University of Potsdam, Germany
Michael zur Muehlen	Stevens Institute of Technology, USA

Executive Committee

General Chair

Flavia Maria Santoro	Federal University of the State of Rio de Janeiro, Brazil

Program Chairs

Marcello La Rosa	Queensland University of Technology, Australia
Peter Loos	DFKI/Saarland University, Germany
Oscar Pastor	Universitat Politècnica de València, Spain

Industry Chairs

Claudia Cappelli	Federal University of the State of Rio de Janeiro, Brazil
Silvia Inês Dallavalle de Pádua	University of São Paulo, Brazil
André Macieira	Elo Group, Brazil
Michael Rosemann	Queensland University of Technology, Australia

Workshop Chairs

Marlon Dumas	University of Tartu, Estonia
Marcelo Fantinato	University of São Paulo, Brazil

Tutorial and Panel Chairs

Manfred Reichert	University of Ulm, Germany
Lucinéia Heloisa Thom	Federal University of Rio Grande do Sul, Brazil

Demonstration Chairs

Leonardo Azevedo	IBM Research/Federal University of Rio de Janeiro State, Brazil
Cristina Cabanillas	Vienna University of Economics and Business, Austria

Doctoral Consortium Chairs

Fernanda Baião	Federal University of the State of Rio de Janeiro, Brazil
Hajo A. Reijers	VU University Amsterdam, The Netherlands

Latin-American BPM Workshop

Juliano Lopes de Oliveira	Federal University of Goiás, Brazil
José Pino	Universidad de Chile, Chile
Pablo D. Villarreal	National Technological University, Argentina

BPM in Public Administration Panel Chair

Carina Frota Alves	Federal University of Pernambuco, Brazil

Publicity Chairs

José Ricardo Cereja	Federal University of the State of Rio de Janeiro, Brazil
Valdemar T.F. Confort	Federal University of the State of Rio de Janeiro, Brazil
Kate Revoredo	Federal University of the State of Rio de Janeiro, Brazil
Ricardo Seguel	BPM LATAM S.A., Chile

Senior Program Committee

Josep Carmona	Universitat Politècnica Catalunya, Spain
Florian Daniel	Politecnico di Milano, Italy
Jörg Desel	Fernuniversität in Hagen, Germany
Avigdor Gal	Technion, Israel
Pericles Loucopoulos	University of Manchester, UK
Heinrich C. Mayr	Alpen-Adria-Universitaet Klagenfurt, Austria
Massimo Mecella	Sapienza Università di Roma, Italy
Jan Mendling	Vienna University of Economics and Business, Austria
Andreas Oberweis	Universität Karlsruhe, Germany
Hajo A. Reijers	VU University Amsterdam, The Netherlands
Stefanie Rinderle-Ma	University of Vienna, Austria
Michael Rosemann	Queensland University of Technology, Australia
Shazia Sadiq	The University of Queensland, Australia
Pnina Soffer	University of Haifa, Israel
Jianwen Su	University of California at Santa Barbara, USA
Farouk Toumani	LIMOS/Blaise Pascal University, France
Boudewijn van Dongen	Eindhoven University of Technology, The Netherlands
Barbara Weber	Technical University of Denmark, Denmark
Matthias Weidlich	Humboldt-Universität zu Berlin, Germany
Mathias Weske	HPI, University of Potsdam, Germany

Program Committee

Mari Abe	IBM Research, Japan
Ahmed Awad	Cairo University, Egypt
Hyerim Bae	Pusan National University, Republic of Korea
Bart Baesens	KU Leuven, Belgium
Seyed-Mehdi-Reza Beheshti	University of New South Wales, Australia
Boualem Benatallah	University of New South Wales, Australia
Giorgio Bruno	Politecnico di Torino, Italy
Fabio Casati	University of Trento, Italy
Francisco Curbera	IBM Research, USA
Massimiliano de Leoni	Eindhoven University of Technology, The Netherlands
Jochen De Weerdt	KU Leuven, Belgium
Patrick Delfmann	ERCIS, Germany
Nirmit Desai	IBM T.J. Watson Research Center, USA
Remco Dijkman	Eindhoven University of Technology, The Netherlands
Marlon Dumas	University of Tartu, Estonia
Schahram, Dustdar	TU Wien, Austria
Johann Eder	Alpen Adria Universität Klagenfurt, Austria
Gregor Engels	University of Paderborn, Germany
Joerg Evermann	Memorial University of Newfoundland, Canada
Dirk Fahland	Eindhoven University of Technology, The Netherlands
Marcelo Fantinato	University of São Paulo, Brazil
Peter Fettke	DFKI, Germany
Walid Gaaloul	Télécom SudParis, France
Luciano García-Bañuelos	University of Tartu, Estonia
Christian Gerth	Osnabrueck University of Applied Sciences, Germany
Chiara Ghidini	FBK-irst, Italy
Guido Governatori	Data61, Australia
Sven Graupner	Hewlett-Packard Laboratories, USA
Gianluigi Greco	University of Calabria, Italy
Daniela Grigori	University of Paris-Dauphine, France
Thomas Hildebrandt	IT University of Copenhagen, Denmark
Richard Hull	IBM T.J. Watson Research Center, USA
Marta Indulska	The University of Queensland, Australia
Stefan Jablonski	University of Bayreuth, Germany
Gabriel Juhas	Slovak University of Technology, Slovakia
Leonid Kalinichenko	Russian Academy of Science, Russian Federation
Dimka Karastoyanova	University of Stuttgart, Germany
Rania Khalaf	IBM T.J. Watson Research Center, USA
Jana Koehler	Hochschule Luzern, Switzerland
Agnes Koschmider	Karlsruhe Institute of Technology, Germany
Jochen Kuester	IBM Research, Switzerland
Akhil Kumar	Penn State University, USA
Geetika Lakshmanan	Audible, USA

Ralf Laue	University of Applied Sciences Zwickau, Germany
Henrik Leopold	VU University Amsterdam, The Netherlands
Chengfei Liu	Swinburne University of Technology, Australia
Rong Liu	IBM Research, USA
Irina Lomazova	National Research University Higher School of Economics, Russian Federation
Heiko Ludwig	IBM Research, USA
Fabrizio Maria Maggi	University of Tartu, Estonia
Marco Montali	Free University of Bozen-Bolzano, Italy
Hamid Motahari	IBM Research, USA
Juergen Muench	University of Helsinki, Finland
John Mylopoulos	University of Trento, Italy
Hye-Young Paik	University of New South Wales, Australia
Dietmar Pfahl	University of Tartu, Estonia
Artem Polyvyanyy	Queensland University of Technology, Australia
Frank Puhlmann	Bosch Software Innovations, Germany
Mu Qiao	IBM Almaden Research Center, USA
Manfred Reichert	University of Ulm, Germany
Manuel Resinas	University of Seville, Spain
Gustavo Rossi	LIFIA, National University of La Plata, Argentina
Maximilian Röglinger	Universität Bayreuth, Germany
Theresa Schmiedel	University of Liechtenstein, Liechtenstein
Heiko Schuldt	University of Basel, Switzerland
Marcos Sepúlveda	Pontificia Universidad Católica de Chile, Chile
Sergey Smirnov	SAP Research, Germany
Minseok Song	Ulsan National Institute of Science and Technology, Republic of Korea
Alessandro Sperduti	University of Padua, Italy
Stefan Strecker	University of Hagen, Germany
Keith Swenson	Fujitsu, USA
Samir Tata	Telecom SudParis/CNRS Samovar Lab, France
Ernest Teniente	Unversitat Politècnica de Catalunya, Spain
Arthur ter Hofstede	Queensland University of Technology, Australia
Lucinéia Heloisa Thom	Federal University of Rio Grande do Sul, Brazil
Peter Trkman	University of Ljubljana, Slovenia
Roman Vaculin	IBM T.J. Watson Research Center, USA
Wil van der Aalst	Eindhoven University of Technology, The Netherlands
Amy Van Looy	Ghent University, Belgium
Irene Vanderfeesten	Eindhoven University of Technology, The Netherlands
Hagen Völzer	IBM Research, Switzerland
Jianmin Wang	Tsinghua University, China
Ingo Weber	Data61, Australia
Lijie Wen	Tsinghua University, China
Karsten Wolf	University of Rostock, Germany

Moe Wynn	Queensland University of Technology, Australia
Eric Yu	University of Toronto, Canada
Liang Zhang	Fudan University, China
Michael zur Muehlen	Stevens Institute of Technology, USA

Additional Reviewers

Kevin Andrews
Vasilios Andrikopoulos
Abel Armas Cervantes
Nour Assy
Vladimir Bashkin
Dina Bayomie
Khalid Belhajjame
Arne Bergmann
Mirela Madalina Botezatu
Federico Chesani
Jan Claes
Raffaele Conforti
Riccardo De Masellis
Johannes De Smedt
Adela Del Río Ortega
Claudio Di Ciccio
Chiara Di Francescomarino
Mortada El Bana
Jonnro Erasmus
Maria Fay
Valeria Fionda
Markus Fischer
Antonella Guzzo
Michael Hahn
Farideh Heidari
Iman Helal
Vatche Ishakian
Anna Kalenkova
Klaus Kammerer
Christopher Klinkmueller
Monika Klun
David Knuplesch
Julius Köpke
Sander Leemans
Patrick Lohmann
Xixi Lu

Annapaola Marconi
Alfonso Marquez-Chamorro
Alexey Mitsyuk
Jorge Munoz-Gama
Chun Ouyang
Jan Recker
Florian Rittmeier
Andrey Rivkin
Carlos Rodriguez
Kristina Rosenthal
Marco Roveri
Marc Schickler
Alexander Schmid
Johannes Schobel
Stefan Schönig
Simon Schwichtenberg
Zhe Shan
Tijs Slaats
Aleksander Slominski
Sebastian Steinau
Sergey Stupnikov
Alexander Teetz
Benjamin Ternes
Lucinéia Heloisa Thom
Sanja Tumbas
Han van der Aa
Sebastian Wagner
Andreas Weiß
Dennis Wolters
Xiwei Xu
Peifeng Yin
Sira Yongchareon
Jian Yu
Nesma Zaki
Jelena Zdravkovi

Contents

Management

Execution

Resource Allocation with Dependencies in Business Process Management Systems

Giray Havur[✉], Cristina Cabanillas, Jan Mendling, and Axel Polleres

Vienna University of Economics and Business, Vienna, Austria
{giray.havur,cristina.cabanillas,jan.mendling,axel.polleres}@wu.ac.at

Abstract. Business Process Management Systems (BPMS) facilitate the execution of business processes by coordinating all involved resources. Traditional BPMS assume that these resources are *independent* from one another, which justifies a greedy allocation strategy of offering each work item as soon as it becomes available. In this paper, we develop a formal technique to derive an optimal schedule for work items that have *dependencies* and *resource conflicts*. We build our work on Answer Set Programming (ASP), which is supported by a wide range of efficient solvers. We apply our technique in an industry scenario and evaluate its effectiveness. In this way, we contribute an explicit notion of resource dependencies within BPMS research and a technique to derive optimal schedules.

Keywords: Answer Set Programming · Optimality · Resource allocation · Resource requirements · Work scheduling

1 Introduction

Business Process Management Systems (BPMS) have been designed as an integral part of the business process management (BPM) lifecycle by coordinating all resources involved in a process including people, machines and systems [1]. At design time, BPMS take as input a business process model enriched with technical details such as role assignments, data processing and system interfaces as a specification for the execution of various process instances. In this way, they support the efficient and effective execution of business processes [2].

It is an implicit assumption of BPMS that work items are *independent* from one another. If this assumption holds, it is fine to put work items in a queue and offer them to available resources right away. This approach of resource allocation, can be summarized as a greedy strategy. However, if there are *dependencies* between work items, this strategy can easily become suboptimal. Some domains like engineering or healthcare have a rich set of activities for which various

Funded by the Austrian Research Promotion Agency (FFG) grant 845638 (SHAPE).

ⓒ Springer International Publishing Switzerland 2016
M. La Rosa et al. (Eds.): BPM Forum 2016, LNBIP 260, pp. 3–19, 2016.
DOI: 10.1007/978-3-319-45468-9_1

resources, human and non-human, are required at the same time. Resource conflicts have often the consequence that working on one work item blocks resources such that other work items cannot be worked on. This observation emphasizes the need for techniques to make better use of existing resources in business processes [3].

In this paper, we address current limitations of BPMS with respect to taking such resource constraints into account. We extend prior research on the integration of BPMS with calendars [4] to take dependencies and resource conflicts between work items into account. We develop a technique for specifying these dependencies in a formal way in order to derive a globally optimal schedule for all resources together. We define our technique using Answer Set Programming (ASP), a formalism from logic programming that has been found to scale well for solving problems as the one we tackle [5]. We evaluate our technique using an industry scenario from the railway engineering domain. Our contribution to research on BPMS is an explicit notion of dependence along with a technique to achieve an optimal schedule.

The paper is structured as follows. Section 2 presents and analyzes an industry scenario. Section 3 conceptually describes the resource allocation problem. Section 4 explains our ASP-based solution and how it can be applied to the industry scenario. Section 5 evaluates the solution. Section 6 discusses related work. Section 7 summarizes the conclusions of the work and the future steps.

2   Motivation

In the following, we describe an industry scenario that leads us to a more detailed definition of the resource allocation problem and its complexity.

2.1   Industry Scenario

A company that provides large-scale technical infrastructure for railway automation requires rigorous testing for the systems deployed. Each system consists of different types and number of hardware that are first set up in a laboratory. This setup is executed by some employees specialized in different types of hardware. Afterwards, the simulation is run under supervision.

Figure 1 depicts two process models representing the setup and run phases of two tests. We use (timed) Petri nets [6] for representing the processes. The process activities are represented by transitions (a_i). The number within square brackets next to the activities indicates their (default maximum) duration in generic time units (TU). The numbers under process names indicate the starting times of the process executions: 8 TU for Test-1 and 12 TU for Test-2. The processes are similar for all the testing projects but differ in the activities required for setting up the hardware as well as in the resource requirements associated with them. Certain resources can only be allocated to activities during working periods, i.e., we want to enforce time intervals (so called *breaks*) where

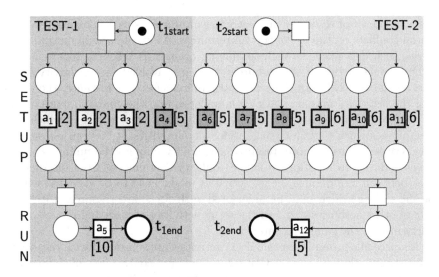

Fig. 1. Workflow for two projects

some resources are not available. In our scenario, no resource is available in the intervals $[0, 8)$, $[19, 32)$, $[43, 56)$, and $[67, 80)$.

For completing tests, the available non-human resources in the organization include 13 units of space distributed into 2 laboratories (Table 1) and several units of 3 types of hardware (Table 2). The human resources of the company are specialized in the execution of specific phases of the two testing projects, whose activities are able to complete in a specific time. Table 3 shows available resources in different process phases and therefore, their ability to conduct certain activities along with their years of experience in the company in square brackets.

The requirements on the use of such resources in the process activities are shown in Table 4. Each process activity requires a specific set of resources for its completion. For instance, three of the activities involved in the setup of Test-1 require 1 employee working on 1 unit of the hardware HW-1 in a laboratory; 1 setup activity requires 1 employee working on 1 unit of the hardware HW-2 in a laboratory; and the run activity requires 4 employees. Besides, a test can only be executed if the whole setup takes place in the same laboratory.

The aim in this scenario is to optimize the overall execution time of simultaneous tests and consequently, the space usage in the laboratories.

2.2 Insights

The resource allocation problem[1] deals with the assignment of resources and time intervals to the execution of activities. The complexity of resource allocation in BPM arises from coordinating the explicit and implicit dependencies

---

[1] Commonly referred as *scheduling*.

across a broad set of resources and activities of processes as well as from solving potential conflicts on the use of certain resources. As we observe in our industry scenario, such dependencies include, among others: (i) resource requirements, i.e., the characteristics of the resources that are involved in an activity (e.g., roles or skills) (cf. Table 3); (ii) temporal requirements. For instance, the duration of the activities may be static or may depend on the characteristics of the set of resources involved in it, especially for collaborative activities in which several employees work together (such as for the activities of the run phase of a testing process). Furthermore, resource availability may not be unlimited (e.g., break calendars). In addition, resource conflicts may emerge from interdependencies between requirements, e.g., activities might need to be executed within a specific setting which may be associated with (or share resources with) the setting of other activities (e.g., all the setup activities of a testing process must be performed in the same laboratory).

A resource allocation is *feasible* if (1) activities are scheduled with respect to time constraints derived from activity durations and control flow of the process model, and (2) resources are allocated to scheduled activities in accordance with resource availability and resource requirements of activities. This combinatorial problem for finding a feasible resource allocation under constraints is an *NP-Complete* problem [7]. However, organizations generally pursue an optimal allocation of resources to process activities aiming at minimizing overall execution times or costs, or maximizing the usage of the resources available. In presence of objective functions the resource allocation problem becomes Δ_2^P [8].

3   Conceptualization of the Resource Allocation Problem

Figure 2 illustrates our conceptualization of the resource allocation problem. We divide it into three complexity layers related to the aforementioned dependencies and resource conflicts. Optimization functions can be applied to all types of allocation problems. This model has been defined from the characteristics identified in our industry scenario as well as in related literature [9].

Table 1. Available space in labs

	LAB − 1	LAB − 2
Space	4	9

Table 2. Available hardware (HW)

Type	Units
HW1	hw1a, hw1b, hw1c
HW2	hw2a, hw2b, hw2c, hw2d
HW3	hw3a, hw3b, hw3c

Table 3. Specialization of employees

	Test − 1		Test − 2	
	Setup	Run	Setup	Run
Glen[7]	✓	✓		
Drew[7]		✓		
Evan[3]		✓		
Mary[5]	✓	✓		
Kate[6]			✓	✓
Amy[8]	✓		✓	✓

Table 4. Activity requirements

	Activities	Requirements
Test-1	$a_1 - a_3$	1 *Employee*:Setup-1, 1 *Hardware*:HW-1, 1 *Lab*:a_1-a_4 same lab
	a_4	1 *Employee*:Setup-1, 1 *Hardware*:HW-2, 1 *Lab*:a_1-a_4 same lab
	a_5	4 *Employee*:Run-1, after execution(a.e.) release the lab for a_1-a_4
Test-2	$a_6 - a_8$	1 *Employee*:Setup-2, 1 *Hardware*:HW-2, 1 *Lab*:a_6-a_{11} same lab
	$a_9 - a_{11}$	1 *Employee*:Setup-2, 1 *Hardware*:HW-3, 1 *Lab*:a_6-a_{11} same lab
	a_{12}	2 *Employee*:Run-2 (hasExp>5), a.e. release the lab for a_6-a_{11}

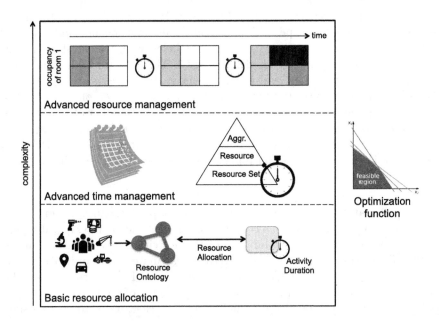

Fig. 2. Resource allocation in business processes

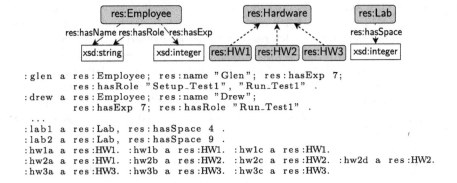

```
:glen  a  res:Employee;  res:name "Glen";  res:hasExp 7;
          res:hasRole "Setup_Test1", "Run_Test1" .
:drew  a  res:Employee;  res:name "Drew";
          res:hasExp 7; res:hasRole "Run_Test1" .
...
:lab1  a  res:Lab, res:hasSpace 4 .
:lab2  a  res:Lab, res:hasSpace 9 .
:hw1a  a  res:HW1.  :hw1b  a  res:HW1.  :hw1c  a  res:HW1.
:hw2a  a  res:HW1.  :hw2b  a  res:HW2.  :hw2c  a  res:HW2.  :hw2d  a  res:HW2.
:hw3a  a  res:HW3.  :hw3b  a  res:HW3.  :hw3c  a  res:HW3.
```

Fig. 3. Resource ontology and example instantiation

3.1 Basic Resource Allocation

Three elements are involved in a basic resource allocation, namely: a model that stores all the information required about the resources available, information about the expected duration of the process activities, and a language for defining the restrictions that characterize the allocation.

Resource Ontology. As a uniform and standardized representation language, we suggest the use of RDF Schema (RDFS) [10] to model organizational information and resources. Figure 3 illustrates a sample RDFS ontology, in which a *resource* is characterized by a *type* and can have one or more *attributes*. In particular, any resource type (e.g. *Employee*) is a subclass of rdfs:Resource. The attributes are all of type rdf:Property; domain (rdfs:domain) and range of attributes are indicated with straight arrows labeled with the attribute name, whereas dashed arrows indicate an rdfs:subclassOf. There are three different types of resources: *Employee*, *Hardware* and *Lab*, where *Hardware* has three resource subtypes. Employees have attributes for their name (*hasName*), role(s) (*hasRole*) and experience level (*hasExp*) in the organization (number of years). Labs provide a certain amount of space for experiments (*hasSpace*). An instantiation of the ontology is described at the bottom of the figure using the RDF Turtle syntax [11]. This instantiation represents Tables 1, 2 and 3 of the industry scenario.

Activity Duration. Resource allocation aims at properly distributing available resources among running and coming work items. The main temporal aspect is determined by the expected duration of the activities. The duration can be predefined according to the type of activity or calculated from previous executions, usually taking the average duration as reference. This information can be included in the executable process model as a property of an activity (e.g. with BPMN [12]) or can be modelled externally. In either case, it has to be accessible by the allocation algorithm.

Resource Allocation. Resource allocation can be seen as a two-step definition of restrictions. First, the so-called *resource assignments* must be defined, i.e., the restrictions that determine which resources can be involved in the activities [13] according to their properties. The outcome of resource assignment is one or more[2] *resource sets* with the set of resources that can be potentially allocated to an activity at run time. The second step assigns cardinality to the resource sets such that different settings can be described, e.g. for the execution of activity a_1, 1 employee with role *setup-1*, 1 hardware of type *HW2*, and 1 unit space of a laboratory are required.

There exist languages for assigning resource sets to process activities [13–16]. However, cardinality is generally disregarded under the assumption that

---

[2] Since several sets of restrictions can be provided, e.g. for activity a_1 resources with either role r_1 or skill s_1 are required.

only one resource will be allocated to each process activity. This is a limitation of current BPMS that prevents the implementation of industry scenarios like the one described in Sect. 2.1.

3.2   Advanced Time Management

This layer extends the temporal aspect of resource allocation by taking into account that: (i) resource availability affects allocation, and that (ii) the resource sets allocated to an activity may affect its duration. Regarding resource availability, calendars are an effective way of specifying different resource availability status, such as available, unavailable, occupied/busy or blocked [9]. Such information must be accessible by the resource allocation module. As for the variable activity durations depending of the resource allocation, three specificity levels can be distinguished:

- *Resource-set-based duration*, i.e., a triple $(activity, resourceSet, duration)$ stating the (minimum/average) amount of time that it takes to the resources within a specific resource set (i.e., cardinality is disregarded) to execute instances of a certain activity. For instance, $(a_1, technician, 6)$ specifies that people with the role *technician* need (at least/on average) 6 TU to complete activity a_1, assuming that *technician* is an organisational role.
- *Resource-based duration*, i.e., a triple $(activity, resource, duration)$ stating the (minimum/average) amount of time that it takes to a concrete resource to execute instances of a certain activity. For instance, $(a_1, John, 8)$ specifies that *John* needs (at least/on average) 8 TU to complete activity a_1.
- *Aggregation-based duration*, i.e., a triple $(activity, group, duration)$ stating the (minimum/average) amount of time that it takes to a specific group to execute instances of a certain activity. In this paper, we use *group* to refer to a set of human resources that work together in the completion of a work item, i.e., cardinality is considered. Therefore, a *group* might be composed of resources from different resource sets which may not necessarily share a specific resource-set-based duration. An aggregation function must be implemented in order to derive the most appropriate duration for an activity when a group is allocated to it. The definition of that function is up to the organization. For instance, a group might be composed of $(John, Claire)$, where *John* has an associated duration of 8 TU for activity a_1 and *Claire* does not have a specific duration but she has role *technician*, with an associated duration of 6 TU for activity a_1. Strategies for allocating the group to the activity could be to consider the maximum time needed for the resources involved (i.e., 8 TU), or to consider the mean of all the durations (i.e., 7 TU) assuming that the joint work of two people will be faster than one single resource completing all the work.

3.3   Advanced Resource Management

The basic resource allocation layer considers resources to be *discrete*, i.e. they are either fully available or fully busy/occupied. This applies to many types of resources, e.g. people, software or hardware. However, for certain types of non-human resources, availability can be partial at a specific point in time. Moreover, they may have other *fluent* attributes. For instance, *cumulative resources* are hence characterized by their *dynamic* attributes and they can be allocated to more than one activity at a time, e.g. in Fig. 2 there is a resource *room 1* whose occupancy changes over time.

We use the ASP solver *clasp* [17] due to its efficiency for our experiments. This allows us to use integer variables as attributes. There are also other extensions of ASP such as FASP [18] that adds the power to model continuous variables.

3.4   Optimization Function

Searching for (the existence of) a feasible resource allocation ensures that all the work items can eventually be completed with the available resources. However, typically schedules should also fulfill some kind of optimality criterion, most commonly completion of the schedule in the shortest possible overall time. Other optimization criteria may involve for instance costs of the allocation of certain resources to particular activities, etc.

Given such an optimization criterion, there are greedy approaches [19] providing a substantial improvements over choosing any feasible schedule, although such techniques depend on heuristics and may not find a globally optimal solution for complex allocation problems.

We refer to [20] for further information on various optimization functions, but emphasize that our approach will in principle allow arbitrary optimization functions and finds optimal solutions – similar in spirit to encodings of cost optimal planning using ASP [21].

4   Implementation with ASP

Answer Set Programming (ASP) [17] is a declarative (logic-programming-style) paradigm. Its expressive representation language, ease of use, and computational effectiveness facilitate the implementation of combinatorial search and optimization problems (primarily *NP-hard*). Modifying, refining, and extending an ASP program is uncomplicated due to its strong declarative aspect.

An *ASP program Π* is a finite set of rules of the form:

$$A_0 \leftarrow A_1, \ldots, A_m, not\, A_{m+1}, \ldots, not\, A_n. \tag{1}$$

where $n \geq m \geq 0$ and each $A_i \in \sigma$ are (function-free first-order) atoms; if A_0 is empty in a rule r, we call r a constraint, and if $n = m = 0$ we call r a fact.

Whenever A_i is a first-order predicate with variables within a rule of the form (1), this rule is considered as a shortcut for its *grounding ground(r)*, i.e., the set of its ground instantiations obtained by replacing the variables with all possible constants occurring in Π. Likewise, we denote by *ground(Π)* the set of rules obtained from grounding all rules in Π. Sets of rules are evaluated in

ASP under the so-called stable-model semantics, which allows several models, so called *answer sets* (cf. [22] for details).

ASP Solvers typically first compute a subset of $ground(\Pi)$ and then use a DPLL-like branch and bound algorithm to find answer sets for this ground program. We use the ASP solver *clasp* [17] for our experiments as it has proved to be one of the most efficient implementations available [23].

As syntactic extension, in place of atoms, *clasp* allows set-like *choice expressions* of the form $E = \{A_1, \ldots, A_k\}$ which are true for any subset of E; that is, when used in heads of rules, E generates many answer sets, and such rules are often referred to as *choice rules*. Another extension supported in *clasp* are optimization statements [17] to indicate preferences between possible answer sets:

$$\#minimize\{A_1 : Body_1 = w_1, \ldots, A_m : Body_m = w_m @p\}$$

associates integer weights (defaulting to 1) with atoms A_i (conditional to $Body_i$ being true), where such a statement expresses that we want to find only answer sets with the smallest aggregated weight sum; again, variables in $A_i : Body_i = w_i$ are replaced at grounding w.r.t. all possible instantiations. Several optimization statements can be introduced by assigning the statement a priority level p. Reasoning problems including such weak constraints are Δ_2^P-complete.

Finally, many problems conveniently modelled in ASP require a boundary parameter k that reflects the size of the solution. However, often in problems like planning or model checking this boundary (e.g. the plan length) is not known upfront, and therefore such problems are addressed by considering one problem instance after another while gradually increasing this parameter k. Re-processing repeatedly the entire problem is a redundant approach, which is why incremental ASP (iASP) [17] natively supports incremental computation of answer sets; the intuition is rooted in treating programs in program slices (extensions). In each incremental step, a successive extension of the program is considered where previous computations are re-used as far as possible.

A former version of our technique is detailed in [5]. We enhance our encoding in three folds: (1) basic resource allocation supporting multiple business processes with multiple running instances, (2) definition of *advanced resource management* concepts, and (3) definition of *advanced time management* concepts. The entire ASP encoding can be found at http://goo.gl/Q7B2t4.

4.1 Basic Resource Allocation

This program schedules the activities in business processes described as timed Petri nets (cf. the generic formulation of 1-safe Petri Nets [5, Sect. 4]) and allocates resources to activities with respect to activity-resource requirements. To achieve this, the program finds a firing sequence between initial and goal places of given processes, schedules the activities in between, and allocates resources by complying with resource requirements. In our program, a firing sequence is represented as predicates `fire(a,b,i,k)`, which means that an activity a of a business process b in instance i is fired at step k. Starting time of each activity in the firing sequence is derived from the time value accumulated at the activity's input place p. A time value at a place p is represented by the predicate timeAt(p,c,b,i,k), where c is the time value.

A *resource set* is defined as a rule that derives the members of the set that satisfy a number of properties. These properties can be class memberships or resource attributes defined in resource ontology(cf. Sect. 3.1). Note that, any resource ontology described in RDF(S) can be easily incorporated/translated into ASP [24]. A resource set is represented with the predicate resourceSet(R,id), where R is a set of discrete resources and id is the identifier of the set. We explain the following resource sets following our industry scenario:

All employees that can take part in the setup phase of Test-1:
resourceSet(R,rs_set1):-employee(R), hasRole(R,setup1).
All employees that can take part in the run phase of Test-2 and have a working experience greater than 5 years:
resourceSet(R,rs_ex2):-employee(R), hasRole(R,run2), hasExp(E), E>5.
All hardware resources of type HW2:
resourceSet(R,rs_h2):-hardware2(R).

After defining resource sets, we define *resource requirements* of an activity a with the predicate requirement(a,id,n) where id refers to a specific resource set and n is the number of resources that activity a requires from this set. For instance, requirement(a_{12},rs_ex2,2) means that activity a_{12} requires 2 resources from the resource set rs_ex2. The resource requirements that we support include typical access-control constraints [13]. In particular, *Separation of duties (SoD)* and *binding of duties(BoD)* are implemented in our program by using the predicate separateDuties(a_1,b_1,a_2,b_2), which separates the resources allocated to the activity a_1 of process b_1 from the resources allocated to a_2 of b_2; and bindDuties(a_1,b_1,a_2,b_2), which binds the resources allocated to the activity a_1 of process b_1 with the resources allocated to a_2 of b_2.

4.2   Advanced Time Management

Default durations of activities are defined in the timed Petri nets and represented as activityDuration(T,D) in our program. This default duration can be overwritten by d when any resource r that belongs to a resource set rs is assigned to a certain activity a of the process b by using the predicate rSetActDuration(rs,a,b,d). In a similar fashion, the default duration can be overwritten by a new value d when a certain resource r is assigned to a certain activity a of the process b by using the predicate resActDuration(r,a,b,d). The order ($>$) preferred in activity time is resActDuration>rSetActDuration>activityDuration. This is especially useful when a resource or a resource set is known to execute a particular activity in a particular amount of time, which can be different from the default duration of the activity.

As one activity can be allocated to a group of resources (cf. Sect. 3.2), an aggregation method might be needed. Our default aggregation method identifies the maximum duration within the group and uses it for allocation. This method can be modified with different aggregation options that fit in the purpose of allocation scenario.

In many real-life projects, certain resources are only available during the working periods (a.k.a. *break calendars*). We model this by break(rs, c_1, c_2) that forbids allocation of resources in the resource set rs between time c_1 and c_2, where $c_1 < c_2$.

For business process instances and their activities, (optionally, max. or min.) starting or ending times can be defined using the following predicates: actStarts(o,a,b,i,c), i.e. activity a in business process b of instance i, starts <o> at c; actEnds(o,a,b,i,c), i.e. activity a in business process b of instance i, ends <o> at c; bpiStarts(o,b,i,c), i.e. business process b of instance i, starts <o> at c; bpiEnds(o,b,i,c), i.e. business process b of instance i, ends <o> at c; where o∈ {strictly,earliest,latest}.

4.3   Advanced Resource Management

A cumulative resource has an integer value attribute describing the state of the resource. This value can increase or decrease when the resource is *consumed* or *generated* by an activity requiring it. Definition of cumulative resource sets have one extra term for this reason: resourceSet(R,V,id), where R is the set of cumulative resources, V is the set of their initial value and id is the identifier of the resource set. For example:

Lab space set:
resourceSet(R,V,lab_space):-lab(R),hasSpace(R,V).

Resource requirements are defined like for discrete resources, where n is the amount of resource consumed or generated. For instance, requirement(a_1,lab_space,1) consumes 1 unit of lab space when a_1 is allocated, whereas requirement(a_{12},lab_space,-6) releases 6 units of space by the time a_{12} is completed.

Resource blocking functionality allows us to block some resources between the execution of two activities in a process. A blocked resource is not allowed to be allocated by an activity in this period. block(a_1,a_2,id,n) blocks n amount of resources in the resource set id from the beginning of a_1 to beginning of a_2.

4.4   Optimization Function

As aforementioned, the ASP solver *clasp* allows defining objectives as cost functions that are expressed through a sequence of #minimize statements. In our encoding, we ensure time optimality of our solutions using a minimization statement. The incremental solver finds an upper-bound time value c_{upper} at step k. A time optimal solution is guaranteed at step k' where k'$= c_{upper}/min(D)$, D is the set of activity durations. In a similar way, any objective that is quantified with an integer value (e.g. cost objectives, resource leveling, etc.) could be introduced. When there is more than one objective, they should be prioritized.

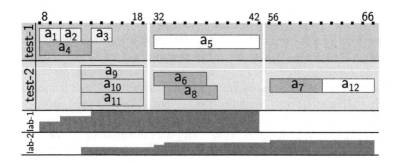

Fig. 4. Optimal resource allocation for our industry scenario

Taking into account all the aforementioned functionality, using the encoding summarized above and detailed in http://goo.gl/Q7B2t4, a time optimal solution for our industry scenario is depicted in Fig. 4. The final allocation of resources to each activity a_i is as follows:

a_1 {Amy, hw1a, lab − 1(1)}

a_2 {Amy, hw1b, lab − 1(1)}

a_3 {Glen, hw1c, lab − 1(1)}

a_4 {Glen, hw2b, lab − 1(1)}

a_5 {Glen, Drew, Ewan, Mary, lab − 1(−4)}

a_6 {Kate, hw2c, lab − 2(1)}

a_7 {Mary, hw2a, lab − 2(1)}

a_8 {Amy, hw2d, lab − 2(1)}

a_9 {Amy, hw3c, lab − 2(1)}

a_{10} {Mary, hw3b, lab − 2(1)}

a_{11} {Kate, hw3a, lab − 2(1)}

a_{12} {Kate, Amy, lab − 2(−6)}

5 Evaluation

Our resource allocation technique not only finds an optimal schedule for activities in our industry scenario but also consequently optimizes the resource utilization. We show the improvement in result quality by comparing an optimal allocation of the scenario (cf. Fig. 4) against a greedy allocation, depicted in Fig. 5. We use the following two criteria for this comparison:

1. *Total execution time (TET)* corresponds to the end time of the last activity for each process (e.g. a_5 for process Test-1).

2. *Average employee utilization (AEU):* For any time unit $c \in C$, c_{start} is the start time, c_{end} is the end time of process execution, $c_{start} \leq c \leq c_{end}$, a function $s : c \to R_b$ returns an ordered set of billable employees R_b respecting Table 3. For each element $s \in R_b$ a function $w_c : r \to \{0, 1\}$ returns whether the employee r is working at time c. In other words, we first sum the ratio between the number of employees allocated and the total number of employees that potentially can

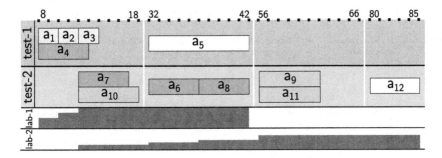

Fig. 5. A greedy (suboptimal) resource allocation for our industry scenario

take part at each time unit, and normalize this sum using the overall execution time. *AEU* is calculated as described by (2).

$$AEU = \frac{\sum_{i=c_{start}}^{c_{end}} \frac{\sum_{r \in s(i)} w_c(r)}{|s(i)|}}{c_{end} - c_{start}} \tag{2}$$

For instance, in Fig. 5, $s(8) = \{Glen, Drew, Evan, Mary, Amy\}$. Note that $Kate$ is not in the set since she only takes part in Test-2 and Test-2 instances have not started due to the deadline constraint `bpStarts(earliest,test-2,12)`. At time 8, only $w_c(Amy)$ and $w_c(Glen)$ have value of 1.

Table 5. Result quality comparison

	Optimal (Fig. 4)	Greedy (Fig. 5)
TET	30	35
AEU	0.61	0.54

Table 5 summarizes the results obtained using the two aforementioned criteria for the two allocation strategies. The execution of our industry scenario finishes 5 TU before under optimal allocation, which corresponds to 14 % of time usage improvement while *AEU* improves 7 %. We refer the reader to [5] for scalability of our technique, where we demonstrated that ASP performs well for resource allocation in the BPM domain.

6   Related Work

Resource allocation has been extensively explored in various domains for addressing everyday problems, such as room, surgery or patient scheduling in hospitals, crew-job allocation or resource leveling in organizations. Table 6 collects a set of recent, representative approaches of three related domains: operating room

Table 6. Representative approaches related to resource allocation

Approach	Basic resource allocation		Advanced time management		Advanced Res. Mgmt.	Objective	Formalism
	Res. Type	A. Level	Calendar	Aggreg.	Dynamism		
[25]	Both	Low	✓	-	-	Usage	MIP
[26]	Both	Medium	✓	-	-	Usage	IP
[27]	Both	High	✓	-	-	Any	Ad-hoc
[28]	Both	Medium	-	✓	-	Time&usage	LIP
[29]	Both	Medium	-	✓	-	Time&usage	CP
[30]	Both	Medium	-	✓	-	Makespan	Ad-hoc
[31]	Both	Medium	-	✓	-	-	CP
[19]	Both	Medium	-	✓	-	Makespan	Petri N.
[5]	Human	Medium	-	✓	-	Time	ASP

scheduling [25–27], project scheduling [28–30] and resource allocation in business processes [5,19,31]. The features described in Sect. 3 are used for comparing them[3]. Specifically, column *Res. Type* specifies the type(s) of resource(s) considered for allocation (human, non-human or both); column *A. Level* indicates the expressiveness of the restrictions that can be defined for the allocation, among: (i) low, when a small range of resource assignment requirements are considered *and* only one individual of each resource type (e.g., one person and one room) is allocated to an activity, i.e., cardinality is disregarded; (ii) medium, when a small range of resource assignment requirements are considered *or* cardinality is disregarded; and (iii) high, when flexible resource assignment *and* cardinality are supported; column *Calendar* refers to whether information about resource availability is taken into account (a blank means it is not); column *Aggreg.* indicates whether the execution time of an activity is determined by the resources involved in it; column *Advanced Res. Mgmt.* shows the support for cumulative resources that can be shared among several activities at the same time; column *Objective* defines the variable to be optimized ; and column *Formalism* specifies the method used for resolving the problem.

The concept of process is not explicitly mentioned in the operating room scheduling problem. Traditional approaches in this field tended to adopt a two-step approach which, despite reducing the problem complexity, failed to ensure optimal or even feasible solutions [27]. It is a property of the surgery scheduling problem that some resources, such as the operating rooms, can only be used in one project at a time [27], so cardinality is disregarded [25,26]. However, it is important to take into account resource availability. The most expressive approach in this domain [27] is an ad-hoc algorithm, whereas integer programming (IP) stands out as a formalism to efficiently address this problem.

Project scheduling consists of assigning resources to a set of activities that compose a project, so the concept of workflow is implicit. The approaches in this domain support cardinality for resource allocation but they rely on only

---

[3] We have adopted the vocabulary used in BPM for resource allocation [19,31].

the resource type for creating the resource sets assigned to an activity. These approaches implement the so-called *resource-time tradeoff*, which assumes that activity completion is faster if two resources of the same type work together in its execution [28,29] (cf. Sect. 3.2). However, they assume a constant per-period availability of the resources [30], hence calendars are overlooked. The project scheduling problem has been repeatedly addressed with formalisms like linear integer programming (LIP) [28] and constraint programming (CP) [29], yet ad-hoc solutions also exist [30].

Finally, in the domain of BPM, the state of the art in resource allocation does not reach the maturity level of the other domains despite the acknowledged importance of the problem [32] and the actual needs (cf. Sect. 2.1). Similar to project scheduling, a constant availability of resources is typically assumed. In addition, due to the computational cost associated to joint resource assignment and scheduling problems [33], the existing techniques tend to search either for a feasible solution without applying any optimizations [31]; or for a local optimal at each process step using a greedy approach that might find a feasible but not necessarily a globally optimal solution [19]. Nonetheless, recently it was shown that global optimization is possible at a reasonable computational cost [5]. Moreover, driven by the limitations of current BPMS, which tend to disregard collaborative work for task completion, cardinality has been unconsidered for allocation, giving rise to less realistic solutions.

In general, the optimization function depends on the problem and the objective of the approach but it is generally based on minimizing time, makespan or cost, or making an optimal use of the resources (a.k.a. resource leveling [34]).

7   Conclusions and Future Work

In this paper we have conceptualized the complex problem of resource allocation under realistic dependencies that affect resources and activities as well as potential conflicts that may arise due to simultaneous requirement of resources. Our implementation based on ASP and its evaluation show that optimal solutions for this problem are possible, which extends the state of the art in BPM research and could contribute to extend the support in existing BPMS. ASP has proved to scale well [23] and can be easily integrated with RDF ontologies [24].

It is not the aim of this work to provide an end-user-oriented but an effective solution. In order to reasonably use our ASP implementation with a BPMS, it is required: (i) to map the notation used for process modeling along with the durations associated with the activities to (timed) Petri nets, for which several techniques have been designed [35]; and (ii) the integration of languages for defining all the requirements which could be used by non-technical users in the system as well as their mapping to ASP. However, to the best of our knowledge, there is not yet such an expressive end-user-oriented language but languages that allow a partial definition of the requirements [14,16].

As future work we plan to compare our technique with existing approaches on other optimal resource allocation techniques, explore the preemptive resource allocation as well as to apply our technique in other domains.

References

1. Rummler, G.A., Ramias, A.J.: A framework for defining and designing the structure of work. In: vom Brocke, J., Rosemann, M. (eds.) Handbook on Business Process Management 1, pp. 81–104. Springer, Heidelberg (2015)
2. Reijers, H.A., Vanderfeesten, I.T.P., van der Aalst, W.M.P.: The effectiveness of workflow management systems: a longitudinal study. Int. J. Inf. Manage. **36**(1), 126–141 (2016)
3. Rosemann, M., vom Brocke, J.: The six core elements of business process management. In: vom Brocke, J., Rosemann, M. (eds.) Handbook on Business Process Management 1, pp. 105–122. Springer, Heidelberg (2015)
4. Mans, R., Russell, N.C., Aalst, W.M.P., Moleman, A.J., Bakker, P.J.M.: Schedule-aware workflow management systems. Trans. Petri Nets Other Models Concurrency **4**, 121–143 (2010)
5. Havur, G., Cabanillas, C., Mendling, J., Polleres, A.: Automated resource allocation in business processes with answer set programming. In: Reichert, M., Reijers, H. (eds.) BPM Workshops 2015. LNBIP, vol. 256, pp. 191–203. Springer, Heidelberg (2016). doi:10.1007/978-3-319-42887-1_16
6. Popova-Zeugmann, L.: Time Petri Nets, pp. 139–140, Springer, Heidelberg (2013)
7. Johnson, D.S., Garey, M.R.: Computers and Intractability: A Guide to the Theory of NP-Completeness. WH Free. Co., San Fr. (1979)
8. Buccafurri, F., Leone, N., Rullo, P.: Enhancing disjunctive datalog by constraints. IEEE Trans. Knowl. Data Eng. **12**(5), 845–860 (2000)
9. Ouyang, C., Wynn, M.T., Fidge, C., ter Hofstede, A.H., Kuhr, J.-C.: Modelling complex resource requirements in Business Process Management Systems. In: ACIS (2010)
10. Brickley, D., Guha, R.: RDF Schema 1.1. W3C Recommendation, February 2014. http://www.w3.org/TR/rdf-schema/
11. Beckett, D., Berners-Lee, T., Prud'hommeaux, E., Carothers, G.: Turtle - Terse RDF Triple Language. W3C Candidate Recommendation, February 2014. https://www.w3.org/TR/turtle/
12. OMG, BPMN 2.0, recommendation, OMG (2011)
13. Cabanillas, C., Resinas, M., Río-Ortega, A., Ruiz-Cortés, A.: Specification and automated design-time analysis of the business process human resource perspective. Inf. Syst. **52**, 55–82 (2015)
14. Aalst, W.M.P., Hofstede, A.H.M.: YAWL: yet another workflow language. Inf. Syst. **30**(4), 245–275 (2005)
15. Stroppi, L.J.R., Chiotti, O., Villarreal, P.D.: A BPMN 2.0 extension to define the resource perspective of business process models. In: CIbS 2011 (2011)
16. Cabanillas, C., Resinas, M., Mendling, J., Cortés, A.R.: Automated team selection and compliance checking in business processes. In: ICSSP, pp. 42–51 (2015)
17. Gebser, M., Kaminski, R., Kaufmann, B., Schaub, T.: Answer Set Solving in Practice. Morgan & Claypool Publishers, San Rafael (2012)
18. Van Nieuwenborgh, D., De Cock, M., Hadavandi, E.: Fuzzy answer set programming. In: Fisher, M., van der Hoek, W., Konev, B., Lisitsa, A. (eds.) JELIA 2006. LNCS (LNAI), vol. 4160, pp. 359–372. Springer, Heidelberg (2006)
19. van der Aalst, W.: Petri net based scheduling. Operations-Research-Spektrum **18**(4), 219–229 (1996)
20. Roose, R.: Automated Resource Optimization in Business Processes. MSc. Thesis

21. Eiter, T., Faber, W., Leone, N., Pfeifer, G., Polleres, A.: Answer set planning under action costs. J. Artif. Intell. Res. (JAIR) **19**, 25–71 (2003)
22. Brewka, G., Eiter, T., Truszczyński, M.: Answer set programming at a glance. Commun. ACM **54**(12), 92–103 (2011)
23. Calimeri, F., Gebser, M., Maratea, M., Ricca, F.: Design and results of the fifthanswer set programming competition. Artif. Intell. **231**, 151–181 (2016)
24. Eiter, T., Ianni, G., Krennwallner, T., Polleres, A.: Rules and ontologies for the semantic web. In: Baroglio, C., Bonatti, P.A., Małuszyński, J., Marchiori, M., Polleres, A., Schaffert, S. (eds.) Reasoning Web 2008. LNCS, vol. 5224, pp. 1–53. Springer, Heidelberg (2008)
25. Castro, P.M., Marques, I.: Operating room scheduling with generalized disjunctive programming. Comput. Oper. Res. **64**, 262–273 (2015)
26. Silva, T.A., Souza, M.C., Saldanha, R.R., Burke, E.K.: Surgical scheduling with simultaneous employment of specialised human resources. Eur. J. Oper. Res. **245**(3), 719–730 (2015)
27. Riise, A., Mannino, C., Burke, E.K.: Modelling and solving generalised operational surgery scheduling problems. Comput. Oper. Res. **66**, 1–11 (2016)
28. Siu, M.-F.F., Lu, M., AbouRizk, S.: Methodology for crew-job allocation optimization in project and workface scheduling. In: ASCE, pp. 652–659 (2015)
29. Menesi, W., Abdel-Monem, M., Hegazy, T., Abuwarda, Z.: Multi-objective schedule optimization using constraint programming. In: ICSC15 (2015)
30. Sprecher, A., Drexl, A.: Multi-mode resource-constrained project scheduling by a simple, general and powerful sequencing algorithm1. Eur. J. Oper. Res. **107**(2), 431–450 (1998)
31. Senkul, P., Toroslu, I.H.: An architecture for workflow scheduling under resource allocation constraints. Inf. Syst. **30**, 399–422 (2005)
32. Arias, M., Rojas, E., Munoz-Gama, J., Sepúlveda, M.: A framework for recommending resource allocation based on process mining. In: BpPM Workshops (DeMiMoP) (in press) (2015)
33. Lombardi, M., Milano, M.: Optimal methods for resource allocation and scheduling: a cross-disciplinary survey. Constraints **17**, 51–85 (2012)
34. Rieck, J., Zimmermann, J.: Exact methods for resource leveling problems. In: Schwindt, C., Zimmermann, J. (eds.) Handbook on Project Management and Scheduling, vol. 1. Springer, Switzerland (2015)
35. Lohmann, N., Verbeek, E., Dijkman, R.: Petri Net transformations for business processes - a survey. Trans. Petri Nets Other Models Concurrency **II** (2), 46–63 (2009)

Parent-Child Relation
Between Process Instances

Luise Pufahl[(✉)] and Mathias Weske

Hasso Plattner Institute at the University of Potsdam, Potsdam, Germany
{Luise.Pufahl,Mathias.Weske}@hpi.de

Abstract. Business process management systems are well equipped to support the enactment of business processes. However, relations between process instances have not sufficiently been taken into account. To improve the execution of related process instances, batch activities have been introduced, which are based on jointly executing process activities. When analyzing real-world business processes, we encountered situations in which activities of specific process instances do not have to be executed at all. To conceptualize these situations, this paper introduces parent-child relationships between instances of a process. The approach is implemented in a cloud-based BPMS, and the technical contribution is embedded in a design methodology. A simulation shows that the cycle time and process execution costs can be significantly reduced by using parent-child relationships between process instances.

Keywords: BPMN · Redesign · Relations of process instances · Parent-child

1 Introduction

Business process management allows organizations to specify, execute, monitor, and improve their business operations [15] using business process management systems (BPMS) [3,6]. In current BPMS, process instances run independently from each other, disregarding relations between them. To improve the execution of related process instance, recent works introduce batch activities for synchronized execution of process instances [9,11,12].

When analyzing real-world business processes, we encountered situations in which activities of specific process instances do not have to be executed at all. An example is an incident process of a large IT service provider. In case of mass disruption, many incidents targeting the same issue arrive in a short period of time. When detected, the first incident of this type becomes a parent incident. Further incidents, the children, can be assigned to this parent. When the parent incident is resolved, its assigned child incidents can take over the result. By re-using results, the assigned children can skip all activities related to solving the incident. These parent-child relations are often already used, but hard-coded in IT systems. We propose to make parent-child relations explicit in process

© Springer International Publishing Switzerland 2016
M. La Rosa et al. (Eds.): BPM Forum 2016, LNBIP 260, pp. 20–37, 2016.
DOI: 10.1007/978-3-319-45468-9_2

models where they are traceable for all stakeholders and can be updated easily in comparison to a hard-coded solution.

This paper introduces parent-child relationships between process instances. As will be shown by a simulation study, this approach leads to an improved process performance. In this work, requirements are elicited based on an interview with a German IT Outsourcing company for integrating parent-child relations into business processes whereby four additional control-flow elements are identified. With these insights, the parent-child relation is integrated into BPMN process models, the industry-standard. A generalized parent-child BPMN process model is given which can be applied to any use case. Additionally, the internal behavior of all introduced activities is described which serves as basis for implementation. This works provides a functional as well as an effectiveness evaluation of the concept. For functional evaluation, the generalized parent-child process is applied to the incident process and its result is implemented in a cloud-based BPMS. The effectiveness evaluation based on a simulation where the basic incident process is compared to the parent-child incident process provides insights in how far a parent-child relation can improve the process efficiency.

The remainder of this paper is structured as follows. Section 2 introduces the motivating example, the incident process, for requirement analysis. Section 3 provides theoretical foundation, based on which we introduce the concept to integrate parent-child relation in BPMN processes in Sect. 4. Section 5 discusses the functional as well as effectiveness evaluation on the incident use case and describes lessons learned. Section 6 is devoted to related work and Sect. 7 concludes the paper.

2   Motivating Example and Requirements

This section presents a motivating example for the parent-child relation, the incident process. For requirement elicitation, an interview was conducted. The interview and the elicited requirements on a process model, which integrates a parent-child relation are discussed in this section.

The process model of Fig. 1 visualizes a simplified version of the incident process described by ITIL V3 [4]. An incident can be received via different channels, e.g. by an email or a call of a user. When an incident is reported, it is logged (i.e., the important information is captured) and categorized. In the next step, the incident is prioritized to define its urgency. Then, the first level support starts with the initial diagnosis. If it is categorized as to be *escalated* by the first level support, it is forwarded for further diagnosis to the 2nd and later maybe also to the 3rd level support. When investigation and diagnosis of the incident is finalized, it is resolved and communicated to the user. Finally, the incident is closed.

In case of massive disruption, incidents that target the same issue arrive, e.g., 100 users call that their email is not working. The handling of massive disruption is currently not captured by ITIL V3. Therefore, we interviewed a German IT outsourcing company to capture the requirements. This outsourcing company

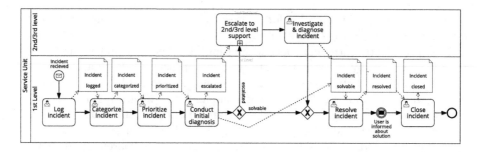

Fig. 1. Simplified incident process as described by ITIL V3.

has hard-coded the incident process in a self-made software for supporting it. If more than two incidents targeting the same issue are identified, they are handled by the outsourcing company as follows: one of them is selected to be the *master incident* to which all others are linked. The master incident is then handled. When it is resolved, the solution is forwarded automatically to all assigned incidents. With this approach, the outsourcing company makes sure that only one solution is followed and streamlines the communication to the user. Further, process performance is improved as the working steps and the solution is only once documented and can be automatically broadcast to similar ones. Currently, this approach is hard-coded in an IT system. Since the master assignment approach is not traceable for the process owner and the participants, its settings cannot be controlled by them and adaptations result in high efforts. We propose to implement it in a process model where it can be accessed and updated by all stakeholders. The process model can be then used for implementation.

From a control flow view point, the described approach requires that the master incident follows the normal flow, but a subset of incidents can skip by re-using the solution of the master all steps after the categorization until sending the message to the user. It has to be ensured that the re-usage of the master solution by the assigned instances only takes place when the master is in a state where its solution is available. For example, the *closed*-state ensures that a solution is available which is not updated anymore. Realizing the parent-child relation for the given example, the process model in Fig. 1 has to be extended with the following four aspects:

(1) An additional activity which checks the existence of a potential master (the parent) after the categorization of the incident
(2) An alternative flow where
(3) child-incidents are assigned to the identified master and can skip all following activities until the solution is communicated to the user
(4) An activity on the alternative flow which applies the result of the master incident and is only enabled, if the master is in state *closed*

In the remainder of this paper, we will present a BPMN diagram serving as template to realize parent-child relations. Thereby, the template will consider the just listed requirements. The following section introduces the foundations for our concept.

3   Foundation

We propose to set up a parent-child relation by means of process data whereby the child instance data references the data of the parent. Therefore, we proceed with introducing formalisms for process and data modeling. Starting with a generic process model definition, we require it to be syntactically correct with respect to the used modeling notation. Behaviorally, we require that it terminates for all execution paths of the model in exactly one of probable multiple end events and that every node participates in at least one execution path, i.e., the process model must be lifelock and deadlock free. Formally, a process model is defined as follows.

Definition 1 (Process Model). A *process model* $m = (N, D, DS, \mathcal{C}, \mathcal{F}, \mathcal{D}, \mathcal{A}, type)$ consists of a finite non-empty set $N \subseteq A \cup E \cup G$ of control flow nodes being activities A, events E, and gateways G (A, E, and G are pairwise disjoint), a finite non-empty set D of data nodes and the finite set DS of data stores used for persistence of data objects (N, D, DS are pairwise disjoint). $\mathcal{C} \subseteq N \times N$ is the control flow and $\mathcal{F} \subseteq (A \times D) \cup (D \times A)$ is the data flow relation specifying input/output data dependencies of activities. $\mathcal{D} \subseteq (D \times DS) \cup (DS \times D)$ is the data persistence of data objects and $\mathcal{A} \subseteq (A \times DS) \cup (DS \times A)$ is the data access relation of activities. Function $type : G \rightarrow \{AND, XOR\}$ gives each gateway a type. $\Diamond$

We refer to a data node $d \in D$ being read by an activity $a \in A$, i.e., $(d, a) \in \mathcal{F}$, as *input data node* and to a data node d being written by an activity a, i.e., $(a, d) \in \mathcal{F}$, as *output data node*. Figure 1 shows a process model in BPMN notation [10] with one start event, one end event, eight activities (one of them with internal behavior – a sub-process), two XOR-gateways, one intermediate message event and multiple data nodes read and written by activities. Each data node has a name, e.g., *Incident*, and a specific data state, e.g., *logged* or *categorized* (can be represented by a short form *Incident[logged]*). An activity $a \in A$ can have several input and output data nodes, grouped into input sets and output sets. Different input/output sets represent alternative pre-/post conditions for $a \in A$. For example, activity *Conduct initial diagnosis* has two output nodes: *Incident[escalated]* and *Incident[solvable]*, each part of an own output set such that only one of them has to be fulfilled. A data store represents any information system or database. A data node $d \in D$ which is connected with a data store $ds \in DS$, i.e., $(d, ds) \in \mathcal{D}$ indicates that all information of it is stored in this location. In contrast, an activity $a \in A$ connected with a data store $ds \in DS$, i.e., (a, ds) or $(ds, a) \in \mathcal{A}$ indicates that the activity requests or updates the data store. Each data node refers to a data class; here: *Incident*.

Definition 2 (Data Class). A data class $c = (J, S)$ consists of a finite set J of attributes and a finite non-empty set S of data states (J and S are disjoint). $\Diamond$

A data class describes the structure of data nodes in terms of attributes and possible data states which are in a logical and temporal order. The function $\chi : D \rightarrow C$ returns for data node d the corresponding data class c. If we want to express that a data node can be in any state, then the corresponding node gets assigned an asterisks as data state acting as placeholder for each possible state described by the data class. On the execution level, an arbitrary set of data objects exits.

Definition 3 (Data Object and Data State). A *data object* $o = (c, s_o)$ references a data class c describing its structure and allowed data states. Let V be a universe of data attribute values. Then, the *data state* $s_o : J_c \rightarrow V$ is a function which assigns each attribute $j \in J_c$ a value $v \in V$ that holds in the current state of data object o. $\Diamond$

At any point in time, each data attribute of an object can get assigned a value. If it is not defined, the value is set to $\perp$.

Executions of process models are represented by process instances with each instance belonging to exactly one process model m. Each instance contains a set of data objects being tied to the life cycle of the process instance and being disposed as soon as the instance terminates [10] (i.e., case data [13]). Data objects can be made persistent if corresponding data nodes are connected via a data persistent relation to a data store (i.e., work-flow data [13]). We assume that data objects referencing the same data class are stored in one data store ds. If an activity a of a process model has reading access to a data store ds, the process instance can access all stored data objects even if they were not created by it. The function $\delta : I \times DS \nrightarrow \mathcal{P}(\mathcal{O})$ returns for an instance i a set of data objects O_i stored in a data store ds on which it is working. Thereby, $\mathcal{P}(\mathcal{O})$ is the power set of data object set O.

Process instance can be grouped based on data characteristics as introduced in [11] by using the concept of *data views*. In the scope of this paper, we ease this concept such that a *data view DV* is a projection on the values of a data object for a list of logically combined data attributes contained by a *single* data class. This list of fully qualified data attributes is called *data view definition DVD* and is provided by the process designer.

4 Formalizing Parent-Child Relations Based on BPMN

This section presents a concept to integrate parent-child relations into BPMN processes. BPMN [10], a rich and expressive modeling notation, is the industry standard for BPM.

We define a parent-child relation depicted in a process model as a dependency between instances of a process where a set of similar instances is assigned to a so-called *parent instance*. Process instances having similar data characteristics, carrying the same data for certain attributes, are considered as being similar. The assigned instances, the *children*, are allowed to skip a set of connected activities by re-using the result of the parent instance as soon as it is in a certain state in which relevant results for the children are available. Thereby, the goal of the parent-child relation is to save processing time and resource cost by avoiding redundant work. We propose to set up a parent child relation by means of case-to-case data interaction (see pattern 13 in [13]) aiming at passing the parent's data to the child instances during their execution.

In Sect. 4.1, we specify how to model a parent-child relation as BPMN template which can be applied to any use case. In Sect. 4.2, it is described how to implement a parent-child relation by documenting the internal activities' behavior of the template.

4.1 Modeling Parent-Child Relation

In Sect. 2, the motivating example shows that the following elements are needed to realize a parent-child relation: (1) an activity checking whether a parent exists, (2) a skipping flow on which (3) an activity assigns the children to the parent and (4) an activity being enabled when the parent is in a defined state to apply the result of the parent. Based on these insights, a BPMN template to establish a parent-child relation is developed given in Fig. 2. All activities with three dots represent activities which can be adapted or extended to a specific business use case. Basically, a parent-child relation is realized by three additional activities (see Fig. 2, all starting with $a\_$) and a flow for skipping certain activities of the usual flow. This is called the parent-child BPMN fragment. The fragment includes also required data nodes and stores to realize the case-to-case data interaction (see pattern 13 in [13]) for passing data of the parent to its child instances. The three additional activities are service activities such that parent-child relation is realized during process execution automatically with no additional effort for the process participants. We could also hide these service activities in a sub-process to abstract from the details of a parent-child implementation. However, this paper will show the details for explanation purposes. In the following, the parent-child process template is presented in more detail.

For realizing a potential parent-child relation, first the activity $a_{checkForParent}$ is needed on the normal flow. This service activity checks for all instances whether a parent exists. If not, the instance follows the normal flow. If yes, it uses the skipping flow on which it is assigned to the parent and waits for the parent's result. The service activity $a_{checkForParent}$ has one input set consisting of the data node $d[s]$ being from type c_d for which a corresponding parent should be identified. By defining the input data node for this activity, the process designer decides based on which data type the parent-child relation is established. Additionally, the activity has access to a data store ds, the central storage for every produced objects of type c_d to realize the access on other case data.

The activity can produce one of the following output sets: $outputset1 = \{d[s]\}$ and $outputset2 = \{d[s], parent_d[*]\}$. As introduced in the foundation, input and output sets represent alternative pre-/post conditions for an activity $a \in A$. The output sets of an activity a are represented by $out_A = \{\{..\}, \{..\}\}$, a set of sets where each element set contains data nodes in specific states presenting an

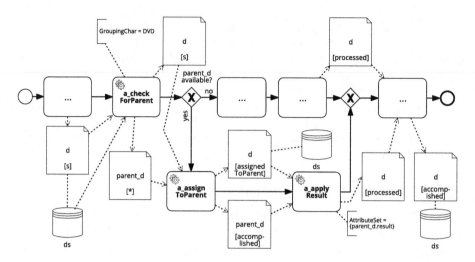

Fig. 2. BPMN process template for a parent-child relation realized by three service activities and a skipping flow.

alternative which can be produced by the activity a. The same applies for input sets of an activity a represented by $in_A = \{\{..\}, \{..\}\}$ where one of the element sets have to be available to enable the activity.

The second output set is only provided if a $parent_d$ – also an object of the data class c_d – was found in the data store ds. The asterisk-state of the parent data object indicates that its state is unknown. For being able to identify the parent data object, every data object d of type c_d has to be available in the data store ds. We assume that previously to or shortly after the activity $a_{checkForParent}$ the data node d is an output data node of any activity and is connected to the data store ds expressing a data persistence relation. In Fig. 2, for example, $d[s]$ is output of the first activity and connected to the data store ds. Further, a data view definition DVD has to be provided by the process designer as grouping characteristic to identify a potential parent. As defined in Sect. 3, a data view definition DVD consists of a qualified set of data attributes of one data class. A parent is identified, if the projection using the attributes of the data view definition on a data object from type c_d, the so-called data view, is equal to the data view of the data object o_i of the currently active process instance i. Here, we assume that the grouping characteristic is designed in a way that the result is in at most one potential parent. If this is not possible, the selection of a parent can be supported by a user decision which can be easily integrated by adding a user activity after this service activity. This user activity presents in its form a list of potential parents and the user can select then either one or no parent.

After identifying whether a parent exists, a splitting OR-gateway is added. It is the decision point between the normal flow and the skipping flow. All child process instances for which a parent was identified, follow the skipping flow. On the skipping flow, the first service activity is $a_{assignToParent}$. It assigns the data object o_i to the parent object o_{parent} by storing a reference to the parent object in the current object and transferring it into the *assignedToParent*-state. Further, it has one input set consisting of the data nodes $d[s]$ and $parent_d[*]$ and produces the following output set with data node d in a new state *assignedToParent* which is in a persistent relation to the data store ds. The persistent relation ensures that the corresponding object can be identified by other new arriving instances as a child object being excluded from the set of potential parents.

Skipping of certain activities by the child instances is only possible, because they apply certain results of the parent. The service activity $a_{applyResult}$ is responsible for this step. It has one input set consisting of the data nodes $d[assignedToParent]$ and $parent_d[accomplished]$. The state *accomplished* of the parent data node is a placeholder and represents the state where a result reusable by the children is available. We assume that each data object is stored in this state such that the parent is accessible in corresponding state. To ensure this, a data node in the state *accomplished* should be output of an activity on the normal process flow – being executed in each case– and should be in a persistent relation to a data store in the process model. For example in Fig. 2, data object d in state *accomplished* is output of the last activity and connected to the data store ds. The corresponding data store ds where the parent data object is stored, has to be requested until the corresponding object o_{parent} has the required state. An implementation of data input conditions is shown for example in the work by Meyer et al. [8]. Further, the activity has one output set consisting of the data node d in the new state *processed*. This output data node indicates that the child object was updated with the values of the parent data object o_{parent} for a set of defined data attributes by the process designer (see text annotation of activity $a_{applyResult}$ in Fig. 2). With termination of this service activity, the child instance can return with the help of a XOR-join gateway to the normal process flow and can follow the process path to the process end.

4.2   Execution Semantics of Parent-Child Relation

In this subsection, the internal behavior of the service activities is described. It serves as implementation support of processes with a parent-child relation. For the description of the internal behavior, pseudo code is used. We start with the first service activity $a_{checkForParent}$ in Algorithm 1.

Algorithm 1 requires a specified data view definition DVD by the process designer, the current process instance i, the input data node $d[s]$ and the data store ds. At first, all data objects being of the same data class as the data node $d[s]$ are retrieved from the data store ds with the help of the auxiliary function $select : DS \times D \nrightarrow \mathfrak{P}(O)$. Thereby, the *select*-function uses χ of the foundations returning for a data node d the corresponding data class c. Further, the local object o_i of the process instance i for the data node $d[s]$ is fetched. Then, for each data object in the set O_d, it is checked whether its data view is equal to the data view of the data object of the current running process instance. Thereby, the auxiliary function $dataView : DVD \times O \to V$ returns the values for the given attributes in DVD for a data object o. In case of equality, the parent o_{parent} is

---

Algorithm 1. Algorithm of the service activity $a_{checkForParent}$.

Require: DVD; // is specified by the process designer
Require: i; // current process instance
Require: $d[s]$; ds; // the input data node and the data store
1. $O_d \leftarrow select(ds, d[s])$; // auxiliary function to retrieve all data objects from ds referencing the same data class as the data node $d[s]$
2. $o_i \leftarrow i.d[s]$; // get local object for given data node $d[s]$ of the process instance i
3. **for all** $o \in O_d$ **do**
4.   **if** $dataView(DVD, o_i) = dataView(DVD, o) \ \&o_i.id \neq o.id$ **then**
5.   // auxilary function dataView returns the projection for the attributes given in DVD on a data object
6. $o_{parent} = o$; // if data view of current data object is equal to one of the data objects, then the parent is identified
7. $i.parent_d = o_{parent}$; // the parent data object is stored as local object of instance i
8. $\delta(i, ds) = \delta(i, ds).add(o_{parent})$; // add the identified parent to the set of persistent data objects accessed by the current instance i
9.   break; // if parent was identified, loop is stopped
10.   **end if**
11. **end for**

---

identified. By additional checking that the *ids* of the two objects are not same, it is ensured that the parent is never the persistent version of the current object. The parent o_{parent} is added to the local data objects of instance i and to the set of persistent data objects $\delta(i, ds)$ in the data store ds on which the process instance i is working by the help of the *delta*-function (see foundation section). In case of successful identification, the loop is terminated.

Algorithm 2. Algorithm of the service activity $a_{assignToParent}$.

Require: i; // current process instance
Require: $d[s]$; $parent_d[*]$; // input data nodes consisting of the child and parent
Require: $d[assignedToParent]$; // output data node
1. $o_i \leftarrow i.d[s]$;
2. $o_{parent} \leftarrow i.parent_d[*]$;
3. $o_i.parentId = o_{parent}.id$; // update current object o_i with a reference to the parent
4. $o_i.state \leftarrow d[assignedToParent].state$; // update state to the output data node state

---

If a parent was identified, the activity $a_{assignToParent}$ is executed. Its internal behavior is described in Algorithm 2. It needs the current process instance i, the input data nodes $d[s]$ and $parent_d[*]$ and the output data node

$d[assignedToParent]$ of the activity. First the local object o_i and the local parent object o_{parent} are retrieved from the process instance. Then, a reference to the parent object o_{parent} is set in o_i, here represented by the attribute *parentId*. Finally, the child object state is changed to *assignedToParent* – the state of the output data node.

After assigning the child to the parent, the solution of the parent is taken over. The service activity $a_{applyResult}$ is enabled only if the parent is in a certain state and uses the algorithm shown in Algorithm 3.

Algorithm 3. Algorithm of the service activity $a_{applyResult}$.

Require: i; // current process instance
Require: $d[assignedToParent]$; $parent_d[accomplished]$; // input data nodes
　　consisting of the child and parent
Require: $d[processed]$; // output data node
Require: ATT; // set of attributes defined by the process designer
　1. $o_i \leftarrow i.d[assignedToParent]$;
　2. $O_i \leftarrow \delta(i, ds)$; // get all stored data object of the instance i in ds with the
　　　δ-function
　3. $o_{parent} \leftarrow O_i.parent_d[accomplished]$// get parent object from the set of stored
　　　objects of i
　4. **for all** $att \in ATT$ **do**
　5. 　　$o_i.att \leftarrow o_{parent}.att$; // update the current object o_i with the results of the
　　　parent object
　6. **end for**
　7. $o_i.state \leftarrow d[processed].state$;

Algorithm 3 needs the current process instance i, the input data nodes $d[assignedToParent]$ and $parent_d[accomplished]$, the output data node $d[processed]$ of the activity and a set of attributes ATT provided by the process designer describing which attributes values are taken over from the parent. With the *delta*-function, all persistent data objects in ds, in which the process instance i is interested, can be retrieved. From this set the parent data object o_{parent} is fetched. For each attribute of the given attribute set ATT, the value is written to the child object o_i. Finally, the child object state is changed to *processed* – the state of the output data node.

5 Evaluation

In this section, the generalized parent-child BPMN process is evaluated by a functional evaluation and an effectiveness evaluation. For the functional evaluation, the parent-child BPMN process is applied to the incident process, discussed in Sect. 5.1 whereby a methodology for the application is deduced and presented. The result is implemented in effektif.com, a cloud-based BPMN, discussed in Sect. 5.2. In Sect. 5.3, the comparison between a simulation of the basic and parent-child incident process is discussed with regards to cycle times and resource costs. In Sect. 5.4, lessons learned of the evaluation are discussed.

5.1   Application of the Concept to the Incident Process

The presented formalization of the parent-child relation in BPMN shown in Fig. 2 is applied for a functional evaluation to the motivating use case, the incident process shown in Fig. 1. During application, five steps[1] were conducted to apply the parent-child BPMN template. The steps are described in detail in the following.

In step (1), it had to be decided where in the process the parent-child template starting with the service activity $a_{checkForParent}$ and ending with the join XOR-gateway should be added. In the incident process, after logging and categorization the most important data for an incident are available. Prioritization information are only important for the actual diagnosis phase, but not for identifying a potential master incident, the parent. Therefore, the parent-child template was added after incident categorization. Next, it has to be decided how many activities can be skipped. In the incident processes, the idea is to apply the diagnosis and the solution of the master incident and to communicate the solution to each user individually. Therefore, the join-gateway for the normal and splitting flow had to be added after the activity *Resolve incident* and before the send-event. The result is shown in Fig. 3.

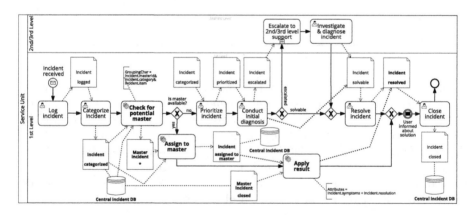

Fig. 3. Incident process extended by the parent-child relation based on the BPMN process template which is adapted to the incident use case.

In step (2), all labels of the template were adapted such that it fits to the use case. Thereby, the service activities, the data nodes with its states and the data stores were relabeled. The service activities were renamed such that the term *master* used by the practitioners is used. For the data nodes, the data class establishing

---

[1] The documented steps are available at http://bpt.hpi.uni-potsdam.de/Public/ParentChild.

the parent-child relation at runtime had to be chosen. Here, the *incident* data class was selected such that the data node *d* in the fragment is called *incident* and the parent node *parent$_d$* is called *master incident*. Also, the states of the data nodes have to be partly adapted. For example, the input state *s* of *d* in the fragment, we relabeled to the output state *categorized* of the categorization activity after which the fragment was added. Similarly, the output state of the fragment *processed* is renamed to the output of the activity *resolve incident* after which normal and splitting flow are joined that is *incident* in state *resolved*. Further, the state of the parent – in the fragment given as *parent$_d$[accomplished]* – in which the results can be taken over has to be defined. As shown in Fig. 3, we selected the *closed*-state of the master incident. It assures that incidents can apply the result although the master was already closed. We assume that the incidents are set later in a follow-up process to *archived* indicating that they are not relevant as a master anymore. The data store for the incidents is the *Central incident DB* such that data store *ds* is adapted accordingly.

In step (3), the grouping characteristic for selecting the right parent and the set of attributes which are taken over by the parent – annotations of the first and last service activity – were adapted. The data view definition consisting of the following incident attributes *category* & *item* & *masterId* was used as grouping characteristic such that the parent is identified based on the categorization information. The attribute *masterId* is also included to make sure that no child instances is selected as master. For an incident, it is important to have finally a description of the symptoms and a resolution. Therefore, *symptoms* and *resolution* are defined as the attributes taken over by the master incident in the annotation of the activity *Apply result*.

In step (4), it had to be assured that data is made persistent at the right spots in the process such that the master can be identified and later the results can be applied. This had to be done at two points: before or right after the check for the potential parent in order to make sure that the parent is available and as soon as the data object is written into the state in which the parent is required. As the most important data is available for an incident after its categorization, the incident output data node is connected to the *Central incident DB*. Additionally, the incident data node in state *closed* is connected to the data base because the child instances require the master in this state (Fig. 3). These are all steps which are needed to design the model with the parent-child relation. In order to execute the model, the internal behavior of the service activities has to be adapted as well in a last step (step (5)). This is discussed in the next sub-section.

The application of the parent-child BPMN process template shows that it is useful to adapt a process easily with a few steps and to make sure that all important elements are included. Based on it, we can summarized that the following important steps:

1. Add the parent-child template at the correct spots in the process,
2. Relabel service activities, data nodes and stores such that it fits to the use case,

3. Adapt annotations of service activities to define a grouping characteristic and
   the set of attributes taken over by the children,
4. Assure data persistence to enable parent identification and re-usage of results,
5. Adapt internal behavior of service activities for implementation purpose.

5.2   Implementation of Incident Process

The goal of the concept is to provide a parent-child process template which can
be used for process design and implementation. Now focusing on the implementation part, we used the incident model of the former subsection and implemented it in effektif.com[2], a cloud-based workflow engine. This workflow engine
was selected, because it offers a user-friendly environment where processes can
be quickly implemented. effektif.com does not handle data nodes annotated in
process models as all current standard BPMS [8], only process variables are
supported. Therefore, data relations had to be handled manually.

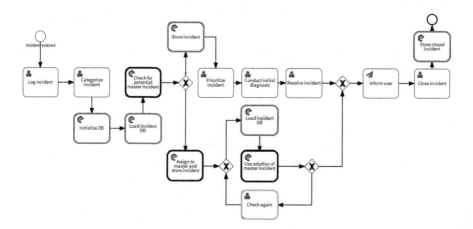

Fig. 4. Implemented incident process in effektif.com with the parent-child relation.

The implemented process is very similar to the incident process of Fig. 3.
Minor differences are highlighted in Fig. 4 with a gray boarder. They are mainly
due to the missing data support: For the implementation, we eased the process
by leaving out the escalation of incidents to focus on the parent-child relation. By
default, effektif.com does not provide a connection to a database system, but has
Java Script service activities. Therefore, we implemented a web service storage
accessible via REST (Representational State Transfer) calls. Due to it, some
additional activities were added in the process implementation, e.g., *Initialize
incident DB* for setting up the data store, if it does not exist or *Load incident
DB* for selecting all data entries. The data input relations for an activity can

---

[2] Please see http://bpt.hpi.uni-potsdam.de/Public/ParentChild for more information.

not be checked automatically with effektif.com. Thus, a loop was implemented where all incidents are loaded from the store and then the activity *Use solution of master* is executed. If the required variables *symptoms* and *resolution* could be not filled because the master incident object is still not *closed*, a user activity is activated which can restart another try. As soon as the variables are filled, the child instance returns to the normal flow and the user is informed, here by an email activity.

The implementation shows that even if the data nodes concept is not supported by a BPMS, the parent-child relation model served as important orientation for the implementation, i.e., which data has to be accessed and where an access to the data store is needed. The pseudo code given in Sect. 4.2 for the three service activities provided support in how to implement the main java script activities to provide a correct execution of the parent-child relation. Small differences were mainly due to the missing support for data annotations and are documented in their comments. Despite the implementation template, it is still some manual work required from an IT specialist. If the methodology of the previous section is detailed further, the adaption of the service activities to the use case could be partly automized.

5.3   Simulation of the Incident Process

In this sub-section, we evaluate the impact of the parent-child relation on the process performance by a single case. Thereby, the simulation results of the basic incident process (see Fig. 1) are compared to the simulation results of the parent-child incident process (see Fig. 3) with regards to cycle times and resource costs. The interview with the German IT Outsourcing company provided us the average number of cases per day, the average processing times of each activity, the probabilities of decisions and information about the resource number and costs. All information can be found in Table 1.

For our evaluation we used the BIMP simulator[3]. The BIMP simulator offers quick creation of multi-instance simulations by importing a BPMN XML file. This is extended by information regarding the inter-arrival times of instances and activity duration distributions. For the inter-arrival time, an exponential distribution with a mean of one minute was selected. We assume here that incidents only arrive between 9:00 am and 5:00 pm (in sum around 500 cases per day). In reality, also incidents outside of this time with other distributions could be received. However, this is not further considered, because it has no huge impact on the comparison between the basic and the parent-child process. For the activity processing times, a normal distribution was selected for activities which are governed by choice fields, e.g., the categorization or prioritization. An exponential distribution was used for activities where open text fields are included and difficult cases can lead to longer processing times, e.g., the initial diagnosis or investigation and diagnosis. The simulation is eased in this regards

---

[3] http://bimp.cs.ut.ee/. The BPMN XML files used for the simulation can be found at http://bpt.hpi.uni-potsdam.de/Public/ParentChild.

Table 1. Average process measures for the incident use case provided in the interview with the German IT Outsourcing company.

Process measures		
	# of cases per day	500
Activity processing time	Log incident	4 min
	Categorize incident/prioritize incident	2 min
	Do initial diagnosis	30 min
	Escalate to 2nd level support	3 min
	Investigate and diagnose incident	21 min
	Resolve incident	12 min
Probabilities of decisions	Solvable\escalated incidents	80 %\20 %
	Master available\not available	20 %\80 %
Resource information	# of resources\cost in 1st level support	90\20 Euro per hour
	# of resources\cost in 2nd level support	20\35 Euro per hour

that an incident is only escalated to the second level support, but not further. For the parent-child incident process, assumptions about the processing times of the service activities has to be made. In general, it is assumed that service times are conducted in a few seconds, but sometimes the service might take longer due to server loads. An exponential distribution with a mean of 5 s was selected. The activity *Apply result* is highly influenced by the time when the master is resolved. As this relation cannot be integrated into the BIMP simulator, the distribution of the activity duration has to reflect the waiting time for the master. Therefore, a simulation of the basic incident process was conducted for all activities from incident prioritization until closing to find the average duration a parent needs until it is *closed*. As a child arrives some time after the parent, we assume that the child waits on average half of the needed time. A normal distribution of 25.5 min (51 min\2) with a deviation of 10 min for providing a high variation in the values was taken.

Table 2. Results of one simulation run of the basic incident process and one simulation run of incident process the parent-child relation.

	Cycle time			Process costs	
	Min	Avg	Max	Average case costs	Total costs
(1) Basic process	11.3 min	57.1 min	5.5 h	20.1 EUR	200719.7 EUR
(2) Parent-child process	2.5 min	50.6 min	5.2 h	15.5 EUR	155485.1 EUR
Difference of (2) to (1) in %	77.9 %	11.4 %	5.4 %	22.8 %	22.5 %

Both simulation were conducted for 10000 instance. The results consisting of cycle time and cost information are represented in Table 2. The results show that the average cycle time is reduced by some minutes, a minor improvement of

11.4 %. The main reason is that child incidents have to wait for the result of the parent incident. Further, the portion of probable child incidents is 20 % in this use case. If the portion is greater, the advantage would be even higher. The minimum cycle time has reduced by 77.9 % to 2.5 min, because if an instance is assigned to a parent which is already in state *closed*, the service activities are conducted in a few seconds. In comparison to the cycle time, the parent-child relation has a higher impact on costs. The average costs could be reduced by 22.8 %, similar to the total costs, because the child instances are handled automatically and does not generate any resource costs. To summarize, the single-case simulation shows that the parent-child relation has a minor impact in reduction of cycle time, but a high impact on reducing process costs, because the children bypass a set of user activities.

5.4   Lessons Learned and Limitations

We will now discuss the lessons leaned from the evaluation and its limitations. The effectiveness evaluation based on the simulation implicates that parent-child relations are useful: They can offer time and costs saving, although the costs saving are higher, because the child instances have still to wait for parent instance. Currently, the results are based on one use case. This should be extended to a validation of further use cases, e.g., complaint management where a set of similar complaints targeting the same issue can reuse the result of a already handled complaint. The application of our proposed concept for the integration of parent-child relations – the parent-child relation BPMN process template – shows that it offers support in integrating a parent-child relation correctly in a business process model in a few steps. The most important advantages of integrating parent-child relations in process models are that a parent-child relation is traceable for the process stakeholders, can be easily adapted and can be used for process validation (e.g. simulation) and implementation. Nevertheless, some manual work by the process designer to adapt the fragment to a concrete use case is still needed. Similar results shows the process implementation: The resulted parent-child process model and the pseudo code description provide an orientation for a correct implementation despite missing support for data annotation in BPMS, but manual work is still needed. However, the proposed methodology, the 5-step approach, deduced from application to the incident use case can be used as a prerequisite for (semi) automation of our concept. An automatized approach could use a basic process model as input and some user inputs to generate a process model extended with the parent-child relation based on them. In future, the first deduced methodology should be detailed and further evaluated.

6   Related Work

The workflow control-flow patterns of [1] are an important standard that describe workflow functionalities with regard to the control-flow as patterns. However, patterns for interrelations between process instances are not considered. A first step in this regard are the multi-instances patterns, but for them it is assumed that multiple instances are created and terminated during the execution of one process instance and does not consider relations between instances in general.

In BPMN, the signal event can be used for intra- and inter-process communication [10]. However, a signal is "like a shot into the sky" where each instance reacts which has subscribed for this signal type. A signal is not instance-specific. Therefore, we realized the parent-child relation between process instances based on the instance data.

Whereas the parent-child relation between instances of a process model received little attention in the BPM research, the batch relation, was discussed in several works e.g., in [2,7,14] and also recently e.g., in [9,11,12]. In a batch relation, instances of a batch are processed together in one step (e.g. the instances' attributes are shown in one user view) whereas in a parent-child relation, the parent executes the normal flow; the children can skip certain activities by using the result of it. In both relations, similar instances have to be identified which can be in a batch or parent-child relation. The process designer has to define on which data attributes process instances can be grouped.

In PHILharmonicFlows [5], a data-oriented modeling approach, it is possible that the user enters form values in one go for multiple data objects. This requires that the set of children is known before the parent can be processed further such that the results can be applied. In our approach, child instances can also use the result of the parent, if it is already terminated. PHILharmonicFlows considers also execution dependencies where certain object instances have to be available for process continuation, but parent-child relation are not discussed in their work.

7   Conclusion

In this paper, parent-child relation of process instances where a set of instances can skip certain activities by reusing results of a parent instance is investigated for the first time. The explicit representation of parent-child relations in process models enables the traceability, validation, optimization and correct implementation of the parent-child relation for the process stakeholders. This work provides requirements for the integration, and further a definition and formalization of the parent-child relation in BPMN, the industry standard. Our contribution consists of a parent-child BPMN process template with all necessary elements to model a parent child-relation and the internal activity specification as prerequisite for implementation. Activities of the parent-child template are all service activities to avoid additional effort for process participants.

The functional evaluation where the parent-child template is applied to a use case shows that the concept helps to adapt a process in a few steps which is then able to correctly execute a parent-child relation. The application identified a five step methodology, a first step in the direction to make the integration of parent-child relations in business processes (semi) automatized. It can be generalized by applying it to other use cases, e.g., the complaint management, to use it for an automatic integration approach. Implementation of the resulted parent-child process shows that despite of missing data support in existing BPMS, the model and the internal behavior provide an important support for a correct parent-child implementation. The results of the effectiveness evaluation by simulating a single use case indicate significant savings in cycle time and costs by a parent-child relation. This single case simulation should be extended in future. Further, we aim to evaluate the usability of our approach in a user study.

References

1. van der Aalst, W.M.P., ter Hofstede, A.H.M., Kiepuszewski, B., Barros, A.P.: Workflow patterns. Distrib. Parallel Databases **14**(1), 5–51 (2003)
2. van der Aalst, W.M.P., Barthelmess, P., Ellis, C.A., Wainer, J.: Proclets: a framework for lightweight interacting workflow processes. Int. J. Coop. Inf. Syst. **10**(4), 443–481 (2001)
3. Camunda: camunda BPM platform. https://www.camunda.org/
4. Großbritannien Office of Government Commerce: Service operation (SO): ITIL. TSO (The Stationery Office) (2007)
5. Künzle, V., Reichert, M.: PHILharmonicFlows: towards a framework for object-aware process management. J. Softw. Maint. **23**(4), 205–244 (2011)
6. Lanz, A., Reichert, M., Dadam, P.: Robust and flexible error handling in the aristaflow BPM suite. In: Proper, E., Soffer, P. (eds.) CAiSE Forum 2010. LNBIP, vol. 72, pp. 174–189. Springer, Heidelberg (2011)
7. Liu, J., Hu, J.: Dynamic batch processing in workflows: model and implementation. Future Gener. Comput. Syst. **23**(3), 338–347 (2007)
8. Meyer, A., Pufahl, L., Fahland, D., Weske, M.: Modeling and enacting complex data dependencies in business processes. In: Daniel, F., Wang, J., Weber, B. (eds.) BPM 2013. LNCS, vol. 8094, pp. 171–186. Springer, Heidelberg (2013)
9. Natschläger, C., Bögl, A., Geist, V.: Optimizing resource utilization by combining running business process instances. In: Toumani, F., et al. (eds.) ICSOC 2014. LNCS, vol. 8954, pp. 120–126. Springer, Heidelberg (2015)
10. OMG: Business Process Model and Notation (BPMN), Version 2.0, January 2011
11. Pufahl, L., Meyer, A., Weske, M.: Batch regions: process instance synchronization based on data. In: EDOC, pp. 150–159. IEEE (2014)
12. Pufahl, L., Weske, M.: Batch activities in process modeling and execution. In: Basu, S., Pautasso, C., Zhang, L., Fu, X. (eds.) ICSOC 2013. LNCS, vol. 8274, pp. 283–297. Springer, Heidelberg (2013)
13. Russell, N., Hofstede, A.H.M., Edmond, D., Aalst, W.M.P.: Workflow data patterns. Queensland University of Technology, Tech. rep. (2004)
14. Sadiq, S., Orlowska, M., Sadiq, W., Schulz, K.: When workflows will not deliver: the case of contradicting work practice. In: BIS, pp. 69–84 (2005)
15. Weske, M.: Business Process Management: Concepts, Languages, Architectures, p. 404, Second Edition. Springer, Heidelberg (2012)

A Hybrid Approach for Flexible Case Modeling and Execution

Marcin Hewelt[(✉)] and Mathias Weske

Hasso Plattner Institute Potsdam, Potsdam, Germany
{marcin.hewelt,mathias.weske}@hpi.de

Abstract. While the business process management community has concentrated on modelling and executing business processes with a known structure, support for processes with a high degree of variability performed by knowledge workers is still not satisfactory. A promising approach to overcome this deficiency is case management. Despite of the work done in the area of case management in recent years, there is no accepted case handling formalism that features a well defined semantics. This paper introduces a novel approach to case management, which is based on dynamically combining process fragments as required by knowledge workers. An operational semantics defines the meaning of case models in detail, using states of data objects and enablement conditions of process fragments.

Keywords: Case management · Business process management

1   Introduction

Business process management concepts and techniques have been successfully applied in a variety of domains to document, analyze, automate and optimize business processes. Processes with a predefined structure are well supported by today's technology. However, this is not true for processes with a high degree of variability, which are conducted by knowledge workers. As a result, data-driven and goal-oriented business processes with a high degree of variability are not well supported.

Increasing the flexibility of business processes has been one of the main drivers in the development of the BPM field, for instance in areas like flexible process management, process variants, declarative and object-centric approaches [12]. Based on these works, the area of case management centers around the concept of cases and knowledge workers [2]. Case Management is not a new concept, but IT support for knowledge work is still limited to specific domains and implemented in an ad-hoc manner.

Case management received attention in the industry [14], however, only few research publications deal with this topic. According to the literature review of Hauder et al. [6] a "solution that aims to support knowledge workers needs to balance between structured processes for repetitive aspects of knowledge work

© Springer International Publishing Switzerland 2016
M. La Rosa et al. (Eds.): BPM Forum 2016, LNBIP 260, pp. 38–54, 2016.
DOI: 10.1007/978-3-319-45468-9_3

and unstructured processes." While case management is an important approach that complements traditional process management, there is no agreed operational semantics for case management. Therefore, Hauder et al. [6] identify the proposal of a case management theory as one of the key challenges.

In this paper we introduce a case management approach, based on [8] that provides an operational execution semantics for cases. Case models are specified by a number of process fragments, which are structured pieces of work that are dynamically combined during case execution based on data objects and their states. At runtime this results in a multitude of valid execution paths from case instantiation to case termination, suiting the flexible nature of knowledge work.

The rest of this paper is structured as follows. We review related work in Sect. 2. The conceptual framework for case management is presented in Sect. 3, followed by the operational semantics in Sect. 4. We discuss our approach in Sect. 5 and then conclude.

2   Related Work

The case handling approach [2] observes that classical WfMS are too rigid for knowledge workers and relaxes the control-flow of processes. Cases, data objects, and activities are the central concepts of case handling. Activities can write a subset of the case's data objects and while some are optional, other data objects are mandatory to complete the activity. Activities can be skipped, when their mandatory data objects are already defined, e.g. by a previous activity. Similarly to the presented approach, case states in [2] depend not only on control-flow, but also on case data. Their approach is formalized by giving generic lifecycles for activities and data objects, as well as event-condition-action rules that describe the execution semantics.

Artifact- or object-centric approaches to process modeling shift the focus from the control-flow to the data perspective. Data objects are considered first-order citizens in the modeling methodology.

The business artifacts approach [4] considers both data and process aspects and represents key business entities as business artifacts. These artifacts have an attached lifecycle specifying states of interest an artifact can be in as well as permissible state transitions, which are realized by services (corresponding to tasks in workflow approaches). In addition, artifacts have an associated information model specifying their attributes similar to a database schema. In [3] the authors present an artifact-centric design methodology, which involves the steps of artifact identification, lifecycle and information model design, service specification and association, operationalization of the logical specification into so-called conceptual flows, optimization of those flows, and implementation. The specification of services includes input and output artifacts as well as which attributes can be written, pre-conditions and effects (post-conditions) of service execution. The association of services to state transitions of artifacts as well as ordering of services is achieved by event-condition-action (ECA) rules.

Triggering events might be external messages, attribute and lifecycle state changes of artifacts, begin and termination of services, and requests by case workers. The condition is specified as a first-order logic formula, although the authors do not clarify over which domain. Possible actions of rules are the performing of services and state changes of artifacts. In addition, rules include constraints on the performers of the service, e.g. requiring certain capabilities. ECA rules prove a powerful and flexible formalism that can simulate both procedural and declarative modeling styles.

Although the methodology is very elaborated it begs the question of rule maintainability. The ECA rules, which contain the business logic to us seem hard to manage and especially modify. The lack of a visual representation has been amended with the introduction of conceptual flows. However, they use an ad-hoc notation, which is harder to understand than for example the BPMN standard. Additionally, it seems that once the flow is optimized and implemented, the flexibility existing on the BOM level is reduced.

The case management modeling and notation (CMMN) is a OMG specification released in 2014 [11] based on the Guard-Stage-Milestone (GSM) approach. CMMN's case plan models structure cases into several stages that are guarded by sentries waiting for certain events to occur and conditions to be fulfilled to enter the stage. The sentries' formulae determine case behavior, however, they are not part of the graphical model. Stages contain tasks that can be repetitive, mandatory or optional, and performed in arbitrary order as long as they are not dependent on another task to terminate. Data is represented as a single case file with multiple items that can be anything from a XML document to a folder hierarchy. The downside of this generic definition is that case data is treated essentially as a black box, and is not used to make automated decisions in the process. Additionally, the graphical presentation of CMMN models to us seems hard to understand compared to BPMN, although only an user study could support this argument.

Declarative process modeling languages follow a different approach. Instead of explicitly specifying the ordering of activities, they use a set of constraints between activities, like precedence or non-coexistence, to exclude possible behaviors. The language framework DECLARE [1] expresses these constraints as LTL formulae over finite traces which are transformed into finite automata to check their satisfaction. In general, constraints are more flexible, i.e. more execution paths are permitted at runtime, however, constraints might also conflict leaving no valid behavior. Therefore, DECLARE verifies the models for dead activities and conflicting constraints. The authors mention that declarative approaches are not suited for prescriptive, strict processes, and become illegible when many constraints have to be expressed. Additionally, the approach in [13] does not handle process data. However, current research on declarative process modeling [9] includes basic support for task data.

3   A Hybrid Framework for Case Management

As the presented approach combines aspects of object-centric models with BPMN, it exhibits quite a few interrelated concepts. We will first provide an overview of this concepts using a sample scenario before we give their formal definitions and discuss operational semantics.

3.1   Overview of Concepts

In our approach, business scenarios are captured in a *case model* that consists of (a) a domain model, (b) a set of object lifecycles, (c) a set of process fragments, and (d) a goal state. A case model is instantiated into a *case*, which represents the scenario at runtime and hence exhibits the notion of *case state* that changes over time, mainly through knowledge workers performing activities. Cases are similar to process instances in traditional workflow systems, however, contrary to those, cases are made up of several fragment instances, as well as data objects.

As a running example we will consider the organization of universitary seminars. This scenario clearly qualifies as knowledge work, as it is variant-rich, goal-oriented, data-driven, and its course unfold over time. A case is usually started during the semester break by finding a suitable theme and assigning teaching staff responsible for organizing the seminar.

Data and Lifecycles. The *domain model* is part of the case model. It defines the business objects relevant for the scenario as a set of data classes and their associations in an UML diagram. Each data class is a named entity that has a set of attributes, which can assume values from a specified domain. For each data class we can specify a data object creation policy that determines whether data objects are created automatically during case instantiation. One of the data classes is designated the *case class* and as such the root class of any associations. In our example the seminar is the case class, as it holds references to the other data classes. Other relevant domain objects in the scenario are the seminar topics, student enrollments, and teaching staff, as is shown in Fig. 1. As topics should be explicitly suggested by staff members during case execution, no data objects of this type are created during instantiation. For the sake of presentation, we will not consider domain objects like presentations given for and by the students, and papers or software artifacts handed-in by the students.

Each data class in the domain model has an associated object lifecycle (OLC) that specifies valid behavior of its instances, i.e. data objects. Object lifecycles are state transition systems consisting of states and state transitions, as well as initial and final states. Whenever a data object is instantiated, an instance of the associated OLC is created. At runtime, each data object is in exactly one of the states defined by the lifecycle, while different objects of the same class can be in different states. Valid states for a seminar object, i.e. an instance of the data class 'Seminar', are for example in `planing`, `prepared`, or `grades submitted`, as depicted in Fig. 2.

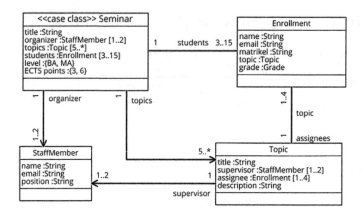

Fig. 1. Domain model for the seminar organization scenario

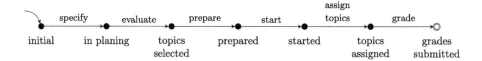

Fig. 2. Lifecycle for data class 'Seminar'

Fragments and Activities. The concept of splitting process models into smaller fragments and combing them dynamically during runtime is the main difference compared to traditional workflow approaches. A process fragment describes a structured part of a business scenario, and thus defines the possible behavior of a case only in unison with the other fragments. Each fragment, just like usual BPMN process models, consists of events, gateways, activities, and data objects[1]. However, our formalization encompasses only a subset of the BPMN specification [10]. Like data classes, fragments have an associated lifecycle that controls the behavior of their instances. Fragment instantiation is controlled by a pre-condition requiring a data object to be in a certain state, and can occur multiple times for the same case, such that multiple instances of the same fragment can be present at the same time and run in parallel.

Our exemplary scenario encompasses several fragments. Fragment `setup`, depicted in Fig. 3, decides on the format of the seminar, asks staff members for topic proposals, and selects among them after the proposal deadline. Fragment `topic proposal`, shown in Fig. 4 can be instantiated multiple times while the seminar is in state `in planing` to create and propose new topics. Due to space limitations the other fragments dealing with student enrollment and assignment, preparation of presentations and student supervision, as well as grading are not depicted in this paper.

---

[1] We need to distinguish between the BPMN modeling construct named data objects used in fragments and the instances of a data class present at runtime. The former represent the latter in the model.

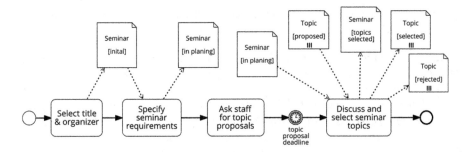

Fig. 3. Fragment for seminar setup

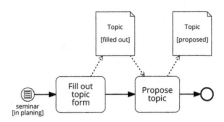

Fig. 4. Fragment for topic proposals

While individual fragments are usually straightforward, their interplay allows for complex behavior. The set of fragments cannot be considered fixed, as case workers might find new ways to deal with certain situations, ways, that were not considered during design of the case model. Therefore, our approach allows to add fragments during runtime. Let us consider that we would like to support cancellation of students. The case worker might add a fragment that specifies how to deal with such a situation.

As usual, activities are the basic units by which work is performed, mainly by creating and manipulating data objects. Activities are only enabled, when their data pre-condition is met, i.e. when a set of specified data objects is in a certain state. Activity instances follow a similar lifecycle like the one defined in [15]. They are instantiated once the fragment they are part of is instantiated.

Termination of a case is defined differently than for workflows, because cases contain multiple fragment instances and data objects. Keeping in mind the goal-orientation of case management, we state that a case is finished, when certain data objects have reached a desired state. In our example the case is terminated, when grades have been submitted to the university. In general, several data objects are involved in the formulation of the termination condition.

3.2 The Domain Model

To formalize our approach we have to formally define the concepts introduced in the last section, i.e. domain model, object life cycle, and fragment. This will be achieved in this section, while the next will instantiate these model-level concepts and discuss the notions of case state and progress.

Definition 1 (Domain Model). *The domain model is a tuple $\mathcal{D} = (DC, AT, D_c, pol, class, dom)$, where $DC := \{D_1, \ldots, D_k\}$ is a set of data classes, $AT := \{\alpha_1, \ldots, \alpha_l\}$ is a set of typed attributes, and $D_c \in DC$ is a mandatory and unique data class, called the* case class. *The function $pol : DC \rightarrow \{true, false\}$ specifies, whether data objects of a data class should be created during case instantiation. The function $class : AT \rightarrow DC$ maps each attribute to exactly one data class it belongs to. The function $dom(\alpha_i) : AT \rightarrow \{Integer, Float, String, Boolean\} \cup DC$ specifies the domain of an attribute, e.g. String or a data class $D_i \in DC$.*

The domain model specifies data classes that represent business entities relevant for the scenario. Basically, a data class is a named set of typed attributes that represents a domain element. Data classes can be associated with each other, however, in this paper we refrain from formalizing associations and multiplicities. Domain models can be expressed as UML class diagrams. The exemplary scenario, shown in Fig. 1, defines data classes 'Seminar', 'Topic', 'Enrollment', and 'StaffMember'.

3.3   Lifecycles

Definition 2 (Lifecycle). *A lifecycle L is a labeled transition system represented by the tuple $(Q, \Sigma, q, \Omega, \rightarrow)$, where Q is a set of states, Σ is a set of actions, $q \in Q$ is the unique initial state, $\Omega \subseteq Q$ is the set of final states, and $\rightarrow \subseteq Q \times \Sigma \times Q$ is the transition relation.*

Lifecycles specify valid states and permissible state transition of model elements. Our framework defines five generic lifecycles L_C, L_F, L_A, L_G and L_E, that are independent of a concrete scenario and used for cases, fragments, activities, gateways, and BPMN events respectively. L_C, the case lifecycle, depicted in Fig. 5, for example determines how case instances behave at runtime. The activity lifecycle L_A, depicted in Fig. 7, governs the behavior of all activity instances. How exactly the interplay of different instances works, is described in Sect. 4 when we discuss the operational semantics of case models. Graphically, lifecycles are represented by the usual notation for state transition systems.

The fragment lifecycle L_F, shown in Fig. 6, is very similar to the case lifecycle, with exception of the `enabled` state, which indicates whether the data precondition of the fragment is fulfilled. Slightly more complicated is the activity lifecycle depicted in Fig. 7. To reach the `enabled` state, activity instances must be both control-flow-enabled (denoted by action `cfe`), and data-flow-enabled (action `dfe`). Because the data objects references by the activities' data preconditions can change their state, an activity instance can be data-flow-disabled (action `dfd`) again. Activity instances can also be skipped in some situations, e.g. when the follow a XOR gateway, by performing the action `skip`.

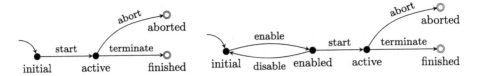

Fig. 5. Lifecycle of a Case   **Fig. 6.** Lifecycle of a Fragment

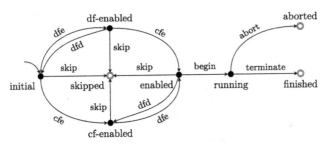

Fig. 7. Lifecycle of an Activity

The gateway lifecycle in Fig. 8 specifies that gateways can be opened, closed, or skipped. Finally, the valid states of BPMN events are defined by the event lifecycle in Fig. 9. Events can either occur directly, e.g. a blank start or an end event, or they are waiting for some external trigger to occur.

In contrast to these generic lifecycles, each data class $D_i \in DC$ in the domain model has its own associated scenario-specific lifecycle $lc(D_i) = L_{D_i}$. The function lc associates lifecycles to elements of the case model, not only to data classes, but also to cases, fragments, activities, gateway, events, and their lifecycles as we will see later. We denote the set of scenario-specific data class lifecycles as L_{DC} for a domain model $\mathcal{D} = (DC, AT, D_c, pol, class, dom)$.

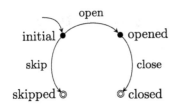

Fig. 8. Lifecycle of a Gateway

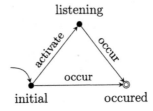

Fig. 9. Lifecycle of an Event

For example, the lifecycle of data class 'Topic' from our introductory scenario is depicted in Fig. 10. For each topic that is prepared in the preparation phase for a seminar, one data object is created as instance of the data class 'Topic'. All these data objects 'topic A', 'topic B', etc. follow the same lifecycle $L_{Topic}, Topic \in DC$. However, different topics might be in different states, e.g. while 'topic A' is proposed, 'topic B' might be already selected.

3.4   Process Fragments

For a domain model $\mathcal{D}$ we define a set $\mathcal{COND}$ of terms called *data object state conditions*. An atomic condition is of the form $D[q]$, where $D \in DC$ is a data class and $q \in Q$ is a state in D's associated lifecycle $lc(D) = (Q, \Sigma, q, \Omega, \rightarrow)$. Any combination of atomic conditions written in disjunctive normal form is also a term $\in \mathcal{COND}$. Data objects state conditions are evaluated in the context of a case state. An examplary data object state condition for our exemplary scenario is `Seminar[in planing]`.

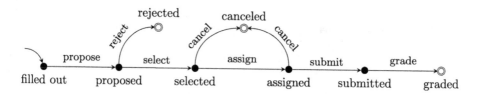

Fig. 10. Lifecycle for data class 'Topic'

Definition 3 (Process Fragment). *Let $\mathcal{G} := \{G_<^\wedge, G_>^\wedge, G_<^\times, G_>^\times\}$ be a set of gateway types, representing AND split, AND join, XOR split, and XOR join. Let $\mathcal{D} = (DC, AT, D_c, pol, class, dom)$ be a domain model as defined in Definition 1.*

Then a process fragment *F is a tuple $(N_A, N_E, N_G, N_D, Cf, Df, \gamma, \delta, \Delta)$, where*

- *N_A, N_E, N_G, N_D are disjunctive sets of activity nodes, event nodes, gateway nodes, and data nodes,*
- *$N = N_A \cup N_E \cup N_G \cup N_D$ is the set of all nodes,*
- *$Cf \subseteq (N \setminus N_D) \times (N \setminus N_D)$ is the control-flow and*
- *$Df \subseteq (N_D \times N_A) \cup (N_A \times N_D)$ is the data-flow relation,*
- *$\delta : N_D \rightarrow \bigcup_{\forall i}(D_i \times Q_i)$ maps each data node to a pair of data class $D_i \in DC$ and one of its states,*
- *$\gamma : N_G \rightarrow \mathcal{G}$ assigns a gateway type to each gateway node,*
- *$\Delta \in \mathcal{COND}$ is the fragment's data pre-condition.*

We use the following usual notions.

- *$°N$ (resp. $N°$) denotes the first (resp. last) element of an ordered set N*
- *$\bullet A := \{B \mid (B, A) \in Cf\}$ denotes the set of A's preceding nodes*
- *$A\bullet := \{B \mid (A, B) \in Cf\}$ denotes the set of A's successive nodes*
- *$\blacksquare A := \{\delta(D) \mid (D, A) \in Df\}$ denotes the data pre-condition of an activity node, consisting of pairs of a data class and one of its lifecycle states.*
- *Similarly, $A\blacksquare$ denotes the data post-conditions of an activity node*
- *$\blacksquare F := \Delta$ is used to refer to the data pre-condition of the fragment F.*

The notion of a *process fragment* formalizes certain aspects of usual BPMN process models, closely following the BPMN specification [10]. However, we focus on the parts relevant for this paper and exclude constructs like pools and lanes, complex gateways, sub-processes, boundary events, as well as message flows.

The BPMN specification provides basic modeling constructs for data modeling, see [10, Section 10.4.1], that are used in fragments to represent data pre- as well as post-conditions of activities. Following [7] we refer to these model elements as *data nodes*. Each data node in the fragment model stands for one data object at runtime that is required for the activity to be enabled (pre-condition) resp. that is produced when the activity terminates (post-condition).

Definition 4 (Well-formed Process Fragment). *A process fragment* $F = (N_A, N_E, N_G, N_D, Cf, Df, \gamma, \delta, \Delta)$ *is called* well-formed, *if the following propositions are true.*

(a) *The first and last nodes regarding the order Cf are unique, i.e.* $|^\circ N| = |N^\circ| = 1$
(b) *The last node is an event node* $N^\circ \in N_E$
(c) *The first node is an activity node* $^\circ N \in N_A$
(d) *Activity and event nodes have exactly one predecessor and one successor,*
   i.e. $\forall X \in (N_A \cup N_E) \setminus (^\circ N \cup N^\circ), |{\bullet}X| = |X{\bullet}| = 1$

As the first and last elements are unique according to (a), we use $^\circ N, N^\circ$ *to refer to the start activity, respectively end event of a fragment. Similarly, because of (d) we overload to notion of* ${\bullet}A$ *and* $A{\bullet}$ *to refer to the unique element rather than the set when talking about activity or event nodes* $X \in N_A \cup N_E$. *According to (c) start events are not part of the formalization. They are used in the graphical presentation of fragments to indicate the data pre-condition of a fragment.*

Now, that all its components are defined, we define the notion of a case model, which captures the essence of a business scenario.

Definition 5 (Case Model). *A case model* $(\mathcal{D}, \mathcal{L}, \mathcal{F}, \mathcal{A}, tc, lc)$ *consists of a domain model* $\mathcal{D}$, *a set of lifecycles* $\mathcal{L} := \{L_C, L_F, L_A, L_G\} \cup \{lc(D_i) = L_{D_i} \mid D_i \in DC\}$, *a set of well-formed process fragments* $\mathcal{F}$, *a set of activities* $\mathcal{A}$, *a termination condition* $tc \in COND$, *and a function* lc *assigning a lifecycle to the other elements.*

4   Operational Semantics of Case Models

This section formally specifies the operational semantics of case models, i.e. their behavior at runtime. To perform a case model it needs to be instantiated into a case that is in an initial state. This is described in Sect. 4.1, while Sect. 4.2 explains how the case state can change according to case progress rules.

4.1   Case State and Instantiation

Cases reside on the instance level and consist of fragment, activity, gateway, and event instances, as well as data objects, i.e. instances of data classes defined in the domain model. Each of these elements is at any time in exactly one lifecycle state and values are assigned to each data object attribute. A case is in flux, new data objects are created, the states of activity instances change, the case finally terminates, however, the case identifier stays the same. Each snapshot in this series is referred to as a *case state*, which is formally defined as follows.

Definition 6 (Case State). *Given a case model $M = (\mathcal{D}, \mathcal{L}, \mathcal{F}, \mathcal{A}, tc, lc)$ multiple cases $c_1, c_2, \ldots$ can be instantiated forming the set of cases $Cases_M$. At any time a case $c \in Cases_M$ is in a certain case state S. A case state S is a tuple (I, in, cs, val), where $I = FI \cup AI \cup GI \cup EI \cup DO$ is a set of instances, partitioned into fragment, activity, gateway, and event instances, as well as data objects, $in \subset (I \times I)$ defines the inclusion among instances and data objects, cs maps instances and data objects, including the case c itself, to their lifecycle states, and $val : (DO \times AT) \to dom(AT)$ assigns values to data object attributes. The (infinite) set of all possible states of instances for a case model M is denoted as $States_M$.*

The inclusion relation *in* gives rise to a directed, acyclic graph called *case graph*. It is rooted in the case identifier $c \in Cases_M$ and specifies which activity instances belong to which fragment instances, as well as which data objects are bound to which activity instance.

New cases can be either manually instantiated by a knowledge worker or automatically when an external event occurs. Instantiation of a case model creates a new case instance, one instance for each fragment, and instances for all activity, gateway, and event nodes in every fragment. The initial state of these instances is determined by their associated lifecycles. For some instances, lifecycle transitions occur during instantiation, e.g. an activity instance belonging to the first activity node of a fragment[2] will be control-flow-enabled by the engine. Activity, gateway, and event instances are in inclusion relation with their respective fragment instance and depending on the data object creation policy of a data class, data objects are created in their initial state.

For our exemplary scenario the initial state is $S_0 = (I_0, in_0, cs_0, val_0)$, where $I_0 = FI_0 \cup AI_0 \cup GI_0 \cup EI_0 \cup DO_0$ and FI_0 contains one instance for the setup fragment (f_1) and one for the topic proposal fragment (f_2). AI_0, GI_0, EI_0 contain instances for all activity, gateway, and event nodes respectively. Those instances are related to their fragment instance via the *in* relation. DO_0 is empty, because data objects of class 'Seminar' and 'Topic' have to be created explicitly during the case according to the data object creation policy. Because DO_0 is empty, there are no attributes to which val_0 could assign values. The state $cs(f_1)$ of

---

[2] When it is clear from the context, we will speak of the first activity, when we mean the activity instance belonging to the first activity. Bear in mind, that cases are on instance level.

the setup fragment instance is *enabled*, while $cs(f_2) = initial$, because the data precondition $\blacksquare F_2 = $ Seminar[in planing] is not fulfilled. The activity instance of "select title & organizer" is enabled, because it is the first activity of a fragment and has no data pre-condition. All other activity instances are either in state `initial` or `df-enabled`, depending on whether they have a data pre-condition.

For cases that are automatically started due to an external event, it would be useful to consider input data for the case derived from the event. To achieve this, data objects would need to be created with attribute values assigned according to the triggering event. However, the mapping of external events to data objects is beyond the scope of the basic formalism.

4.2 Case Progress

Knowledge workers progress a case by performing activities, in addition automatically performed system activities, as well as external events can drive the case's progress. These state changes, called global transitions, are governed by a set of rules that together define the operational semantics of our approach. Because a case c consists of many component instances – fragment, activity, gateway, and event instances, as well as data objects – its state S is compounded of the component instances' states, which are captured by their associated lifecycle and changed through lifecycle transitions. However, these transitions cannot occur on their own in isolation, but only when triggered by a rule due to a global transition. The following definition introduces triggering of lifecycle transitions.

Definition 7 (Lifecycle transitions). *Let $M = (\mathcal{D}, \mathcal{L}, \mathcal{F}, \mathcal{A}, tc, lc)$ be a case model and $S = (I, in, cs, val) \in States_M$ be the state of a case c of M. Let further $i \in I$ be an instance with associated lifecycle $lc(i) = (Q, \Sigma, q, \Omega, \rightarrow)$ in state $cs(i) = q_s$, $q_s \in Q$. We write action(i) to denote the triggering of lifecycle transition $(q_s, action, q_t) \in \rightarrow$. This lifecycle transition results in changing the instance's state from $cs(i) = q_s$ to $cs'(i) = q_t$.*

Take for example fragment instance f in state $cs(f) = active$ and activity instance $a, (a, f) \in in$ in state $cs(a) = running$. Let us assume further that the activity node, a is an instance of, is the final activity node in its fragment. Although the fragment lifecycle L_F allows a transition $(active, terminate, finished)$, this transition is taken only when the end event of that fragment occurs. When the case worker terminates the final activity through the frontend, several lifecycle transitions are executed by the engine. First, the lifecycle state of the terminated activity instance changes. As a result, the succeeding end event performs the lifecycle transition `occur`, which triggers the lifecycle transition `terminate` of the fragment instance. As a result of the global transition the case is in state S' with $cs'(a) = cs'(f) = finished$.

To ease definition of progress rules we define some helper functions. $type : DO \rightarrow DC$ maps data objects to their data class. $node$ maps activity, gateway, and event instances to the node they are instances of. $frag : FI \rightarrow \mathcal{F}$ maps fragment instances to the fragment they are instances of. The notion of pre/post-set of nodes is extended to instances, i.e. $i \in AI, i\bullet = \{x \mid node(x) \in node(i)\bullet \wedge$

$(i, f), (x, f) \in in\}$, analogously for $\bullet i$. Also, data pre/post-conditions of activity nodes are extended to instances, i.e. $a \in AI, a\blacksquare = node(a)\blacksquare$.

Data object state conditions as well as data expressions are evaluated in the context of a case state, yielding either true or false. An atomic condition $D[q] \in COND$ holds true in a state S, if and only if there exists a data object of type D that is in state q, i.e. $\exists d \in DO : type(d) = D \wedge cs(d) = q$. Compound formulae are evaluated according to the usual rules of conjunction and disjunction. Data pre-conditions of activities are evaluated in a similar fashion.

Definition 8 (Fulfilled data pre-conditions). *Let $M = (\mathcal{D}, \mathcal{L}, \mathcal{F}, \mathcal{A}, tc, lc)$ be a case model and $S = (I, in, cs, val) \in States_M$ be the state of a case c of M. Let further $a \in AI$ be an activity instance of activity node $node(a) = A$, and $\blacksquare A = \{(D_1, q_1), \ldots, (D_n, q_n)\}$ be the data pre-condition of A. A subset $B = \{b_1, \ldots, b_n\} \subseteq DO$ fulfills the data pre-conditions of A in state S, if $type(b_i) = D_i$ and $cs(b_i) = q_i$. If $\blacksquare A = \emptyset$ the empty set fulfills the data pre-conditions. B is said to be* unbound, *if $\forall b \in B, \nexists x \in I : (b, x) \in in$.*

An unbound subset of data objects that fulfills the data pre-conditions of an activity instance, can be bound to that instance, once it becomes control-flow-enabled and is started by the user. In our running example, in the case state after terminating activity "select title & organizer" the data object set $\{sem\}$ with $type(sem) = Seminar$ is unbound and fulfills the pre-condition of activity "specify requirements". This leads to the first progress rule.

Rule 1 (Activity Start). *Let $M = (\mathcal{D}, \mathcal{L}, \mathcal{F}, \mathcal{A}, tc, lc)$ be a case model and $S = (I, in, cs, val) \in States_M$ be the state of a case c of M. Let $a \in AI$ be an activity instance in state $cs(a) = enabled$, let $f \in FI$ be a fragment instance with $(a, f) \in in$, and $B \subseteq DO$ be an unbound set of data objects, potentially empty, that fulfills the data pre-conditions of a.*

Then S can make a global transition to $S' = (I', in', cs', val)$ with

(a) $in' = in \cup \{(b_i, a) \mid b_i \in B\}$, i.e. data objects are bound to activity instance a
(b) cs' is defined by the following lifecycle transitions: $begin(a)$ and
(c) If f is not yet active, i.e. $cs(f) = enabled$,
  (i) $start(f)$, i.e. start the fragment instance f
  (ii) $FI' = FI \cup f'$ where f' is a new fragment instance with $frag(f') = frag(f)$, initialized as described in Sect. 4.1

According to Rule 1(c) a fragment instance f stays in state enabled until one of its activity instances begins execution, only then it makes the lifecycle transition $start(f)$. At the same time a new fragment instance f' of fragment F is created in its initial state (although $enable(f')$ will be performed when $\blacksquare f'$ is empty or fulfilled). This allows to create new fragment instances at the moment they are required, ensuring that arbitrarily many instances are available.

Activity Termination with User Input. Running activities can be terminated by knowledge workers when they finished working on that activity, leading to a new global case state. If the activity manipulates data objects, i.e. its data post-set is non-empty, users can enter attribute values for those data objects through a form. This input determines the valuation of the attributes of those data objects. We formalize the input as a valuation function defined for all bound data objects. When an activity terminates, the state of data objects in its data post-set is changed according to the model and all of its successors are triggered.

Rule 2 (Activity Termination). *Let M, S be defined as before. Let $a \in AI$ be an activity instance in state $cs(a) = running$ included in fragment instance $f \in FI$, i.e. $(a, f) \in in$. Let $B = \{b \,|\, (b, a) \in in\}$ be the data objects bound to a and val_{in} be the valuation function provided by the user.*

Then S can make a global transition to $S' = (I, in', cs', val')$ with

(a) cs' is defined by the following lifecycle transitions: $terminate(a)$ and
(i) a's successor is triggered, i.e. if $a\bullet \in AI$ then $cf\text{-}enable(a\bullet)$, if $a\bullet \in GI$ then $open(a\bullet)$, if $a\bullet \in EI$ then $occur(a\bullet)$
(ii) The lifecycle states of all bound data objects $b \in B$ are changed according to the data post-conditions of $node(a)$.
$type(b) = D_i \wedge (D_i, q_t) \in a\blacksquare \wedge (cs(b), action, q_t) \in \rightarrow_i \implies action(b)$
(iii) new data objects d are created in the state $cs'(d) = q_0$,
$DO' = DO \cup \{d \,|\, type(d) = D \wedge (D, q_0) \in a\blacksquare \setminus a\blacksquare\}$
(iv) Attribute value assignment val' is pieced together from the previous valuation val and the user input val_{in}.
(v) $terminate(c)$, if the termination condition is fulfilled
(b) $in' = in \setminus \{(b, a) \,|\, b \in B\}$, i.e. data objects in B are released

Following this rule cases terminate immediately, once their termination condition becomes true. On the other hand, nothing prevents the knowledge worker to continue working on a case that is terminated. The frontend should display that the termination condition is fulfilled and offer the possibility to close the case.

Rule 3 (Event Occurence). *When an event $e \in EI$ occurs in a state S, it triggers its successor $x = e\bullet$, by performing the appropriate lifecycle transition.*
$occur(e) \implies cf\text{-}enable(x), x \in AI \vee open(x), x \in GI \vee occur(x), x \in EI$

Rule 4 (Gateway Behavior). *Let M, S be defined as before and let $g \in GI$ be a gateway instance.*

(a) When a XOR split opens it triggers its successors, i.e. $open(g) \wedge \gamma(g) = G_<^\times \implies cf\text{-}enable(x_i), x_i \in AI \vee open(x_i), x_i \in GI \vee occur(x_i), x_i \in EI$, for all $x_i \in g\bullet$
(b) A XOR split closes and skips all alternatives when one activity begins, i.e. $begin(x_i) \wedge \gamma(g) = G_<^\times \implies close(g) \wedge skip(x_j), x_j \neq x_i$
(c) When AND splits and XOR joins open, they trigger their successors and close, i.e. $open(g) \wedge \gamma(g) \in \{G_<^\wedge, G_>^\times\} \implies close(g) \wedge (cf\text{-}enable(x_i), x_i \in AI \vee open(x_i), x_i \in GI \vee occur(x_i), x_i \in EI)$, for all $x_i \in g\bullet$
(d) An AND join closes when its last predecessor terminates, i.e. $terminate(y_i) \wedge \forall y_j \in \bullet g \setminus \{y_i\} : cs(y_j) = finished \wedge \gamma(g) = G_>^\wedge \implies close(g) \wedge (cf\text{-}enable(x_i), x_i \in AI \vee open(x_i), x_i \in GI \vee occur(x_i), x_i \in EI)$

If there exist paths from a XOR split to a XOR join without activities in between, activities on alternative paths are called optional. Optional activities are enabled, when the XOR split opens, but have to be skipped explicitly.

Rule 5 (Fragment Termination). *If the end event of a fragment instance occurs, that fragment instance terminates.*

$$occur(N^\circ) \wedge (N^\circ, f) \in in \implies terminate(f)$$

Application of the rules to an initial case state S_0 yields the structure of all reachable case states. However, as rule applicability depends on user input and selection of activity bindings, the state space of a case can grow tremendously.

5   Discussion

In this section we explore whether and how our approach eases modeling and execution of flexible processes. The central idea of our approach is to model business scenarios as a set of small fragments and use data object states to combine them at runtime. The alternative would be to express the complex flows that ensue through dynamic fragment combination in one BPMN model. Imagine, the scenario allows to cancel a seminar before the semester started. A BPMN model would necessitate many gateways to allow for cancelation at the right places in the model and hence would become too large to be manageable.

Our fragment approach makes it easy to add fragments and keeps the fragments simple, because fragment combination is based on data objects instead of gateways. This fits naturally for flexible processes in knowledge work, where different courses of action can be expressed by different fragments. One could add a fragment for canceling seminars after they have started, another one for dealing with students who quit their enrollment. While the fragments are much simpler there can be quite many of them and the flows resulting from their combination pose a threat for model comprehension.

Therefore, it is essential for our approach to answer questions about possible flows, e.g. how can I reach a case state satisfying the termination condition. The formalization lays the foundation for this kind of formal analysis of case models. Without the presented operational semantics for cases, analysis techniques would not be able to generate the state space. Thus, the provided formalization is a precondition for verification of cases, e.g. to find deadlocks and reachable states.

Finally, the formal background of our approach helped in implementing a prototypical engine for executing case models [5]. The implementation closely follows the formal definitions by using state machines to control the state of instances and implementing the progress rules.

6   Conclusion

Driven by the deficits of traditional process management technology in supporting knowledge intensive processes, since about a decade there is interest in case management. As discussed in the related work section, several approaches have been presented with different assumptions, notations, and limitations.

In the approach presented in this paper, we have tried to balance the structured parts of cases with the unstructured, flexible ones. We did so by following a hybrid approach in which process fragments expressed in BPMN support the structured part, while enablement conditions based on data objects and their states support the variability aspects.

To validate the approach in general and the operational semantics in particular, they have been prototypically implemented in a software system called Chimera. Initial user tests show the appropriateness of the modeling approach and the effectiveness of the defined execution semantics. However, a thorough empirical analysis involving a formal user study is not in the scope of this paper. On the other hand, this paper provides the technical results of our research which provide the basis for a future empirical evaluation.

References

1. van der Aalst, W.M.P., Pesic, M., Schonenberg, H.: Declarative workflows: balancing between flexibility and support. Comput. Sci. Res. Dev. **23**(2), 99–113 (2009). http://link.springer.com/article/10.1007/s00450-009-0057-9
2. van der Aalst, W.M.P., Weske, M., Grünbauer, D.: Case handling: a new paradigm for business process support. Data Knowl. Eng. **53**(2), 129–162 (2005)
3. Bhattacharya, K., Gerede, C.E., Hull, R., Liu, R., Su, J.: Towards formal analysis of artifact-centric business process models. In: Alonso, G., Dadam, P., Rosemann, M. (eds.) BPM 2007. LNCS, vol. 4714, pp. 288–304. Springer, Heidelberg (2007)
4. Cohn, D., Hull, R.: Business artifacts: a data-centric approach to modeling business operations and processes. IEEE Data Eng. Bull. **32**(3), 3–9 (2009)
5. Haarmann, S., Podlesny, N., Hewelt, M., Meyer, A., Weske, M.: Production case management: a prototypical process engine to execute flexible business processes. In: Proceedings of the BPM Demo Session, pp. 110–114 (2015)
6. Hauder, M., Pigat, S., Matthes, F.: Research challenges in adaptive case management: a literature review. In: Enterprise Distributed Object Computing Conference Workshops and Demonstrations (EDOCW), pp. 98–107. IEEE (2014)
7. Meyer, A.: Data perspective in business process management. Dissertation, Universität Potsdam (2015)
8. Meyer, A., Herzberg, N., Puhlmann, F., Weske, M.: Implementation framework for production case management: modeling and execution. In: Enterprise Distributed Object Computing (EDOC). IEEE (2014)
9. Montali, M., Chesani, F., Mello, P., Maggi, F.M.: Towards data-aware constraints in DECLARE. In: Proceedings of the 28th Annual ACM Symposium on Applied Computing, pp. 1391–1396 (2013)
10. Object Management Group: Business Process Model and Notation (BPMN), Version 2.0.2 (2013). http://www.omg.org/spec/BPMN/2.0.2/
11. Object Management Group: Case Management Model and Notation (CMMN) (2014). http://www.omg.org/spec/CMMN/1.0
12. Reichert, M., Weber, B.: Enabling Flexibility in Process-Aware Information Systems. Springer, Heidelberg (2012)
13. Schonenberg, H., Weber, B., van Dongen, B.F., van der Aalst, W.M.P.: Supporting flexible processes through recommendations based on history. In: Dumas, M., Reichert, M., Shan, M.-C. (eds.) BPM 2008. LNCS, vol. 5240, pp. 51–66. Springer, Heidelberg (2008)

14. Swenson, K.D.: Mastering the Unpredictable - How Adaptive Case Management Will Revolutionize the Way that Knowledge Workers Get Things Done. Meghan-Kiffer Press, Tampa (2010)
15. Weske, M.: Business Process Management, 2nd edn. Springer, Heidelberg (2012). http://link.springer.com/10.1007/978-3-642-28616-2

Software Process Performance Improvement Using Data Provenance and Ontology

Gabriella Castro Barbosa Costa[1(✉)], Cláudia M.L. Werner[1],
and Regina Braga[2]

[1] Systems Engineering and Computer Science Department,
Federal University of Rio de Janeiro COPPE, Rio de Janeiro, RJ, Brazil
{gabriellacbc,werner}@cos.ufrj.br
[2] Computer Science Department, Federal University of Juiz de Fora,
Juiz de Fora, MG, Brazil
regina.braga@ufjf.edu.br

Abstract. Organizations are investing on process definition and improvement in order to enhance their products' quality. In the software processes context, this is not different. A practice to support software processes continuous improvement is to reuse the knowledge acquired in previous process executions. After defining measures to the software processes performance, an analysis of process execution data can be done, in order to detect process enhancement points. One way to capture these process execution data is using data provenance models. Thus, these data can be analyzed, using information derivation mechanisms, such as inference engines for ontologies. This paper aims to describe and evaluate an approach to support software process execution analysis to improve process performance, using data provenance and ontologies. A pilot case study was conducted with software processes used in two software development companies. With this study, implicit information was derived and can be used for improving process performance.

Keywords: Software process · Data provenance · Ontology

1 Introduction

Based on the principle that software product quality is strongly related to the software process quality, organizations have increasingly invested on improving processes definition and management [6].

In order to enable software processes improvement, it is necessary to define processes performance measures. Thus, after defining these measures (such as time, productivity and stress, for example), an analysis of process execution data, necessary for obtaining the previously defined measures, should be done, aiming to detect process improvement points. One way to capture and analyze these data is by using data provenance models and techniques [3].

After collecting provenance data, one possible way to analyze these is by using ontology and inference mechanisms offered by it, enabling the discovery of information that can help to improve the software process.

© Springer International Publishing Switzerland 2016
M. La Rosa et al. (Eds.): BPM Forum 2016, LNBIP 260, pp. 55–71, 2016.
DOI: 10.1007/978-3-319-45468-9_4

Aiming to enhance software process performance in future executions, this paper proposes an approach to support the reuse of experience in previous executions of software processes, using data provenance and ontology.

The remainder of this paper is structured as follows. Section 2 covers the background. The proposed approach is described in Sect. 3 and a pilot case study is presented in Sect. 4. Section 5 discusses related works and, finally, in Sect. 6 conclusions and acknowledgments also presented.

2   Background

Software process can be defined as a set of activities, methods, practices and transformations that people use to develop and maintain software and associated products [16]. This set of activities, methods, practices and transformations can be arranged in a software process lifecycle. In our approach, the lifecycle was adapted to encompass software process enactment, monitoring, analysis and improvement using data provenance and ontology.

Buneman et al. (2001) define data provenance as the description of the origins of a piece of data. Thus, data provenance can be used in the context of software process development in order to provide additional information about it. Then, during the process lifecycle, data provenance can be captured. To capture the origin of process data, it is necessary to capture the process flow specification (prospective provenance) and process execution data (retrospective provenance) [5] in order to have the information regarding the success, failure, delays and errors, during process execution. Provenance models, such as PROV [14], can be used to provide a standard model to capture and store these process execution data. The goal of PROV provenance model is to enable the publication and interchange of provenance information in heterogeneous environments. This model has three vertices to represent *entities*, *activities* and *agents* and also causal relationships between them, such as *wasGeneratedBy*, *used*, *wasInformedBy*, *wasStartedBy*, *wasEndedBy*, *wasInvalidatedBy*, *wasDerivedFrom*, *wasAttributedTo*, *wasAssociatedWith*, *actedOnBehalfOf*, *alternateOf*, *specializationOf*, *hadMember*.

In our approach, data provenance is used with ontology in order to derive implicit information. An ontology defines a formal and explicit specification of a shared conceptualization. It allows capturing the common understanding of objects and their relationships in a particular domain [7]. The PROV model also offers an ontology called PROV-O [11] to represent the PROV Data Model using the Web Ontology Language (OWL2). It provides a set of classes, properties and restrictions to represent provenance information. Furthermore, OWL2 is based on logic specification, then, it is possible to use inference mechanisms in this language. With this mechanism we can derive new information and relationships that were previously implicit. Thus, process data provenance captured using PROV can be analyzed by using ontology and inference mechanisms offered by it, enabling the discovery of implicit information.

3   Approach Overview

The systematic approach to software process enactment, monitoring and analysis improvement using data provenance and ontology is divided into four distinct layers (Fig. 1): (1) **Client Layer**: It is the interface between process members and the approach; this layer is a web application, developed using JavaJSF and PrimeFace and allows for users interaction and visualization of all process lifecycle. This layer also comprises a manager layer, to provide information only to process managers; (2) **Integration Layer**: Integrates the Client Layer to all other layers of the approach, allowing the exchange of data/information between them; (3) **Measure Layer**: Is responsible for storing and capturing the measures related to the process to be executed and (4) **Provenance Layer**: Prospective and retrospective data provenance are captured during process lifecycle and imported to this layer, which has a database based on PROV specification for process provenance data. Also in this layer, process provenance data are imported into an ontology in order to make inferences using these data. This layer can also be called PROV-Process [4].

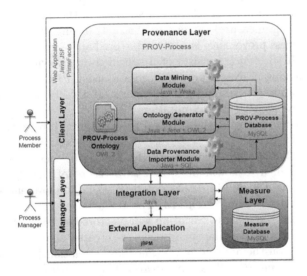

Fig. 1. Approach architecture. (Color figure online)

This approach also uses an external application called jBPM [19]. It is a free Business Process Management System (BPMS) with an extensible workflow engine that allows processes execution using BPMN 2.0 [15][1].

---

[1] It should be noted that SPEM 2.0 (Software and Systems Process Engineering Meta-Model) [20] has great potential for software process modeling, however, it does not provide concepts to address process simulation, execution, monitoring and analysis.

The process to use the proposed approach has four distinct phases: (1) **Process Measurement Definition**; (2) **Process Execution and Monitoring**; (3) **Process Execution Analysis**; and (4) **Process Information Feedback**. The first phase starts after process modeling, using BPMN 2.0 [15], and creation of a new process instance. After defining the process model and process instance, which is stored as prospective provenance, the four phases detailed in sequence can be conducted.

Phase 1: Process Measurement Definition: In this phase, the measures to be collected and stored should be established. The project manager will be able to define measures aligned to the organization's business goals. The definition of new measures is made according to [18] and an example of this definition is shown in Table 1. Routines are incorporated to the process flow model (a web service is incorporated to the process flow in order to capture provenance data) that will enable the capture of information needed for these measures in an automated way (Phase 2).

Phase 2: Process Execution and Monitoring: Process execution was implemented using a BPMS, like jBPM [19]. Then, the capture/storage of measures data can be done in an automated way. In addition to the data required for the establishment of the measures set out in Phase 1, during Phase 2, data from retrospective process provenance is captured, stored and analyzed using PROV-Process approach [4], which consists of a specified architecture for capturing, storing and analyzing processes provenance data, using PROV [14]. PROV was adopted in this approach assuming its elements are closely linked to elements that can be represented by BPMN notation.

The main criteria for using the PROV-Process approach to software process execution data are: (1) All tasks performed in a process specific instance will be stored in the *Activity* table, according to the flow model described in BPMN; (2) The executor of a task will be stored as a record of the *Agent* table, in addition to creating a record in *wasAssociatedWith* table representing the relationship between *Activity* and *Agent*; (3) The artifacts generated and consumed by the tasks during the process execution will be stored as *Entity* table records. The relationships between artifacts and tasks are created in accordance with the action carried out on the artifact at runtime. These relationships can be: *used, wasStartedBy, wasEndedBy, WasGeneratedBy.* The *wasAttributedTo* ratio must be used to establish that an artifact was used by a particular agent; (4) *wasRevisionOf* and *wasDerivedFrom* relationships are captured when new artifacts are created during process execution, if these are revisions of existing artifacts or derived from existing artifacts. The developer, when creating a new artifact, should inform these relationships.

In addition to allowing the storage of provenance data, the PROV-Process approach offers an interface to build an OWL (Ontology Web Language) file with the captured provenance data of a software process using an extension of PROV-O ontology [11], named PROV-Process Ontology. All the captured process provenance data is added to this ontology as individuals. These individ-

Table 1. Process runtime measurement

1	Name:	Process runtime
2	Definition:	Measure used to quantify the duration of process execution
3	Mnemonic:	PR
4	Measure Type:	Base Measure
5	Measured Entity:	Change Request Process
6	Measured Property:	Time
7	Measurement Unit:	Hours
8	Scale Type:	Absolute
9	Values Range:	Positive real numbers, using two decimal places of precision
10	Range Expected Data:	-
11	Calculation Formula:	PR = FT ST, where: FT= final time (date and time of process completion) ST = start time (date and time to when process starts)
12	Measurement Procedure:	Calculate the duration of process execution, using the measurement calculation formula
13	Measurement Moment:	At the start and end of any process execution instance
14	Measurement Frequency:	Whenever initialized and finalized a process execution
15	Measurement Responsible:	Will be held in an automated way
16	Analysis Procedure:	Compare obtained value with other process runtime, using a graph, verifying if the value obtained in this measure has the same behavior as in previous executions. If it does not, the causes of instability need to be investigated
17	Measurement Analysis Moment:	After process execution
18	Frequency Analysis:	After each process execution
19	Analysis Responsible:	Project Manager

uals are represented in the relational database as activities, agents and entities, in addition to the relationships between them, according to the process execution data.

An example of how process provenance data were imported in ontology can be seen in Fig. 2. It shows that the task *Opening_the_Request_for_Change_1* was established as an individual of the *Activity* class and it is associated with the actor *Client_1* (for this, we used the property *wasAssociatedWith* to represent this PROV relationship), since, according to the process execution data of this task, it was performed by the actor *Client_1*. Also related to this task, there were its start time and end time, using the properties *startedAtTime* and *endedAtTime*.

After process execution and collection of process provenance data to calculate process metrics, Phase 3 can be performed.

Phase 3: Process Execution Analysis: This phase comprises reporting to the project manager mechanisms to analyze process execution metrics and provenance data previously captured.

In this phase, the captured metrics can be analyzed through graphs generated with the amounts collected/calculated at runtime, allowing the verification of values and a comparison of these with other implementations of the same process.

Regarding process provenance data, they may be used by a process manager through node-link graphs visualization, generated by the captured retrospective provenance, in order to make decisions about the process evolution. In addition, as a differential of our research, we can mention the derivation of implicit information, which can improve future process executions. This can be accomplished by means of ontology inference mechanisms, using data captured during Phase 2.

Fig. 2. Process provenance data in ontology.

An example of how these mechanisms may be useful for the analysis of performance data is presented in Fig. 3. After running the inference engine on the PROV-Process Ontology, with the respective individuals and relationships created from the process provenance data, we obtained information derived from the established relationships that were not explicit in process data. Figure 3 shows, for example, that activity *Solution_Implementation_11* was done by actor *VB_6* but it was also influenced by *DotNet_5* actor.

Phase 4: Process Information Feedback: After process execution, considering the collection of provenance data and the possibility of analysis, the process manager can observe possible improvements and adjustments to do in the process. Thus, this approach proposes a phase that will allow the process feedback with information that can improve next process executions. Examples of this information may be team members that should work together, or separately, or tasks to be removed from the process, as they have never been executed. Therefore, this provenance data could be used while driving the process

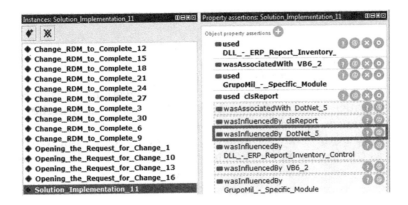

Fig. 3. Inferences in ontology.

and allocation of tasks to actors to optimize the total time of process execution and/or reduce the number of 'cycles' (i.e., repetitions) of the task, concerning the implementation of the solution.

The storage of software process execution data and its provenance into a MySQL database (Phase 2) and these data analysis (Phase 3) can be done automatically, with tool support (all technologies used in this tool are presented in red, in Fig. 1). We are still working in this tool to support phases 1 and 4.

4 Pilot Case Study

A pilot case study considering the application of the approach in two real industry processes was performed, in order to get suggestions/information that could provide feedback to newer executions of the software process promoting its performance improvement. These processes represent an actual implementation of the process in industry and all the processes models created were previously validated by the company. However, due to space limitation, only one of these processes executions is presented in this paper.

The objective of the case study has been: **Analyze process execution data in order to improve its performance with respect to the previously defined metrics from the manager's point of view in the context of software processes.**

Based on the proposed goal, the hypothesis (H1) is: *the storage and further analysis of software process performance data using a data provenance model, with an ontology, is able to provide information to be used to improve the performance of newer instances of this process*, and the null hypothesis (H0) is: *the storage and further analysis of software process performance data using a data provenance model, with an ontology, is NOT able to provide information to be used to improve the performance of newer instances of this process.*

4.1   Planning and Execution

To perform the pilot case study, real industry processes were used. One of them
is a process to manage changes requests in a 19 year old Brazilian software
company that deals with business management software.

Using this pilot study, we sought to **obtain suggestions to reduce the
process instances runtime when this runtime was much higher than
in other instances of the same process.**

For conducting this study, the process specification was done using the BPMN
notation, as can be seen in Fig. 4. After that, the approach phases were conducted.

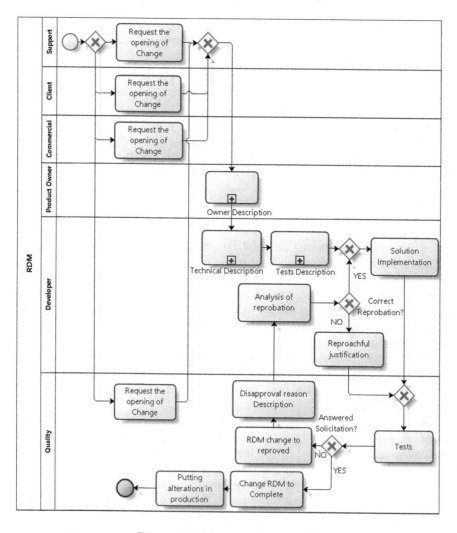

Fig. 4. BPMN process flow model.

Phase 1: Process Measurement Definition: In this phase, three measures to be collected and stored during Phase 2 were established: (1) process runtime, (2) process runtime average, and (3) percentage of process executions that were derived from other executions. Table 1 shows how the first measure was defined, as proposed in [18]. The other two measures follow the same measure definition, with their specific parameters.

Table 2. Example of execution data.

Number	Derived	Opened in		Type	Origin	Team	Closed in	
30006	0	10/03/2013	14:54	Module liberation	Client	VB6	10/03/2013	22:06
30006	1	06/11/2014	17:18	Module liberation	Client	VB6	06/12/2014	10:41
111044	0	01/27/2012	11:14	New resource	Comercial	VB6	01/31/2012	17:52

Phase 2: Process Execution and Monitoring: In this phase, ten process instance executions that had been fully completed were analyzed.

Regarding the obtained data, the following were used: (1) Change request (RDM) number; (2) Information if a process execution was derived from another (3) Date/time of RDM opening; (4) Type of RDM; (5) Responsible for opening the RDM (Origin); (6) Changed modules and components during the deployment task; (7) Team responsible for implementation of the solution; (8) Date/time of RDM completion.

Part of the obtained data can be seen in Table 2, for example. Each row of this table represents a distinct execution of an instance to request and change management. All these data were imported into the relational repository of PROV-Process.

Phase 3: Process Execution Analysis: During this phase, the three measures identified in Phase 1 were analyzed, based on process execution data, which allows checking out values and comparing them with other implementations of the same process. This analysis is described in the following, for each of the three measures:

1. Measure 1: Process Runtime - values obtained for this measure of 10 executed instances are illustrated in the first chart in Fig. 5;
2. Measure 2: Process Runtime Average - values obtained for this measurement, after each of the 10 executed instances, is listed in the second chart of Fig. 5; and
3. Measure 3: Percentage of process execution that was derived from other executions - To obtain this measure, process execution data were analyzed (RDM number and process instance identifier). If any instance of execution has the same RDM number and different process instance identifier, we adopted the instance with the highest value for process instance identifier corresponding to a process execution that was derived from another execution. The data obtained for this measurement, after each of the 10 execution instances, were 50 %, as can be seen in the third chart of Fig. 5.

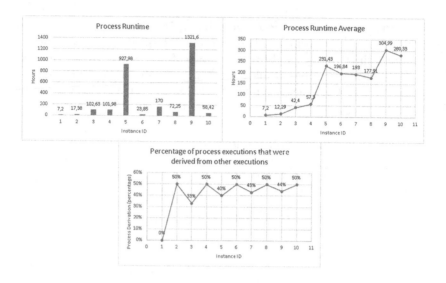

Fig. 5. Process graphs.

Besides the values obtained for the measures defined in Phase 1, through the inference engine used in the ontology (which was populated with individuals created from the process execution data), the discovery of implicit information is possible.

As obtained information from retrospective data coming from this process with the ontology, we can highlight four types: (1) Tasks that influenced the generation of other tasks, i.e., as can be seen in red in Fig. 6: the task *Opening_the_Request_for_Change_1* influenced the task *Opening_the_Request_for_Change_4*; (2) Agents that could be associated to the solution of the deployment task, considering that they already handled the artifacts involved in this task in any other execution of the process. Figure 7 shows that the task *Solution_Implementation_11* was influenced by *DotNet* agent (id = 5), given that this agent handled artifacts common to this task in other instances of this process; (3) A list of all the tasks in which an agent was involved, as well as the artifacts handled by the same; (4) A list of all the tasks in which an artifact was used.

Phase 4: Process Feedback: Based on the measures defined in Phase 1 and obtained in Phase 2, information inferred from the use of ontology and data provenance could help in improving the process performance. As an example, when analyzing the results obtained for measures 1 and 2 (Fig. 5), it is observed that executions 5 and 9 considerably raised the values obtained. Thus, these two instance executions require a further analysis in order to prevent further executions of this process with this high runtime value. When analyzing these two executions using ontology and the inferred data, the following information can provide feedback about the process:

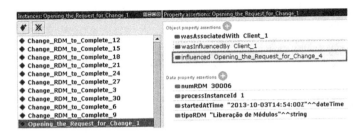

Fig. 6. Tasks that influenced other tasks. (Color figure online)

(1) When assessing tasks and agents involved in instance 5, no relevant information has been inferred, however, when artifacts manipulated during the execution of this process instance were analyzed, it was found that *arApuracaoPisCofins03* and *frelApuracaoPisCofins* were handled only by the task *Solution Implementation* with id = 14 (as can be seen in Figs. 8 and 9). Thus, this information could provide feedback about the process, stating that manipulation of artifacts *arApuracaoPisCofins03* and *frelApuracaoPisCofins* may result in a considerable increase in the process runtime.

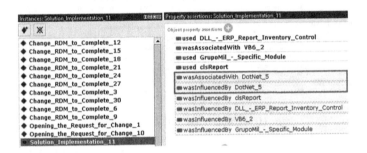

Fig. 7. Agents that influenced a task.

Fig. 8. Artifact *arApuracaoPisCofins03*.

(2) When assessing the *Solution Implementation* task held in instance 9, information that *VB_6 Agent* (id = 2) influenced this task (see Fig. 10) was

Fig. 9. Artifact *fRelApuracaoPisCofins*.

inferred, considering that they already handled the artifacts involved in its execution in some other process, which could perhaps influence the process execution time reduction. Thus, the process could provide feedback using notes next to artifacts with the agents that have already manipulated it. Then, during the execution of a process that starts handling a particular artifact, the executor of the task could include new agents to the solution of that task, since they have used that device in some previous run and therefore could share some knowledge concerning this, which could possibly contribute to the reduction of the task runtime.

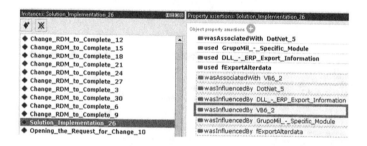

Fig. 10. Agents that influenced a task.

In order to check if the types of information obtained from the application phase of the proposal process are the same ones obtained in other processes, a study of another process was conducted. This process is related to requesting and implementing new features and error handling in an ERP PROJECT of a Brazilian software development company. However, as mentioned before, due to space limitation, it is not presented in this paper.

4.2 Hypothesis Review

When performing the pilot case studies, we could identify four distinct types of information that arise using inference mechanism: (1) Tasks that influenced the generation of other tasks; (2) Agents that might be associated with a task; (3) Tasks in which an agent was involved and artifacts manipulated by him, and (4) Tasks in which a particular artifact was used. Considering these types of information, which were obtained from the proposed approach in conjunction with metrics previously established for the process, there is evidence that it may contribute to the improvement of the process in subsequent runs. Information obtained during the analysis of the process using inference mechanism can be classified into two types: (1) Information related to the artifacts that are manipulated by the process, which helps to considerably increase the runtime of new process instances, and (2) Information related to agents who already manipulated artifacts; thus, during the execution of a process, when a certain artifact is to be handled, the process manager can include new agents to the solution, given that they have used that artifact in some previous run and therefore can share some knowledge concerning it, possibly contributing to the reduction of the task runtime. Therefore, considering the analysis presented above, it is possible to obtain some evidence of the validation of the hypothesis H1. However, additional quantitative and qualitative evaluation studies must be conducted in order to completely validate the proposal.

4.3   Limitations Found

When running the pilot case study with the processes obtained from the organizations, some limitations have been identified: (1) Not all process execution data were informed. Only a worksheet with process execution data was provided, which can interfere with the results shown in Phase 3 of the proposed approach; (2) In the reported process execution data, the information of the actors who, in fact, performed the tasks was not provided. It was only informed the team that carried out certain task.

4.4   Threats to Validity

There are four validity types about the results of an experiment: (1) Completion Validity: Related to the ability to obtain a correct conclusion about the relationship between treatment and the outcome of the experiment; (2) Internal Validity: whether the relationship observed between the treatment and the result is causal, and is not the result of influence of another factor that is not controlled or was not measured; (3) Construction Validity: considers the relationships between theory and observation, i.e. whether treatment reflects the cause and the result reflects the effect and (4) External Validity: defines the conditions that limit the ability to generalize the results an experiment for the industrial practice. In the conducted pilot case study, the following threats to validity can be mentioned:

1. Completion Validity: Both the total number of cases (2) used in this PoC as the number of running instances used for PoC (10 instances of the processes) is not ideal from a statistical point of view. Thus, the results should be considered only as indications.
2. Internal validity: The processes used in organizations have been refurbished using the notation of this work proposal (BPMN), from interviews/meetings with knowledgeable people of this process in the company, but in spite of

the models have been approved by the respective managers of the process. It was not verified if, in fact, the company, the process took place exactly as specified. The fact that organizations did not provide information on the implementation of the processes as a whole but only some tasks is another threat to internal validity.

3. Construction Validity: Despite showing information that can be used to help improve process performance, it was not possible to assess whether, from this information, the manager of the process could, in fact, improve the performance of process, given that were not obtained/performed executions of the process, after the initial analysis of performance data that were provided.

4. External Validity: Using only two processes, it was not possible to represent all possible situations of a software process and the source of information that can be useful after executions of the same to improve their performance. Although the examples presented are realistic, it is still necessary to check that the approach of the objectives will be achieved in other industrial software processes.

5   Related Work

There is no consensus about tools used to software process execution, monitoring, analysis and improvement. Among the analyzed approaches, they either suggest to use a generic tool for process management, such as BPMS (Business Process Management Suite or System) and PSEEs (Process Centered Software Engineering Environment), or adopt proprietary solutions that meet the specific needs of the approach, such as Opsis System [2], GENESIS [1] or PSEE for MDA software processes [12]. GENESIS platform is the only that allows, in fact, the evolution of processes using policy change operations.

Missier et al. (2013) present D-PROV, an extension of PROV model specification, with the aim of representing process structure, i.e., to enable the storage and query using prospective provenance. It shows an example of using D-PROV in the context of scientific workflows. This work was used as basis to capture prospective provenance in our approach, with adaptations to software process.

A technique, called PRiME [13], was proposed to adapt application projects to interact with a provenance layer. The authors specify the steps involved in applying PRiME and analyze its effectiveness through two case studies. Based on this work, Wendel et al. present a solution to failures in software development processes using PRiME [21]. It also uses the Open Provenance Model and SOA architecture.

Junaid et al. propose an approach where a provenance system intercepts the actions of users, processes and stores these actions to provide suggestions on possible future tasks for the workflow project. These suggested tasks are based on the actions of the current user and are calculated based on the stored provenance information. Similar to the related work mentioned above, the proposed approach aims to improve processes based on data provenance. However, our approach is focused on supporting software process execution, monitoring and analysis phases to improve software processes [10].

Gunther et al. use techniques for mining process change logs to obtain information about when and why process changes become necessary and to provide an aggregated overview of all changes that happened so far. Differently from they, our proposal investigates process provenance data using ontology and inference mechanisms, aiming to improve the process based on previously defined metrics [8,9].

The use of ontology reasoning for business activity monitoring has already been investigated in [17]. They proposed a tool, called SENTINEL, based on semantic technologies, which includes ontology for metrics and tools for computation and analysis of these metrics. We also propose the use of ontology, considering that by using inference mechanisms offered by it, we can find implicit information in the software process provenance data, as for example, implicit relations between users and manipulated artifacts in the process. However, we use ontology in conjunction with a data provenance model, in order to capture more relations/information about the software process execution data.

6   Conclusions

This paper presents an approach to use process provenance data and ontology to analyze process data execution in order to improve future process executions. This approach has four phases (1) Definition of process measures; (2) Implementation and monitoring of the process; (3) process execution analysis; and (4) feedback process that can improve process performance.

A pilot case study has been presented, in order to indicate the advantages of the proposed approach. It shows that source data, together with ontologies, can provide implicit information to be used for improving process performance using previously defined metrics. From the conducted study, we obtained information from execution data of two industrial processes, which can be classified in two types: (1) Information related to the artifacts that are manipulated by the process, which helps to decrease runtime of new process instances; and (2) Information related to agents who already manipulated artifacts; thus, during the execution of a process, when a certain artifact is handled, the executor of the task could include new agents to the solution, given that they have used that artifact in some previous run and, therefore, could share some knowledge concerning it, which could possibly contribute to the reduction of the task runtime.

The proposed approach is focused on software development processes and the pilot case study was applied in this area. However, we believe that it can be adapted and used in general processes, but this has not been evaluated yet.

For obtaining information from process, as future work, we have the development of an intelligent agent to assist, in an automated manner, the provision of process feedback information to process improvement. Furthermore, an analysis of new types of information that can be derived from processes provenance data is under development.

Acknowledgments. We would like to thank CEOsoftware and Projetus TI, for kindly sharing their data, and CNPq, for their financial support.

References

1. Aversano, L., Lucia, A.D., Gaeta, M., Ritrovato, P., Stefanucci, S., Villani, M.L.: Managing coordination and cooperation in distributed software processes: the genesis environment. Softw. Process: Improv. Pract. **9**(4), 239–263 (2004)
2. Avrilionis, D., Belkhatir, N., Cunin, P.Y.: A unified framework for software process enactment and improvement. In: Proceedings of International Conference on the Software Process, pp. 102–111 (1996)
3. Buneman, P., Khanna, S., Tan, W.-C.: Why and where: a characterization of data provenance. In: Van den Bussche, J., Vianu, V. (eds.) ICDT 2001. LNCS, vol. 1973, pp. 316–330. Springer, Heidelberg (2000)
4. Dalpra, H.L.O., Costa, G.C.B., Sirqueira, T.F.M., Braga, R.M.M., Campos, F., Werner, C.M.L., David, J.M.N.: Proceedings of the Brazilian Seminar on Ontologies, ONTOBRAS 2015, São Paulo, Brazil, pp. 10–21 (2015)
5. Davidson, S.B., Freire, J.: Provenance and scientific workflows: challenges and opportunities. In: Proceedings of the 2008 ACM SIGMOD International Conference on Management of Data, SIGMOD 2008, pp. 1345–1350. ACM, New York (2008)
6. Fuggetta, A.: Software process: a roadmap. In: Proceedings of the Conference on the Future of Software Engineering, ICSE 2000, pp. 25–34. ACM, New York (2000)
7. Guarino, N.: Proceedings of the 1st International Conference on Formal Ontology in Information Systems, Trento, Italy. IOS Press (1998)
8. Günther, C.W., Rinderle, S., Reichert, M., van der Aalst, W.: Change mining in adaptive process management systems. In: Meersman, R., Tari, Z. (eds.) OTM 2006. LNCS, vol. 4275, pp. 309–326. Springer, Heidelberg (2006)
9. Gunther, C.W., Rinderle-Ma, S., Reichert, M., Aalst, W.M., Recker, J.: Using process mining to learn from process changes in evolutionary systems. Int. J. Bus. Process Integr. Manage. **3**(1), 61–78 (2008)
10. Junaid, M.M., Berger, M., Vitvar, T., Plankensteiner, K., Fahringer, T.: Workflow composition through design suggestions using design-time provenance information. In: IEEE International Conference on E-Science Workshops, pp. 110–117 (2009)
11. Lebo, T., Sahoo, S., McGuinness, D.: PROV-O: The PROV Ontology (2013). http://www.w3.org/TR/2013/REC-prov-o-20130430/
12. Maciel, R.S.P., Silva, B.C.d., Magalhães, P. F., Rosa, N.S.: An integrated approach for model driven process modeling and enactment. In: Brazilian Symposium on Software Engineering, SBES 2009, pp. 104–114 (2009)
13. Miles, S., Groth, P., Munroe, S., Moreau, L.: Prime: a methodology for developing provenance-aware applications. ACM Trans. Softw. Eng. Method. (TOSEM) **20**(3), 8 (2011)
14. Missier, P., Belhajjame, K., Cheney, J.: The W3C prov family of specifications for modelling provenance metadata. In: Proceedings of the 16th International Conference on Extending Database Technology, EDBT 2013, pp. 773–776. ACM, New York (2013)
15. OMG: Business Process Model and Notation (BPMN) Version 2.0. Technical report (2011)
16. Paulk, M.C.: A history of the capability maturity model for software. ASQ Softw. Qual. Prof. **12**(1), 5–19 (2009)
17. Pedrinaci, C., Lambert, D., Wetzstein, B., van Lessen, T., Cekov, L., Dimitrov, M.: SENTINEL: a semantic business process monitoring tool. In: Proceedings of the First International Workshop on Ontology-supported Business Intelligence, New York, USA, pp. 1–12 (2008)

18. Rocha, A.R., Santos, G., Barcellos, M.P.: Software measuring and process statistical control. Science, Technology and Innovation Ministry, Brasília - DF, Brazil (2012) (in Portuguese). http://nemo.inf.ufes.br/files/Livro_Medicao_CEP.pdf
19. Salatino, M.: jBPM Developer Guide. Packt Publishing, Olton (2010)
20. Software Process Engineering Metamodel (SPEM) 2.0 Specification, April 2008. http://www.omg.org/spec/SPEM/2.0/PDF/
21. Wendel, H., Kunde, M., Schreiber, A.: Provenance of software development processes. In: McGuinness, D.L., Michaelis, J.R., Moreau, L. (eds.) IPAW 2010. LNCS, vol. 6378, pp. 59–63. Springer, Heidelberg (2010)

Estimating the Cost for Executing Business Processes in the Cloud

Vincenzo Ferme[✉], Ana Ivanchikj, and Cesare Pautasso

Faculty of Informatics, USI Lugano, Lugano, Switzerland
vincenzo.ferme@usi.ch

Abstract. Managing and running business processes in the Cloud changes how Workflow Management Systems (WfMSs) are deployed. Consequently, when designing such WfMSs, there is a need of determining the sweet spot in the performance vs. resource consumption trade-off. While all Cloud providers agree on the pay-as-you-go resource consumption model, every provider uses a different cost model to gain a competitive edge. In this paper, we present a novel method for estimating the infrastructure costs of running business processes in the Cloud. The method is based on the precise measurement of the resources required to run a mix of business process in the Cloud, while accomplishing expected performance requirements. To showcase the method we use the Bench-Flow framework to run experiments on a widely used open-source WfMS executing custom workload with a varying number of simulated users. The experiments are necessary to reliably measure WfMS's performance and resource consumption, which is then used to estimate the infrastructure costs of executing such workload on four different Cloud providers.

Keywords: Cloud resource cost · Cloud BPM · Business process execution · Performance benchmarking · Workflow management system

1 Introduction and Motivation

According to the recent trend of Cloud Business Process Management [16], users may move the execution of their Business Processes (BPs) to the Cloud, by deploying a Workflow Management System (WfMS) on rented Cloud infrastructure, a Cloud model known as Infrastructure as a Service (IaaS). A WfMS deployed in the Cloud (i.e., a Cloud WfMS) can deliver elastic scalability in response to dynamic workload changes, which is one of the main motivating factors for moving to the Cloud. In the IaaS context, it is not only important to determine the inherent performance of the WfMS executing the BPs, but also to measure and analyse the corresponding resource consumption, so that an expected level of performance can be guaranteed while keeping costs to the minimum. The focus of this paper is not on optimizing the BP execution in the Cloud, which has received its due attention [1,24]. Instead, we focus on analysing Cloud WfMS's performance [21,25] and resource consumption [11]. Both aspects are relevant for estimating the infrastructure costs of running BPs in the Cloud.

M. La Rosa et al. (Eds.): BPM Forum 2016, LNBIP 260, pp. 72–88, 2016.
DOI: 10.1007/978-3-319-45468-9_5

Cloud providers introduce cost models [13] with different sizing of the available resources, granularity of the utilization period, and performance guarantees [15]. In this paper, we present a novel method for estimating Cloud infrastructure costs based on precise measures of the resources (CPU, RAM, Database (DB) Size) consumed to run a mix of realistic BPs with a variable number of simulated users. Such measures are necessary for in-depth analysis of WfMS's efficiency in using Cloud resources and to map how well WfMSs can fit into existing Cloud cost models. To show-case the proposed method, we apply it on workloads executed on Camunda[1], a wide-spread open-source WfMS with numerous customers in different sectors. Previous experiments [25] with three open-source BPMN2.0 WfMSs have indicated Camunda's stable behaviour, both in terms of performance and resource utilization, which makes it a good candidate for Cloud deployment, thus motivating us to use it as the System Under Test (SUT) in this work. Then we map its resource utilization to the expected cost of renting it on four different Cloud providers, i.e., Amazon EC2, Microsoft Azure, Google Cloud and Springs.io, implementing five diverse cost models.

Given the inherent variability of the IaaS Cloud providers' performance [23], we run the experiments in a private Cloud, whose controlled environment makes it possible to guarantee performance measurements' reliability and replicability [9], providing, what can be considered, a baseline for the results obtained in the Cloud. Our assumption is that we have obtained sufficient information for an initial estimation of Cloud costs, and for reducing the set of experiments one would have to perform directly on the best matching Cloud instances.

The remainder of the paper is structured as follows. Sect. 2 explains the proposed Cloud infrastructure cost estimation method, while Sect. 3 defines some useful metrics to be used in the proposed method. Sect. 4 describes the performed experiments in terms of their setup and the experiment environment, while Sect. 5 presents the results from the calculated metrics. Sect. 6 offers an in depth discussion and mapping of those results to the costs of running BPs on the Cloud. Sect. 7 presents related work and Sect. 8 describes the threats to validity of the proposed method. Sect. 9 concludes the paper.

2 Cloud Infrastructure Cost Estimation Method

Before estimating any costs, it is necessary to determine what influences them. In the case of Cloud infrastructure, the direct influence comes from the Cloud providers' pricing policy which uses computing resources (e.g., CPU, RAM) to distinguish among different pricing packages. When executing BPs in a Cloud infrastructure, the necessary resources are determined by: (a) the WfMSs input, i.e., the complexity and size of the executed BPs as well as the number of users and the frequency with which they instantiate the BPs, and (b) the end user's execution performance requirements, e.g., reducing latency or improving throughput might require higher computational resources.

---

[1] https://camunda.org/.

Having this in mind, the cost estimation method we propose is comprised of the following steps: (1) determine the mix of BPs, i.e., the workload mix you plan to execute in the Cloud (Sect. 4.1.1), (2) determine the number of users and the frequency in which they will start the business process instances (BPIs) (Sect. 4.1.2), (3) decide the execution performance requirements you are interested in and how you can measure them (Sect. 3.1, Sect. 4.2.3), (4) run experiments in a stable and noise protected environment using the input determined in steps one and two (Sect. 4.2), (5) analyse experiments' results to determine the resources necessary to achieve the desired performance indicators (Sect. 5), (6) map the necessary resources to the pricing packages of Cloud providers (Sect. 6), (7) select the Cloud providers' offerings that minimise your costs while maximising your resource usage efficiency (Sect. 6), and (8) test and analyse in detail the narrowed selection of IaaS offerings. In the rest of the paper we will show-case the applicability of the proposed method by using BenchFlow, a dedicated performance framework [8], for running a set of realistic experiments on Camunda and mapping the results to a selected set of Cloud IaaS providers.

3 Measurements and Metrics

Performance requirements have to be measurable. Thus, selecting and defining both performance metrics and resource consumption metrics is necessary before applying the method described in Sect. 2. In this section we present a non-exhaustive list of possible metrics to use during the experiments, derived from our experience in benchmarking the performance of BPMN2.0 WfMSs [25]. In order to obtain statistically relevant and reliable results, each experiment is comprised of multiple trials. Thus, the raw data for the metrics are gathered separately for each trial and then aggregated to compute experiment-level metrics.

3.1 Performance Metrics

When testing a WfMS, its performance can be evaluated at the BPI level or at workload mix level. At **BPI level** we obtain as raw data from the DB used by the WfMS, the duration of each BPI execution (D) in milliseconds (ms), which we use to calculate the aggregated metrics among different trials of the experiment. Such metrics include: (1) the *weighted average of the duration* - $wavg(D)$, where the weights are computed based on the number of executed BPIs in each trial; (2) the *minimum, maximum duration* - $min(D), max(D)$ across trials; and (3) the *range of the quartiles of the duration* - $Q1(D), Q2(D), Q3(D)$ which is calculated as the minimum, maximum value of the quartiles among the different trials. The Q1, Q2 and Q3 quartiles show under which value does 25 %, 50 % and 75 % of the data fall [18, Chapter 6].

The performance metrics that we evaluate at **workload mix level** based on raw data from the DB are: (1) the *number of BPIs* - $avg(N)$ executed during the experiment; and (2) the *throughput* - $avg(T)$, i.e., the number of executed

BPIs per second (s). For each of these metrics we calculate the average among
the experiment trials with 95 % confidence interval (ci), as well as the standard
deviation (sd). The ci is used to set up a range of likely values for the analysed
metric in which we can be 95 % confident [18, Chapter 8].

Based on data from Faban[2], one of BenchFlow's components [8], we additionally calculate the *weighted average of the requests sent by the users per second -
wavg(REQ/s)* using the number of requests per trial as weights and the *weighted
average response time - wavg(RT)* to the BP instantiation requests in millisec-
ond, where the weight is based on the number of BP instantiation requests in
the different trials.

3.2   Resource Consumption Metrics

The resource consumption metrics are particularly important for Cloud deployment due to the Cloud providers' pricing models which uses them as billing
base, with CPU, RAM and Disk space being the most frequently used ones [13].
Since BenchFlow [8] uses Docker containers to deploy the WfMS, we obtain
the raw data regarding the resource utilisation from the Docker Stats API[3].
CPU and RAM are continuous variables, thus we calculate the expected value
of their total usage per trial using the *integral over time - avg(itg(CPU))*,
$avg(itg(RAM))$ [18, Chapter 4]. We apply the trapezoidal rule to approximate
the definite integral.

To analyse the WfMS's resource allocation efficiency we use the *weighted
average of the efficiency of CPU and RAM usage - wavg(e(CPU))*,
$wavg(e(RAM))$. The efficiency is computed as the ratio between the $itg(CPU)$,
$itg(RAM)$ and the product of the $max(CPU)$, $max(RAM)$ and the number
of data points used to calculate that integral, respectively for CPU and RAM.
The weighting per trial is based on the mentioned number of data points. This
ratio has values between 0 and 100 %, with values closer to 100 % indicating bal-
anced and thus efficient use of the CPU and RAM without significant changes
over time. We also compute the *weighted average CPU, RAM - wavg(CPU)*,
$wavg(RAM)$ among different trials in percentage (%) for the CPU and in MB
for the RAM. The weights are calculated based on the number of CPU, RAM
data points per trial.

To observe the dynamics of the CPU/RAM change over time we provide
the *maximum CPU, RAM - max(CPU), max(RAM)* metric. Furthermore,
we present the *range of the quartile - Q1(CPU), Q2(CPU), Q3(CPU) and
Q1(RAM), Q2(RAM), Q3(RAM)* calculated as described in the BPI level performance metrics.

The Disk space refers to the occupied space to store the execution data in the DB
of the WfMS. We obtain the raw data from the DB information schema by adding
the space occupied by the data to the space occupied by the DB indexes used by the

---

[2] http://faban.org.
[3] https://docs.docker.com/engine/reference/api/docker_remote_api_v1.22/#
get-container-stats-based-on-resource-usage.

WfMS. This is feasible given that Camunda uses MySQL. We calculate the *average Disk space - $avg(DS)$* among trials with 95 % *ci* and *sd*.

4   Experiments Definition

Setting up a performance experiment requires defining: (1) the workload, i.e., the necessary input to the WfMS, and (2) the execution environment of the experiments, i.e., the private Cloud infrastructure and the minimal resources required to execute the workload [9]. This means defining the factors that influence the resource consumption, and the infrastructure costs as mentioned in Sect. 2.

4.1   Workload Definition

The parameters of the workload (workload mix, load functions, and test data) are generic and applicable to different SUTs. However, their specific characteristics depend on SUT's functionality, as well as the experiments' goals. When the SUT is the WfMS, the workload mix refers to the BP models to be executed in the WfMS during the experiments, the load functions define the frequency of BP instantiation and the distribution of executed control flow paths, while the test data might be necessary to start a BPI or during its execution, depending on the BP model characteristics [9].

4.1.1   The Workload Mix

In practice, it is challenging to obtain BP models from industry due to their confidentiality. Alternatively, using a workload mix comprised of workflow patterns would result in very simple models, while the synthesis of arbitrary models would not result in a realistic workload. Therefore, we decided to reuse models included in the demonstrations and performance benchmarking suites conducted by vendors, in particular Camunda[4] and Activiti[5]. In order to stay focused on the WfMS's performance, we needed to adjust vendor's models by removing data flows and replacing any external interaction elements (such as message events, pools, Web service tasks, user tasks) with control flow elements internal to the BPs. Within the original control flow structure, Web service tasks and user tasks have been replaced with empty script tasks, except for the scripts necessary to randomly determine the execution path following branching gateways. The duration of timer events has been arbitrarily set to one minute. Message flows have been replaced with control flows to isolate the impact of external interaction. In models where messages are used as boundary events, they have been replaced with exclusive or inclusive gateways, depending on whether an interrupting or non-interrupting boundary event had been used. Furthermore, since loops introduce non-deterministic behaviour which can impact the average duration of the

---

[4] https://github.com/camunda/camunda-consulting.
[5] http://www.slideshare.net/alfresco/introduction-to-activiti-bpm.

BPI execution and the resources it uses, we limit, using a counter, the number of iterations to a minimum of zero and a maximum of two.

In real-world usage the WfMS deploys concurrently different BP models with different level of complexity. Thus, we use a workload mix comprised of five realistic models with different complexity and different set of used BPMN 2.0 constructs. The smallest BP model is presented in Fig. 1, while all the executable models part of the workload mix are available at http://benchflow.inf.usi.ch/bpm2016 for reproducibility purposes. All models use what zur Muehlen and Recker [20] call the BPMN Common Core constructs (i.e., normal flow, tasks, start/end event and exclusive gateway), while pools have been deliberately omitted to ensure executability of the models. In addition, some of the models also use sub-processes, loops, timer events, terminate end events, inclusive, and parallel gateways. The smallest BP model has 21 elements (both nodes and edges) as evident in Fig. 1, while the largest one has 84 elements, thus they are coherent with findings of empirical studies on modeling practices [5]. Previous experiments with running only individual models vs. running a mix of individual models have revealed comparable execution results [25], thus we have decided to only run experiments where the five models are uniformly represented in the workflow mix: each model is used to instantiate approximately 20 % of the BPIs.

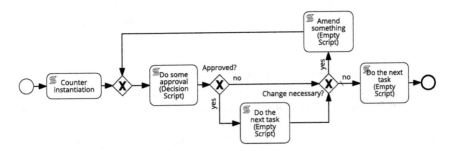

Fig. 1. The smallest business process model in the workload mix

4.1.2   The Load Functions

With WfMS as SUT there are two types of load functions: the load start and the load distribution functions [9]. Due to the unavailability of execution logs for these particular models, in the **load distribution function** we use random load distribution for the diverging paths with equal probability of choosing among alternative paths. The **load start function**, on the other hand, is defined by the load time (or steady state), the ramp-up period, the number of users and the think time. We use 10 min of load time and 30 seconds of ramp-up period. This means that all users become gradually active within 30 seconds, while the BP instantiation requests are being sent for 10 min. The load time decision is based on the fact that some Cloud service providers charge a minimum of 10 min of

Virtual Machine (VM) usage with 1 min increments thereafter. Furthermore, as described by Skouradaki et al. in [25], such a short load time was appropriate to find significant performance bottlenecks, thus making it suitable for realistic tests that provide insight on the WfMS performance behaviour. The actual duration of the experiment depends on the execution time of the started BPIs, and thus might be longer than 10 min. Previous work [8] has shown that changing the number of simulated users impacts the WfMS's performance behaviour. Thus, to reflect realistic usage of WfMSs by differently sized companies or companies which are evaluating their growth strategy, we have decided to simulate 50, 500 and 1'000 users. The think time is the waiting time between a new request the user issues to the SUT, and the time in which the response to the previous request has been received. In this case, the requests refer to instantiation of a new BPI. We use a think time of 1 second, which may or may not reflect real-world workloads, but it serves the purpose of stressing the SUT.

4.2   Experiments Environment

To ensure reliability of the results and more vast exploration of the cost analysis space, automation of the experiments' execution is required. For that purpose we have developed BenchFlow, a dedicated framework for benchmarking WfMSs performance [8], which we use for running the experiments. It automates the configuration and the deployment of the benchmarked WfMSs and its DB. Faban is used to generate the workload.

4.2.1   Execution Environment Configuration

To ensure reproducible initial conditions and minimal interferences, the WfMS, the DB and Faban, are all deployed in Docker images [17] on dedicated servers using the Docker Engine 1.9.1 and Ubuntu 14.04.3 LTS (GNU/Linux 3.13.0-40-generic x86_64) as operating system. They interact through two networks of 10Gbit/s each, one dedicated to the communication between the WfMS and the DB and the other one dedicated to other interactions (e.g., issuing the load). The WfMS and the DB run on exclusively dedicated servers. The WfMS on a server with 64 Cores (2 threads) and a clock speed of 1'400 MHz mounting 128 GB of RAM and a magnetic disk with 15'000 rpm. The DB on a server with 64 Cores (2 threads) and a clock speed of 2'300 MHz mounting 128 GB of RAM and a SSD SATA disk. Faban's Load Drivers are placed on three servers: one with 64 Cores (2 threads) and a clock speed of 2'300 MHz mounting 128 GB of RAM, the second with 48 Cores (2 threads) and a clock speed of 2'000 MHz mounting 128 GB of RAM, and the third with 12 Cores (1 thread) at 800 MHz mounting 64 GB of RAM. With this resource allocation we have ensured and verified that the DB would not become a performance bottleneck during the experiment.

4.2.2   Workflow Management System Configuration

The experiments are run on Camunda 7.4.0. placed in a Docker container with Ubuntu 14.04.01 as operating system and the Oracle Java Server 7u79 VM, run

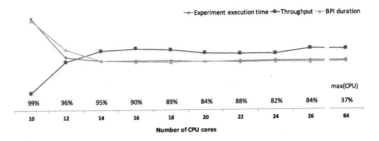

Fig. 2. Normalized performance over number of CPU cores with 500 Users

Table 1. Bounded and Unbounded resource limits

	Users	WfMS CPU	WfMS RAM	DB CPU	DB RAM
B	50	6 Cores	1 GB	6 Cores	2 GB
	100	16 Cores	2 GB	16 Cores	10 GB
	1'000	24 Cores	2 GB	24 Cores	12 GB
U	50, 500, 1'000	64 Cores	128 GB	64 Cores	128 GB

using the host network to avoid performance overhead in the network communication [7]. Standalone deployment is used and the WfMS is configured in accordance with Camunda's web-site suggestions, using Camunda's official Docker image[6]. MySQL Community Server 5.7.10 is used as a DB and is installed on a separate Docker container[7]. WfMS's connection to the DB is through the MySQL Connector/J 5.1.33 with minimum 10 idle connections, maximum 100 connections and an initial thread pool size of 10. The history is set at full level.

4.2.3   Experiments Setup: Resource Allocation Limits

While the experimental testbed provides enough capacity to process the workload, deploying the system in the Cloud requires precise definition of the resources (e.g., CPU, RAM, Disk space) needed by the system to operate under the expected workload and in accordance with the expected performance behaviour. To do so, we first run an **unbounded resource experiment (U)** using the full available capacity (64 CPU cores and 128 GB RAM) for both the WfMS and the DB, for each of the numbers of simulated users (50, 500, 1'000). The purpose is to determine a baseline for WfMS's performance under different workloads without saturating the system, i.e., step three of the proposed cost estimation method: determining the execution performance requirements (Sect. 2).

Since RAM usage was relatively stable during the **U** experiments, we set it to the amount of GB closest (round half to even) to the maximum used during the **U** experiments and then kept it as a fixed variable when searching for the minimum CPU cores required for obtaining a comparable performance to the one

---

[6] https://hub.docker.com/r/camunda/camunda-bpm-platform/.

[7] https://hub.docker.com/_/mysql/.

Table 2. Performance metrics results

Business Process Instance Level Metrics							Workload Mix Level Metrics			
Users	wavg(D) [ms]	min(D) [ms]	max(D) [ms]	Q1(D) [ms]	Q2(D) [ms]	Q3(D) [ms]	avg(N) [bpi]	avg(T) [bpi/s]	(REQ/s)	wavg(RT) [ms]
U 50	8'238.13	0	84'568	[1-1]	[2-2]	[3-3]	30'623±22	44.45±0.13	48.85	22.97
500	9'148.13	0	143'006	[1-1]	[2-2]	[3-3]	272'910±6'024	395.90±8.47	434.14	152.18
1'000	64'023.83	0	888'118	[1-1]	[2-2]	[3-3]	323'783±5'643	329.81±2.73	512.71	946.27
B 50	8'337.41	0	82'855	[1-1]	[2-2]	[3-3]	30'590±43	44.38±0.18	48.84	24.53
500	9'079.07	0	191'536	[1-1]	[2-2]	[3-3]	273'116±3'063	396.21±4.79	435.27	149.21
1'000	65'772.55	0	899'168	[1-1]	[2-2]	[3-3]	328'248±2'268	329.80±3.83	519.14	921.57

with unbounded resources. We run the experiments with the workload described in Sect. 4.1.1 and in Sect. 4.1.2. We start from the minimum required CPU cores, verified from the fact that the system is saturated with peaks of maximum CPU usage which reach 99 % of the available CPU. Then we gradually increment the available CPU Cores and compare the WfMS's performance results as well as the number of requests per second and the response time to the ones from the **U** experiments. We set the bound at the number of CPU Cores at which the performance metrics start to converge towards the **U** experiments performance results, while the maximum CPU usage is no more than 90 % of the available CPU. By doing so we provide a 10 % buffer given the intrinsic variability of the system behaviour and the low, but still present non-determinism of the choices of executed paths in the workflow mix. For space reasons we only show the decision graph (Fig. 2) for the experiments run with 500 users, but the same method has been used with 50 and 1'000 users as well. The selected CPU and RAM limits for the **bounded resource experiment (B)** are presented in Table 1.

5   Experiments Results and Discussion

Each of the experiments described in Sect. 4 is comprised of three trials. In each trial, to consider only the steady state of the WfMS, we discard all data for the first five BPIs of each model in the mix, since they have higher duration caused by the warming up of the SUT. We report the results of the experiments in Table 2 (performance metrics of Sect. 3.1) and Table 3 (resource consumption metrics of Sect. 3.2). Results related to the resource utilization efficiency are reported in Table 4. As evident from the tables, the method for identifying the resource boundaries for the **B** experiments (see Sect. 4.2.3), allowed us to obtain comparable performance between the **B** and the **U** executions. The same applies for the resources utilization. In the **B** experiments we see an increased, but not yet high CPU efficiency utilization, while for the RAM it is comparable to the one experienced in the **U** experiments.

Regarding the WfMS resource utilization, the disk utilization, as expected, grows with the number of executed BPIs, as evident from the $avg(N)$ and the

Table 3. Resource consumption metrics results

	Users	wavg(CPU) [%]	max(CPU) [%]	Q1(CPU) [%]	Q2(CPU) [%]	Q3(CPU) [%]	avg(DS) [MB]
U	50	1.61	23.45	[0.64-0.64]	[1.00-1.10]	[2.46-2.54]	840.08±27.68
	500	10.41	36.81	[0.00-0.01]	[14.13-14.27]	[16.06-16.20]	7'012.21±150.97
	1'000	8.92	38.51	[0.83-0.85]	[3.80-4.45]	[18.01-18.39]	8'505.81±236.15
B	50	9.06	98.73	[5.26-6.94]	[6.33-8.31]	[8.06-11.19]	836.92±14.01
	500	33.00	94.17	[0.07-0.11]	[43.63-45.61]	[49.22-50.16]	7'305.91±164.49
	1'000	21.41	84.29	[2.13-2.20]	[8.82-10.98]	[43.44-44.15]	8'962.10±170.36
		wavg(RAM) [MB]	max(RAM) [MB]	Q1(RAM) [MB]	Q2(RAM) [MB]	Q3(RA) [MB]	sd(avg(DS))
U	50	706.74	823.38	[638.38-652.39]	[672.44-695.44]	[793.72-806.34]	23.97
	500	998.55	1'163.00	[871.87-878.01]	[998.45-1027.59]	[1'120.07-1'131.58]	130.74
	1'000	1'100.73	1'199.59	[1'031.25-1'053.59]	[1'131.85-1'172.45]	[1'132.37-1'173.28]	204.51
B	50	720.07	870.58	[643.66-683.78]	[679.18-716.48]	[759.07-776.83]	12.13
	500	998.97	1'157.24	[876.00-900.38]	[1'000.98-1'011.42]	[1'120.86-1'129.12]	142.45
	1'000	1'100.46	1'189.20	[1'033.29-1'044.38]	[1'150.02-1'165.71]	[1'150.73-1'167.72]	147.53

$avg(DS)$ metrics. The RAM has a more stable utilization than the CPU, as evident from the $Q1, Q2, Q3$ quartiles of the distribution of the weighted average utilization of the two resources. For the RAM the mentioned quartiles are close to the maximum $(max(RAM))$ value. This means that the distribution of RAM usage during the experiment is comparable to the maximum amount needed by Camunda to handle the constant load issued during the experiment. The achieved efficiency of RAM utilization is greater with greater number of users. In Table 4 we also report the efficiency of CPU utilization. It ranges from 10.41 to 36.31 over the **B** experiments, largely far from what can be considered a good efficiency. This is also evident from the CPU quartiles' values, that are distant from the $max(CPU)$ values, meaning that the CPU utilization has spikes leading to a very high maximum utilization, while the average utilization is much lower. This behaviour is more evident with the **B** workload with 50 users, where Camunda experiences spikes of CPU utilization over 98 % while the average value is 10.41 %. High efficiency in resource utilization is very relevant in the Cloud context, since it enables the selection of cheaper resources that are efficiently utilized. CPU spikes are particularly deleterious because they require buying more resources that are not efficiently utilized. We have analysed the CPU utilization during the entire load issued to the WfMS, and we have noticed that the spikes occur when the load starts, and the system is warming up, thus

Table 4. Resource utilisation results

	Users	avg(itg(CPU)) [%*s]	sd(avg(itg(CPU)))	wavg(e(CPU)) [%]	avg(itg(RAM)) [MB*s]	sd(avg(RAM)))	wavg(e(RAM)) [MB]
U	50	1'149.12±14.51	12.56	7.16	508'873.29±4'274.71	3'702.01	86.89
	500	9'397.68±252.41	218.59	29.13	902'479.20±26'337.98	22'809.36	86.81
	1'000	11'343.29±243.09	210.52	23.41	1'400'305.12±35'146.50	30'437.76	92.95
B	50	6'502.40±947.91	820.92	10.41	519'663.08±15'952.49	13'815.26	83.66
	500	29'014.12±549.12	475.56	36.31	878'879.99±7'452.63	6'454.17	86.49
	1'000	26'902.98±128.00	110.85	26.56	1'384'193.35±25'070.42	21'711.62	95.43

needing more resources to execute the requests. The CPU utilization then stabilizes, but still shows some spikes during the entire execution time. Investigating the reasons behind it requires more invasive techniques that go beyond the scope of this paper. However, it is worth mentioning that the experienced spikes, other than the warm up ones, are unexpected given the characteristics of the workload mix, which regardless of some non deterministic choices, is expected to have a constant resource demand under constant load.

Regarding the scalability in the number of users, we can see that Camunda, using the default configuration, experiences a decrease in performance when the number of users increases. This is evident from the $wavg(D)$ metric that increases marginally between 50 and 500 users, and significantly between 500 and 1'000 users. The main reason behind this behaviour is the increase in response time ($wavg(RT)$) that leads to a reduced number of issued start requests per second ($wavg(REQ/s)$). The identified scalability bottleneck clearly does not depend on the unavailability of resources, since as evident from the CPU and RAM quartiles metrics in Table 3, the WfMS had sufficient resources to handle the issued workload. Moreover, we have also verified that the same was true for the DB connected to the WfMS, and that the network was not saturated.

6   Cloud Providers Costs for Various Workloads

Now that we have determined the minimal necessary resources for executing our workload, and analysed Camunda's performance behaviour (see Sect. 5), we can go on with mapping them to Cloud providers' offerings. In the analysed Cloud providers we include what Gartner defines as "leaders" in its 2015 Magic Quadrant for Cloud IaaS report, i.e., Amazon EC2 and Microsoft Azure, as well as the "visionary" Google Cloud, and the newcomer Springs.io. They all use slightly different cost models, offering different flexibility both in renting resources and in the time unit used for billing. The frequently used term "pay-as-you-go" can be misleading on what is actually charged. Amazon[8] and Azure[9] offer "instances" with predefined allocated resources, billed per hour, in the case of Amazon, and per minute, in the case of Azure. Google[10], in addition to the predefined instances, also enables customers to define their custom instance, which although more flexible, is not entirely elastic given that the number of CPUs (or virtualized CPUs) must be even, and the RAM memory per CPU must be between 0.9 GB and 6.5 GB, while being a multiple of 256 MB. Google charges per minute for both types of instances, however, the minimal time that can be charged is set to 10 min. Springs.io[11], on the other hand, charges by hour, but with less limitations on the selected resource bounds. It charges for CPU speed which can be incremented in steps of 50 MHz within the range between

---

[8] https://aws.amazon.com/ec2/pricing/.
[9] https://azure.microsoft.com/en-us/pricing/details/virtual-machines.
[10] https://cloud.google.com/compute/pricing.
[11] http://springs.io/pricing-list/.

500 MHz and 20'000 MHz, while the RAM can be incremented in steps of 128 MB within the range between 256 MB and 32'768 MB.

The mapping of providers' offerings to the resource requirements has been mainly driven by the minimal WfMS's CPU requirements as defined with the bounded resource experiments. This means that the instances presented in Table 5 offer at least the same CPU and RAM as used in the experiment. The prices are on per hour basis, as per provider's official websites[12], for Linux operating system and based on West US region. When multiple instances satisfied the minimal CPU requirement, the most economical one was selected. Since Springs.io uses a concept of simulated core in MHz (core-MHz), core-2 GHz of speed are mapped to 1 CPU Core based on the processor used as per Springs.io's documentation. This translates to a maximum of 10 CPU Cores given its limit in maximum number of MHz available. The limit of 10 CPU Cores is not sufficient computational power for running the workloads with 500 and 1'000 users. Thus, Table 5 only contains Springs.io's cost for 50 simulated users. The stated prices do not include any additional charges for storage or data transfer, since we only focus on the CPU and RAM needed by the WfMS.

Table 5. Selected Cloud Providers' Instances: Resources and Prices[13]

	Cloud Provider	Instance type	CPU	Memory (GB)	Price (USD/hr)
50 Users	Actually used	N/A	5.92 Cores	0.85	N/A
	Amazon (Am)	Compute Optimised - c4.2xlarge	8 Cores	15	0.419
	Azure (Az)	General purpose - basic tier - A4	8 Cores	14	0.376
	Google Predefined (Gp)	High-CPU - n1-highcpu-8	8 Cores	7.2	0.232
	Google Custom (Gc)	N/A	6 Cores	5.4	0.25827
	Springs.io (S)	**N/A**	**12 GHz**	**1**	**0.107**
500 Users	Actually used	N/A	15.07 Cores	1.13	N/A
	Amazon (Am)	Compute Optimised - c4.4xlarge	16 Cores	30	0.838
	Azure (Az)	Compute Optimised - D5 v2	16 Cores	56	1.17
	Google Predefined (Gp)	**High-CPU - n1-highcpu-16**	**16 Cores**	**14.4**	**0.464**
	Google Custom (Gc)	N/A	16 Cores	14.4	0.68872
	Springs.io (S)	N/A	N/A	N/A	N/A
1'000 Users	Actually used	N/A	20.23 Cores	1.16	8.75
	Amazon (Am)	Compute Optimised - c4.8xlarge	36 Cores	60	1.675
	Azure (Az)	Performance optimized compute - G5	32 Cores	448	8.69
	Google Predefined (Gp)	**High-CPU - n1-highcpu-32**	**32 Cores**	**28.8**	**0.928**
	Google Custom (Gc)	N/A	24 Cores	21.6	1.03308
	Springs.io (S)	N/A	N/A	N/A	N/A

Additionally, for each provider we have calculated the CPU usage efficiency as a ratio between the actual used CPU during the experiments, mentioned in Table 5, and the CPU in the provider's instance. As was to be expected for the smallest workload of 50 users, the most flexible provider, Springs.io, offers the best price and the most efficient CPU usage, but it is interesting to see that the

---

[12] The prices in Table 5 are from March 2016 and are subject to change.

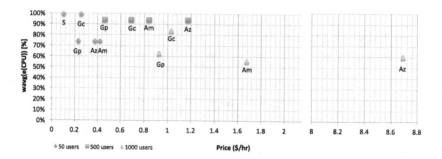

Fig. 3. Usage efficiency vs cloud provider costs per workload

custom instances of Google, which offer greater CPU usage efficiency, are less expensive than the predefined instances of Amazon and Azure. The CPU usage efficiency shown in Fig. 3 in relation to the Cloud provider costs for different workload sizes, is also an indicator of how flexible the existing Cloud offerings are. It is evident that for big workload with 1'000 concurrent users, only with the Google custom instance the CPU is used efficiently, since the predefined instances are not flexible enough and do not offer any instances which have between 16 and 32 CPU Cores. As the size of the workload doubles from 500 to 1'000 users, so does the price of the best offer for the minimal required instances. On the other hand, when going from 50 to 500 users, i.e., a ten-fold workload increase, the price becomes three times higher. Thus, the increase in the best offered price, marked in bold in Table 5, is not linear to the increase in the number of users while keeping the workload mix fixed. The most significant spread of costs is noticeable for the largest workload where Azure only offers one type of instance, which is over eight times more expensive than competitors' offerings due to the high RAM and Disk space available, which are actually not needed for the executed workload. For the 500 users workload, although the CPU usage efficiency is equal among all the providers since they all offer instances with 16 CPU Cores, the ratio between the highest and the lowest price is 1.5 times. In addition to CPU usage differences, from Table 5 it is evident that all analysed Cloud providers, except for Springs.io, are not flexible with the available amount of RAM, which for all workloads is much higher than the actually needed one. If Springs.io increases the CPU it offers, it might be the case that its cost model would be the most convenient one in the future, both in terms of resource usage efficiency and in terms of costs.

Although the duration of our experiments is less than one hour and the hardware is different from what is offered by Cloud providers, we expect similar trends of CPU, RAM usage for longer running experiments in the Cloud. Thus, we find the price per hour in relation to the efficiency of CPU usage calculated based on the experiments, an appropriate indicator for selecting the most suitable Cloud providers for further analysis directly on the selected providers.

7   Related Work

Cloud BPM - In the context of Cloud BPM, users pay for the sustained usage of the Cloud BPM solution, or for renting the IaaS on which they install the WfMS of interest. All Business Activity Monitoring (BAM) measures related to "process instance times" [19] have been already applied in the literature to improve the performance of BP and scientific workflows execution in the Cloud, especially for what concerns the performance of service based and/or computationally intensive processes [1,14,24]. Janiesch et al. [6] rely on the BPI execution time information to propose a BPM-aware scaling mechanism to scale the resources available to services connected to the BPI, with the goal of improving the turnaround time of executed BPs. The proposed scaling mechanism monitors Cloud resources (mainly the CPU) and performance/Service Level Agreement (SLA) measures, to optimize the execution of service-based BPs. It is evident from the discussed literature that the recent trends towards Cloud WfMSs [4] have introduced many challenges [2], such as the need of a comprehensive evaluation of WfMS's and BP's performance, to better quantify and evaluate the effectiveness of moving the BP execution to the Cloud. To optimise time and cost savings by moving to the Cloud, Han et al. [12] propose a Hybrid architecture of Cloud BPM, where depending on activity's computational-intensity and data sensitivity, an optimisation algorithm determines the place of its execution, i.e., the Cloud or an on premises server. More recently, Gómez Sáez et al. [11] have started evaluating the cost of running scientific workflows on different Cloud providers using a similar cost model. However, they use a scientific WfMS and a workload comprised of a single workflow and 10 simulated users, while we use a more diverse workload mix and simulate a variable number of users. In addition to latency, we compute more detailed metrics not only concerning the resource consumption, but also the WfMS's performance. Furthermore, we do not go into analysing the different categories of instances offered by the Cloud providers, but limit our analysis to the cheapest instance per provider that would be sufficient to provide a sufficient amount of resources for the given workload.

WfMS Performance Benchmarking - In the performance benchmarking area, we refer to the work on benchmarking as means to improve WfMS's performance, and the work on reporting WfMSs' resource usage metrics. Weikum et al. [10] propose a benchmark for comparing the performance of different commercial WfMSs by measuring their throughput to study the impact of the database component. They also derive some useful lessons learned for better characterization and improvement of the benchmarked WfMSs performance. Roller [22] proposes a comprehensive study on an internally developed WfMS, with focus on WfMS's throughput. The author relies on benchmarking and proposes different optimization and caching techniques to improve system's performance. Most of the remaining related work on WfMS performance benchmarking, refers to performance benchmarking using black box approaches and considers WfMS's throughput and latency as performance metrics. Only few of them present performance metrics in terms of resource consumption for executing BPs [21,25].

Brebner and Liu [3] analyse costs of using Cloud IaaS for a service application. However, they only obtain data on the CPU resource consumption, later used to map the consumption to the cost for different instance types offered by the analysed Cloud providers. Our goal is not comparing the costs of different Cloud providers for an arbitrary application. We target a specific middleware, the WfMS, and investigate the relation between the diverse performance and resource consumption of different workloads and the costs of deploying them on different Clouds. To do so, we rely on performance benchmarking research and technologies to benchmark the performance of the WfMS's core components and their intrinsic resource consumption as a system running processes. We rely on BAM research and technologies, outside and inside the Cloud, to define the relevant metrics for characterizing the performance, the resource consumption, and consequently the cost of the WfMSs which are part of our study.

8   Threats to Validity

Construct Validity - We conduct our experiments on one WfMS in its default configuration, since it is the first one utilized by practitioners to evaluate system's performance, a standalone deployment, a single workload mix and different workloads. In the analysis, we only consider the WfMS resources, but a similar approach can be followed for the corresponding DB. To reduce measurement noise, we perform experiments using lightweight Docker containers that are not deployed in a virtualized environment.

Internal Validity - The experiments we perform are inherently subject to variability in obtained metrics value, due to the many factors impacting the runtime of a software system. We mitigate this variability by performing multiple trials for each of the experiments, and we verify the variance among trials in order to provide reliable measures validated by descriptive statistics.

External Validity - The method we propose for estimating the cost of executing the BPs on the Cloud by precisely measuring the resources needed by the WfMS running them, is limited in generalizability by the performance variability in a public Cloud and the different hardware on the Cloud instances compared to the one we have used. Cloud prices and cost models are frequently changed by competing Cloud providers. This may affect the obtained ranking. We are aware of this limitation, and thus we propose the current method as only the first step towards evaluating the cost of running BPs in the Cloud which reduces the set of experiments to be performed directly on the Cloud.

9   Conclusion and Future Work

In this work we have introduced a novel method for estimating the costs of running BPs in the Cloud. We have applied it by running experiments with different workloads on Camunda, a widely used open-source BPMN 2.0 WfMS.

Considering the CPU and RAM bounds determined with the experiments we have surveyed four Cloud providers for best fitting offers. A lack of flexibility concerning resource size and granularity in the offerings has been noted, especially for the largest workload of 1'000 concurrent users, where predefined Cloud instances are too big, while the offerings with real flexibility in terms of CPU vs. RAM combinations include maximum CPU bounds that are too low.

Due to the extreme variability of public Cloud performance [23] and the difference in hardware of the rented Cloud resources, our approach contributes the necessary first step towards measuring the actual cost of executing BPs in the Cloud, and limiting the number of Cloud instances to be involved in actual experiments in the Cloud. In the near future we aim to perform additional experiments in the identified Cloud instances using Cloud benchmarking techniques [3, 23], so that we can validate our method Moreover, we plan to apply the proposed method to other BPMN 2.0 WfMSs and to different deployment alternatives, in order to observe differences in resource utilization among the WfMSs, which might lead to different Cloud providers being suitable for different WfMSs subject to different workloads. Lastly, we plan to extend the workflow mix to include Web service calls, events and human tasks to provide a more comprehensive evaluation of the resource needed by all WfMS components.

Acknowledgments. This work is partially funded by the Swiss National Science Foundation with the BenchFlow - A Benchmark for Workflow Management Systems (Grant Nr. 145062).

References

1. Alkhanak, E.N., Lee, S.P., Khan, S.U.R.: Cost-aware challenges for workflow scheduling approaches in Cloud computing environments: Taxonomy and opportunities. Future Gener. Comput. Syst. **50**, 3–21 (2015)
2. Baeyens, T.: BPM in the cloud. In: Daniel, F., Wang, J., Weber, B. (eds.) BPM 2013. LNCS, vol. 8094, pp. 10–16. Springer, Heidelberg (2013)
3. Brebner, P., Liu, A.: Modeling cloud cost and performance. In: Proceedings of Cloud Computing and Virtualization Conference (CCV 2010), Singapore (2010)
4. Cantara, M.: The state of the bpm platform cloud market (id: G00209943) (2011). https://www.gartner.com/doc/1520715/state-bpm-platform-cloud-market
5. Chinosi, M., Trombetta, A.: Bpmn: An introduction to the standard. Comput. Stan. Interfaces **34**(1), 124–134 (2012)
6. Euting, S., et al.: Scalable business process execution in the Cloud. In: Proceedings of IC2E 2014, pp. 175–184, March 2014
7. Felter, W., Ferreira, A., Rajamony, R., Rubio, J.: An updated performance comparison of virtual machines and linux containers. Technical report, IBM, July 2014
8. Ferme, V., et al.: A framework for benchmarking BPMN 2.0 workflow management systems. In: Proceedings of BPM 2015, pp. 251–259. Springer (2015)
9. Ferme, V., et al.: A container-centric methodology for benchmarking workflow management systems. In: Proceedings of CLOSER 2016. Springer (2016)
10. Gillmann, M., Mindermann, R., Weikum, G.: Benchmarking and configuration of workflow management systems. In: Scheuermann, P., Etzion, O. (eds.) Cooperative Information Systems. LNCS, vol. 1901, pp. 186–197. Springer, Heidelberg (2000)

11. Gómez Sáez, S., et al.: Performance and cost evaluation for the migration of a scientific workflow infrastructure to the cloud. In: Proceedings of CLOSER 2015, pp. 1–10. SciTePress, May 2015
12. Han, Y.B., Sun, J.Y., Wang, G.L., Li, H.F.: A cloud-based BPM architecture with user-end distribution of non-compute-intensive activities and sensitive data. J. Comput. Sci. Technol. **25**(6), 1157–1167 (2010)
13. Höfer, C., Karagiannis, G.: Cloud computing services: taxonomy and comparison. J. Int. Serv. Appl. **2**(2), 81–94 (2011)
14. Janiesch, C., et al.: Optimizing the performance of automated business processes executed on virtualized infrastructure. In: Proceedings of HICSS, pp. 3818–3826 (2014)
15. Lenk, A., et al.: What are you paying for? performance benchmarking for infrastructure-as-a-service offerings. In: Proceedings of CLOUD 2011, pp. 484–491 (2011)
16. Liu, X., Yuan, D., Zhang, G., Li, W., Cao, D., He, Q., Chen, J., Yang, Y.: The design of Cloud workflow systems. Springer, Heidelberg (2011)
17. Merkel, D.: Docker: Lightweight linux containers for consistent development and deployment. Linux J. **2014**(239), 2 (2014)
18. Montgomery, D.C., Runger, G.C.: Applied Statistics and Probability for Engineers. Wiley, New York (2003)
19. zur Muehlen, M., Shapiro, R.: Business process analytics. In: Handbook on Business Process Management 2, pp. 137–157. Springer (2010)
20. Muehlen, M., Recker, J.: How much language is enough? theoretical and practical use of the business process modeling notation. In: Bellahsène, Z., Léonard, M. (eds.) CAiSE 2008. LNCS, vol. 5074, pp. 465–479. Springer, Heidelberg (2008)
21. Röck, C., et al.: Performance benchmarking of BPEL engines: A comparison framework, status quo evaluation and challenges. In: Proceedings of SEKE, pp. 31–34 (2014)
22. Roller, D.H.: Throughput Improvements for BPEL Engines: Implementation Techniques and Measurements applied in SWoM. Ph.D. thesis, USTUTT (2013)
23. Schad, J., et al.: Runtime measurements in the cloud: observing, analyzing, and reducing variance. Proc. VLDB Endowment **3**(1–2), 460–471 (2010)
24. Baeyens, T.: BPM in the cloud. In: Daniel, F., Wang, J., Weber, B. (eds.) BPM 2013. LNCS, vol. 8094, pp. 10–16. Springer, Heidelberg (2013)
25. Skouradaki, M., Ferme, V., Pautasso, C., Leymann, F., van Hoorn, A.: Micro-benchmarking BPMN 2.0 workflow management systems with workflow patterns. In: Nurcan, S., Soffer, P., Bajec, M., Eder, J. (eds.) CAiSE 2016. LNCS, vol. 9694, pp. 67–82. Springer, Heidelberg (2016). doi:10.1007/978-3-319-39696-5_5

Modeling

Identifying Variability
in Process Performance Indicators

Bedilia Estrada-Torres[✉], Adela del-Río-Ortega,
Manuel Resinas, and Antonio Ruiz-Cortés

Departamento de Lenguajes y Sistemas Informáticos,
Universidad de Sevilla, Av. Reina Mercedes s/n, 41012 Seville, Spain
{iestrada,adeladelrio,resinas,aruiz}@us.es

Abstract. The performance perspective of business processes is concerned with the definition of performance requirements usually specified as a set of Process Performance Indicators (PPIs). Like other business process perspectives such as control-flow or data, there are cases in which PPIs are subject to variability. However, although the modelling of business process variability (BPV) has evolved significantly, there are very few contributions addressing the variability in the performance perspective of business processes. Modelling PPI variants with tools and techniques non-suitable for variability may generate redundant models, thus making it difficult its maintenance and future adaptations, also increasing possibility of errors in its managing. In this paper we present different cases of PPI variability detected as result of the analysis of several processes where BPV is present. Based on an existent metamodel used for defining PPIs over BPs, we propose its formal extension that allows the definition of PPI variability according to the cases identified.

Keywords: Business process variability · Process performance indicators · Variability in PPIs

1 Introduction

A business process (BP) may vary according to its specific context [1,2], due to changes in original process requirements [3], by the evolution of its environment of application [4], to reflect new allocation of responsibilities, new strategic and business goals, or by changes in general inputs of the BP [5]. The modelling of business process variability (BPV) focuses on identifying variable and invariable parts of a BP (e.g., its control-flow, data or resources) with the aim of managing different versions of the same process together [6–8]. Managing BPV promotes reuse and reduce maintenance efforts and costs of change in BPs [9,10].

This work has received funding from the European Commission (FEDER), the Spanish and the Andalusian R&D&I programmes (grants TIN2015-70560-R (BELI), P12–TIC-1867 (COPAS) and P10-TIC-5906 (THEOS)).

© Springer International Publishing Switzerland 2016
M. La Rosa et al. (Eds.): BPM Forum 2016, LNBIP 260, pp. 91–107, 2016.
DOI: 10.1007/978-3-319-45468-9_6

The performance perspective of BPs is concerned with the definition of performance requirements, usually as a set of Process Performance Indicators (PPIs) that address different dimensions like time, cost and quality [11]. PPIs provide valuable insights about the performance of processes and organizations, facilitate decision-making tasks and identify possible improvement areas [12]. Their management is part of the whole BP lifecycle, from the design and definition of PPIs together with BPs, to the configuration and implementation of both of them, the monitoring of PPIs after execution phase during which PPI values were gathered, and finally the evaluation of the values obtained [12].

Consequently, like other BP perspectives such as control-flow or data, there are cases in which PPIs are subject to variability. This variability can be related to variations that take place in other perspectives (e.g., if an activity measured by a PPI does not appear in a certain variant), but it can also be related to variations in PPIs themselves regardless of the other perspectives (e.g., the target value for a PPI in an incident management process may change depending on the criticality of the incident without this involving any changes in the control-flow).

Unfortunately, as far as we are concerned, there are no studies that deal with the modeling of variability in the performance perspective of BPs. This is undesirable because, like with other BP perspectives, the definition and modification of PPI variants can be a repetitive, laborious and error-prone task. In contrast, having an explicit model of the variability of PPIs together with the other perspectives of the BP helps to guarantee consistency and correctness across PPI variants and can reduce maintenance efforts and costs of change.

In this paper we analyse how variability affects the performance perspective of BPs from the definition of PPIs. To this end, processes to manage incidents in the *Andalusian Health Service (SAS)* and *SCOR processes* have been analysed to identify how PPIs change depending on the variability in the BP and by changes in the requirements for specifying its own attributes. As a result, we come up with several dimensions in which PPIs and their attributes (like measure definitions) can vary. Based on this analysis, we extend the PPINOT Metamodel [12], a metamodel for the definition of PPIs over BPs, to model the variability on PPIs together with the other perspectives of the BP. Furthermore, we define the syntactic validity of this variable PPIs model and we formalize how to obtain the PPI model for each business process variant (PV).

The remainder of this paper is structured as follows. Section 2 introduces background information about variability in BPs and PPIs. The motivating scenario of this approach is presented in Sect. 3. Section 4 identifies dimensions of change to explain how variability affects PPI definitions, and those are related to a real case in Sect. 5. Section 6 shows the PPINOT Metamodel and its extension to manage variability in PPIs. Finally, Sect. 7 draws conclusions and outlines our future work.

2   Related Work

This paper addresses three main areas: (i) the variability in business processes, (ii) PPIs, and (iii) the variability in performance indicators. Below we describe related work on those areas.

2.1   Variability in Business Process

Business processes may exist as a collection of different variants [9,13,14] that share a common base structure and some strategic and business goals. When this variability is not explicitly managed, each variation in the process is modelled as an independent process of each other. This ensures the representation of all information, but depending on the amount of PVs to be defined, a long amount of models could be generated, introducing redundancy and making future adaptations difficult. The lack of control over these multiple PVs usually causes each variant takes more time to be designed, configured and modified. It also may introduce errors from the definition of variants to the evaluation of its performance [2,6].

To solve this issue, many approaches to manage the variability in BPs have been proposed. Most of them focus on the *design and analysis* phase of the BP lifecycle [4], wherein new *Business Process Modeling Languages (BPML)* or expansion for existing ones are proposed. These languages are aimed at avoiding redundancy through *reuse* of some parts of BP flow, identifying common parts of the flow and modeling a BP block only once [15]. This favors reducing duplicated information, thus decreasing design-time and maintenance-time of models [16]. Provop [1,17], C-EPC [18], C-iEPC [8] and BPFM [14] are some examples of proposals for managing variability.

Although, most related work about BPV is focused on variability of control-flow [1,17,19], there are proposals that address variability in data or resources [8,19]. However, as far as we are concerned, there are no studies on the variability in the performance perspective of BPs.

2.2   Process Performance Indicators (PPIs)

A *Process Performance Indicator (PPI)* can be defined as a quantifiable metric focused on evaluating the performance of a BP in terms of efficiency and effectiveness. They are measured directly by data generated within the process flow and are used for process controlling and continuous optimization [20]. These PPIs are managed together with the BP lifecycle [12]. In design and analysis phase, PPIs are modelled together with the BP. During the configuration phase, the instrumentation of the processes that are necessary to take the measures must be defined. During BP enactment, PPIs should be monitored taking into account the PPI values obtained from execution data. Finally, during the evaluation, monitoring information obtained in the enactment phase will help to identify correlations and predict future behaviors.

Different approaches have been proposed for measuring the performance of BPs using PPIs. Some of them include domain-specific languages, metamodels, rules, techniques and notations, to address different phases in the PPI lifecycle. *MetricM* [21] and *PPINOT* [12] are examples of these approaches.

Regardless of the notation used, a *PPI* is defined by means of a set of attributes that specifies relevant aspects to establish what and how to measure [12,22]. The most relevant and recurrent attributes, besides the attributes required to identify the PPI (name, id, description, etc.) are: a *Process* in which the *PPI* is defined, a set of *Goals* indicating the relevance of the PPI, a *Measure definition* that specifies how to calculate the *PPI*, *Target* values to be reached indicating the consecution of the previously defined goals, the *Scope* that is used to define the subset of instances to be considered to calculate the *PPI* value, and the *human resources* involved.

2.3   Variability in Performance Indicators

As far as we know, there are no approaches addressing the variability of PPIs. However, in [23] some concepts about variability and indicators are treated. In this paper the variability is managed using design patterns (composite pattern), defining entities to gather goals, categories, indicators for individual, units for sets of indicators or single indicators, associated to different persons o academical units. The model proposed is based on [24], where each entity is modeled by decorator patterns, to add many features and functions dynamically.

However, unlike in our proposal, the authors do not deal with the traceability between PPIs and BPs and how they can vary together. In addition, they do not detail how the variability model is configured for a specific variant. Finally, the variability in KPIs are described just at a high level of abstraction and it is hardly applicable in different scenarios.

3   Motivating Scenario

The *Supply Chain Operation Reference* model (SCOR) [25] is a process reference model for supply chain management. It enables users to address, improve, and communicate supply chain management practices within and between all interested parties in the enterprise. We focus on two elements of its structure: *processes* and *measure definitions* (called *metrics* in *SCOR*).

SCOR processes identify a set of unique activities within a supply chain. These activities are described at a high level of abstraction because implementation of processes requires internal and specific definitions of activities of each organization, which are out of the scope of SCOR. *SCOR measure definitions* are defined as a standard for measuring the process performance.

Due to its structure and the definition of its components, *SCOR processes* have variability. *Deliver process (D)*, for instance, is defined as the processes associated with performing customer-facing order management and order fulfillment activities. It can be implemented in four different ways depending on the selected strategy: *D1-Stocked Product, D2-Make to Order Product, D3-Engineering to Order Product* and *D4-Retail Product*. Each of them is a PV of Deliver. An excerpt of those PVs are shown in Fig. 1. They have a set of common tasks among them, but also have differences depending on the strategy selected. PV-2 varies in 13 % with regard to activities defined for PV-1 (PV-1 has 15 activities), PV-3 and PV-4 differ in 33 % and 100 % respectively. For simplicity, we only focus on the three first PVs, because *D-4* is totally different from the other PVs.

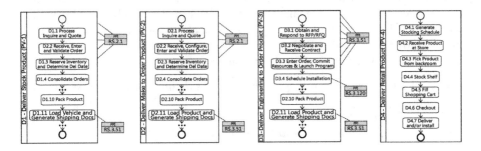

Fig. 1. Four variants of *Deliver* Process

Variability is also reflected in SCOR through its *measure definitions*, due (i) to their dependence on the BP flow in which they are defined or (ii) by specific requirements of the measures defined for each variant. Measures like *RS.3.120 Schedule Installation Cycle Time* reflect the first case. The measure is defined only in a PV, because it is connected to the task *D3.4 Schedule Installation* that only appears in PV-3. The second case is manifested in measures that vary regarding the required components to calculate its value. For example, in PV-1 and PV-2 the *RS.2.1 Source Cycle Time* measure requires 5 different time values from 5 process tasks, while in PV-3 this measure requires 7 different time values.

Currently, although there are BPMLs that allow us to model BPV, there do not exist tools and techniques to model variability in PPIs. In SCOR, for example, Deliver process defines 100, 96 and 96 measures for PV-1, PV-2 and PV-3 respectively, and almost half of them are repeated for all or some PVs. If we want to model them, it would be necessary to model independently the PPIs of each variant, making it a laborious and time-consuming task. Furthermore, if in the future, a PPI changes, we must modify one by one each variant involved, which does not ensure the PPI integrity through all variants, because we could forget to make some changes. If these errors are not detected, they may be carried throughout the whole lifecycle process leading to new problems like monitoring poorly defined PPIs and collecting inaccurate information that will be used in decision-making, to name a few.

In summary, modeling the variability in PPIs brings similar advantages than modeling the variability in the other perspectives of the BPs. Consequently, PPIs should be defined by means of tools and techniques that allow us to represent variability aspects in the BP performance perspective, taking into consideration all dimensions that affect their variability.

4   Variability in Definitions of PPIs

In order to identify variability in PPIs, we studied several BPV cases and analysed differents model to represent PPIs. First, we modeled the SCOR processes with their PVs. Then, we selected those with more similar activities in the control-flow of their PVs: *Deliver* and *Make*. After, we modeled, compared and classified the measures defined for those PVs in the SCOR model. Finally, we compare all PPI attributes among PVs, to identify cases of variation on PPIs. Similar study was made for PPIs of the SAS processes. As a result, we identified two dimensions of change in PPI definitions, namely:

Dim-1: *A PPI varies depending on whether it is defined for all process variants or not.*

Dim-2: *A PPI varies depending on attributes required to define it, which may change depending on the variant in which it is defined.*

Suppose a BP family that has more than one PV. If a PPI is defined for all those PVs and all its attributes do not change, there is no variability. Instead, if a PPI is defined in only one or some of its PVs, regardless of whether their attributes change or not, we are representing the variability expressed by **Dim-1**.

In addition, a PPI, regardless of the behavior derived from *Dim-1*, may vary depending on the changes applied over the value of one or more of its attributes. In Sect. 2.2 we mentioned a set of attributes that conform a PPI, and here we list some cases where the PPI variability is reflected, considering that a PPI varies if at least one of the following attributes changes:

Target *(T)* changes when the target value to be reached changes. For example, the *Andalusian Health Service* defines a PPI for measuring the percentage of resolved incidents in a period of time and in which its target values depend on the priority established for the measured service. If priority is very high, the target value is very high (resolved incidents $>= 95\%$); if priority is high, the target value changes (resolved incidents $>= 90\%$) and if priority is normal, the target value also changes (resolved incidents $>= 82,5\%$).

Scope *(S)* changes when the set of instances to be evaluated changes. For example, if we have one PV that applies during weekdays and another one that applies in weekends (e.g., due to limited availability of resources available on weekends), we might define two variants of the same PPI, one that evaluates instances that take place on weekdays, and another one that evaluates those that take place on weekends.

Human resources *(HR)* may change by two attributes: **responsible** and **informed**. For example, taking up the previous example, depending on the priority of an incident, the person responsible for the PPI or the person informed about its value might change, e.g., because high priority incidents are resolved by a different team.

Measure definition *(M)* is through which a PPI is calculated. In this case, there are two dimensions of change, one related to the measure definition itself and another one related to the relationship with the BP:

Dim-2.M1: *A measure definition maintains its structure, but may vary depending only on the business process elements to which it is connected.*

Dim-2.M2: *A measure definition changes its structure and may vary depending on the requirements of the process variant.*

Dim-2.M1 might occur when a PPI is connected to a task that is not available for all PV where the PPI is defined, or because the definition requirements change and the PPI is assigned to a different task depending on the PV where the PPI is defined. An application example of **Dim-2.M1** is the PPI defined over the SCOR measure *RS.3.51 - Load Product &Generate Shipping Documentation Cycle Time*, which is defined in the Deliver process over the task 11. In *PV-1* this PPI is computed over the task *D1.11 Load Vehicle &Generate Shipping Documents*, but in *PV-2* and *PV-3* this task is not available (See Fig. 1). For this reason the same PPI is defined over an equivalent task, *(D2.11, D3.11) Load Product &Generate Shipping Docs.*

Dim-2.M2 might occur when a PPI is defined in two PVs (or more) as the sum of some measures, but in PV-1 needs to explicitly use a set of measures that differs from the set of measures defined for PV-2. An example is the *Source Cylce Time* measure definition described in Sect. 3.

5   PPI Variability in Two Case Studies

Considering the dimensions of change introduced in Sect. 4, we have analysed case studies to confirm that variability of PPIs is covered by the dimensions proposed. Tables 1 and 2 summarize and classify according to the dimensions proposed, the variability of two SCOR processes (*Deliver* and *Make*) and on the PPIs to manage incidents in the *SAS processes*, respectively.

Both tables include: a column indicating the *Dimension* of change; on its right, the ✗ mark and ✓ mark indicate whether or not there is variability in that dimension. Numbers under marks indicate sub-dimensions fulfilled in each case. The next column *describes* the dimensions and the last one shows the *number of measures* detected according each pair of possible dimensions.

For *SCOR processes*, six scenarios were identified: the first and the most common, indicates that there is no variability in 69 measures; in the following five, variability is reflected in one dimension or in both. In the last case, variability is reflected in **Dim-2** by both sub-dimensions. In these processes, for **Dim-2**, only sub-dimensions of measures are considered *(M1, M2)*, because *SCOR* does not specify attributes like target, scope or human resources, since these depend on specific requirements of each organization.

Instead, in our second example the variability of other PPI attributes is evidenced. Specifically, values of targets *(T)* or other attributes of the PPI change frequently depending on the priority of the incident (very high, high or normal)

Table 1. Classification of SCOR measures according to dimensions of change.

Dimension	Description	Total
Dim-1 ✗ Dim-2 ✗	- Measure is defined in all process variants - Measure is defined in the same way in all process variants	69
Dim-1 ✗ Dim-2 ✓$_1$	- Measure is defined in all process variants - *Dim-2.M1:* The PPI is connected to different BPElements	8
Dim-1 ✗ Dim-2 ✓$_2$	- Measure is defined in all process variants - *Dim-2.M2:* The PPI is calculated using different values	4
Dim-1 ✓ Dim-2 ✓$_1$	- Measure is defined in some process variants - *Dim-2.M1:* The PPI is connected to different BPElements	8
Dim-1 ✓ Dim-2 ✗	- Measure is defined in some process variants - Measure is equal defined in all PV where the PPI appears	24
Dim-1 ✗ Dim-2 ✓	- Measure is defined in all process variants - *Dim-2.M1, Dim-2.M2:* The PPI is connected to different BP Elements and is calculated using different values	7
Total of measures		*120*

Table 2. Classification of SAS PPIs according to dimensions of change.

Dimension	Description	Total
Dim-1 ✗ Dim-2 ✗	- Does not vary with regard to the PV - *(Dim-2.T)* Target does not vary	9
Dim-1 ✗ Dim-2 ✓	- Does not vary with regard to the PV - *(Dim-2.T)* Target varies depending on the priority value	8
Dim-1 ✗ Dim-2 ✓$_o$	- Does not vary with regard to the PV - *(Dim-2.T)* Target does not vary. Other attributes vary (priority)	1
Total of PPIs		*18*

that is being handled by the process. Table 2 classifies those PPIs in accordance with our dimensions of change.

6   Defining Variability of PPIs in PPINOT

As mentioned in Sect. 2, there are no proposals that allow PPIs to be associated with more than one PV or with various types of measures. To overcome this problem, following the same approach that has been followed in other proposals focused on control-flow such as C-EPC, one can extend an existing model to define PPIs in order to support the dimensions of change identified in the previous section. In this paper, we extend the PPINOT Metamodel[1], which is a

---

[1] More details available at http://www.isa.us.es/ppinot/.

metamodel for the definition of PPIs first introduced in [12]. However, the same ideas can be applied to any other PPI metamodel.

Before introducing our proposal, we define and present a formal definition for the original PPINOT Metamodel. Next, on the base of those definitions, we built a set of definitions that introduces the dimensions of change (Sect. 4).

6.1   The PPINOT Metamodel

PPINOT has been developed on the basis of the *PPINOT Metamodel* [12], which is depicted in Fig. 2. The metamodel allows the definition of a performance model composed of a set of *PPIs*. A PPI is linked with a measure definition and the list of attributes described in Sect. 2.2 can be specified for each PPI. PPINOT allows the definition of a wide variety of measures, namely: *base measures*, which represent a single-instance measure that measures values of time, count, conditions or data; *aggregated measures*, which are defined by aggregating one of the base measures that measures several process instances; and *derived measures*, which represent either a single-instance or a multi-instance measure whose value is obtained by calculating a mathematical function over other measures. The traceability with a BP model is kept by means of *conditions* that link measures with the elements of a BP (i.e., activities, events, data objects). Figure 3 provides more details about elements the of the metamodel.

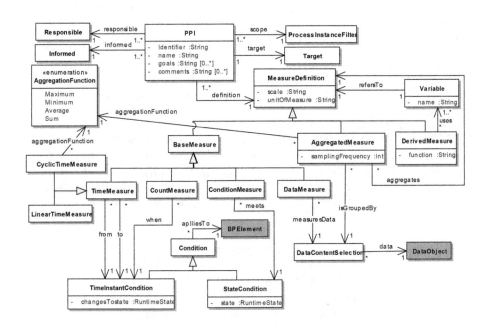

Fig. 2. Excerpt of the *PPINOT Metamodel*

PPI	Containing the measure that defines the PPI. A scope, a target, measures and human resources like responsible and informed, are attributes associated to it.

Measures	Base Measure: It measures each process separately.
	Aggregated Measure: It measures several process instances by aggregating them through an aggregation function: MIN, MAX, AVG, SUM.
	Derived Measure: It performs a mathematical function over several process instances or process measures. *Uses* condition indicates measure values required in the derived function.

Type of measures			
⏱ **Time measure:** measures the duration between two instant conditions. If the time measure is taken between elements located within a loop, the measure may be *linear* or *cyclic*, depending on whether only the first occurrence is considered, or values are aggregated for more than one process instance. Time measure requires a pair of time instant conditions: *from* and *to*, to indicate the *start* and *end* point of the measuring.	⊞ **Count measure:** indicates the number of times that certain instant condition is met. It requires a *time instant condition*: *when*, that indicates the point when something happens and should be measured (start, end and other state).	☑ **Condition measure:** Checks wheather an activity, a pool, a data object or certain events are in a given state (ready, cancelled, completed, etc.) It is related with the BP Elements by a state condition: *meets*, that indicates the condition whose fulfillment is being measured.	🗋 **Data measure:** obtains the value of certain part of a data object. *measureData* selects the part of the data object that is being measured and data stablish the connection with the BP element.

Fig. 3. Description of *PPINOT* elements

In order to formally define a PPINOT performance model, we first need to formalise the concept of *Condition*, which is the link between the performance model and the other elements of the business process.

Definition 1 (Condition). *Let bp be a business process, $\mathcal{A}$ be a not empty set of activities for bp, $\mathcal{S}_\mathcal{A}$ be a set of activity states of $\mathcal{A}$, $\mathcal{D}$ be a finite set of data objects for the bp, $\mathcal{S}_\mathcal{D}$ be a finite set of data object states of $\mathcal{D}$, $\mathcal{A}_\mathcal{D}$ be a nonempty set of data object attributes of $\mathcal{D}$, $\mathcal{E}$ be a non-empty set of events for the bp, $\mathcal{S}_\mathcal{E}$ be a set of event states of $\mathcal{E}$. $\mathcal{C}_{bp} = \mathcal{A} \times \mathcal{S}_\mathcal{A} \cup D \times \mathcal{S}_\mathcal{D} \cup \mathcal{E} \times \mathcal{S}_\mathcal{E}$ is the set of all possible Conditions that can be defined over bp.*

For example, a condition $\mathcal{C} = (D1.1, active)$ represents the moment when activity $D1.1$ becomes *active* in a given running instance.

Now, a PPINOT performance model can be defined as follows.

Definition 2 (PPINOT Performance Model). *Let bp be a business process, $\mathcal{C}_{bp}$ be the set of all possible conditions defined over bp, $\mathcal{S}$ be the set of scopes that can be defined for a PPI, $\mathcal{T}$ be the set of targets that can be defined for a PPI, $\mathcal{HR}$ be the set of human resources that can be related to the PPI, $\mathcal{F}_{agg} = \{MIN, MAX, AVG, SUM, \dots\}$ be a set of aggregation functions. A performance model PM over $\mathcal{S}$, $\mathcal{T}$, $\mathcal{HR}$, $\mathcal{C}_{bp}$ and $\mathcal{F}_{agg}$ is a tuple $PM = (P, M, L_P, L_M)$, where:*

- *P is the set of process performance indicators of a bp;*
- *$M = BM \cup AggM \cup DerM$ is a set of measure definitions, where:*
  - *$BM = TimeM \cup CountM \cup StateM \cup DataM$ is a finite set of base measures, where: $TimeM$, $CountM$, $StateM$, $DataM$, are the set of time, count, state condition and data measures defined by PM, respectively.*
  - *$AggM$ is the set of aggregated measures defined by PM;*
  - *$DerM$ is the set of derived measures defined by PM;*
- *$L_P = sco \cup tar \cup res \cup inf \cup mes$ is the set of links between a PPI $p \in P$ and its attributes, where:*

○ $sco \subseteq P \times S$ is the set of scope links assigned to each PPI;

○ $tar \subseteq P \times T$ is the set of target links assigned to each PPI;

○ $res \subseteq P \times \mathcal{HR}$ is the set of human resource links to indicate the person responsible of the PPI;

○ $inf \subseteq P \times \mathcal{HR}$ is the set of human resource links to indicate the people informed about the PPI;

○ $mes \subseteq P \times M$ is the set of links with the measure that defines each PPI;

● $L_M = cond \cup data \cup agg \cup cyclic \cup uses \cup derfun$ is the set of links between measure definitions and its attributes, where:

○ $cond = from \cup to \cup when \cup meets$ is a set of links among measures and conditions, where:

◇ $from \subseteq TimeM \times C$ is the set of links to time conditions, from;

◇ $to \subseteq TimeM \times C$ is the set of links to time conditions of to type;

◇ $when \subseteq CountM \times C$ is the set of links to time condition, when;

◇ $meets \subseteq StateM \times C$ is the set of links to state conditions, meets;

○ $data \subseteq DataM \times \mathcal{D} \times \mathcal{S_D} \times \mathcal{A_D}$ is the set of links to data conditions;

○ $cyclic \subseteq TimeM \times \mathcal{F}_{agg}$;

○ $agg \subseteq AggM \times (BM \cup DerM) \times \mathcal{F}_{agg}$ is the set of functions to measure a set of process instances when an aggregated measure is used;

○ $uses \subseteq DerM \times M \times \mathbb{N}$ is the set of links between a derived measure and the set of measures involved with it;

○ $derfun \subseteq DerM \times F$ is the set of links between derived measures and its functions, where: F is the set of all possible functions that could be resolved using derived measures;

Given a connector link $lm \in L_M$, $\Pi_M(lm)$ represents the measure involved in lm and $type_M(lm) \in T_M$, where $T_M \in \{from, to, when, meets, cyclic, data, agg, uses, derfun\}$ represents the type of the link. For instance, let $lm = (m_1, c_1) \in from$, $\Pi_M(lm) = m_1$ and $type_M(lm) = from$.

Similarly, given a connector link $lp \in L_P$, $\Pi_P(lp)$ represents the PPI where the attribute has been assigned and $type_P(lp) \in T_P \in \{sco, tar, res, inf, mes\}$ represents the type of the link. We also define $L_P[p, t]$ as the subset of L_P whose PPI is p and whose type is t, i.e., $L_P[p, t] = \{lp \in L_P \mid \Pi_P(lp) = p \wedge type_P(lp) = t\}$. Likewise, $L_M[m, t]$ is the subset of L_M whose measure definition is m and type is t, i.e., $L_M[m, t] = \{lm \in L_M \mid \Pi_M(lm) = m \wedge type_M(lm) = t\}$.

We can now define a syntactically correct PPINOT performance model PM. This is based on the metamodel specification introduced in [12] and displayed in Fig. 2. We mainly specify restrictions about relationships of measuring elements and define link constraints between PPIs and its attributes and between measures and its connectors.

Definition 3 (Syntactically correct PPINOT performance model). *Let* $PM = (P, M, L_P, L_M)$ *be a performance model,* PM *is syntactically correct if it fulfills the following requirements:*

(1) There is at least one PPI p in the performance model $|P| > 0$.

(2) Each PPI attribute can only have exactly one single value linked to the PPI, except for the informed attribute. $\forall p \in P, t \in T_P \setminus \{inf\}(|L_P[p,t]| = 1)$

(3) Measures have at most one link for each possible type of link in L_M except for uses: $\forall m \in M, t \in T_M \setminus \{uses\}(|L_M[m,t]| \leq 1)$

(4) Depending on its type, measures have at least one element of their links:
- $\forall tm \in TimeM(\exists(tm, c_i) \in from \wedge \exists(tm, c_j) \in to)$
- $\forall cm \in CountM(\exists(cm, c) \in when)$
- $\forall sm \in StateM(\exists(sm, c) \in meets)$
- $\forall dm \in DataM(\exists(dm, d, s, a) \in data)$
- $\forall am \in AggM(\exists(am, m) \in agg)$
- $\forall dm \in DerM(\exists(dm, f) \in derfun)$
- $\forall dm \in DerM(\exists(d, m, x) \in uses)$

(5) A derived measure cannot be related to more than one measure with the same identifier: $\forall(d, m_i, x) \in uses \; \neg\exists(d, m_j, y) \in uses \; (x = y \wedge m_i \neq m_j)$

(6) The identifiers used for a derived measure should be sequential, which is ensured if the highest identifier is equal to the number of uses links for such derived measure: $\forall(dm, m_i, x) \in uses(x \leq |L_M[dm, uses]|)$.

(7) For all $(d, f) \in derfun$, $f \in F$ must be a function defined over the Cartesian product of the set of all possible values of the set of measures linked to d $(\{m \in M \mid (d, m, x) \in uses\})$, ordered according to x

6.2   Extending the PPINOT Metamodel

The PPINOT performance model cannot model the variability identified in Sect. 4. To solve it, we introduce a *variable performance model* as an extension of a PPINOT performance model PM where PPIs, measures and connectors for linking measuring elements with bp elements or amongst them vary depending on the process variant to which they are applied. However, we need first to formally define what we understand as a process family and process variant.

Definition 4 (Process family). *A process family $PF = \{bp_1, \ldots, bp_n\}$ is a set of business processes that share some common elements. Each $bp_i \in PF$ is called a process variant.*

This definition do not intend to be complete, but it just focuses on the elements that are relevant for variable performance models.

With this definition of process family, a variable performance model can be defined as follows.

Definition 5 (Variable performance model). *Let $PF = \{bp_1, \ldots, bp_n\}$ be a process family, $\mathcal{PF} = \mathcal{P}(PF) \setminus \emptyset$ be the power set of PF without the empty set, and $\mathcal{C}_{PF} = \mathcal{C}_{bp_1} \cup \ldots \cup \mathcal{C}_{bp_n}$ be the set of possible conditions defined over any process in the process family, a variable performance model is a tuple $PM^V = (P, M, L_P, L_M, P^V, L_P^V, L_M^V)$, where:*

- P, M, L_P, L_M refer to elements of a performance model defined over $\mathcal{C}_{PF}$.
- $P^V : P \to \mathcal{PF}$ defines the process variants to which each PPI applies.
- $L_P^V : L_P \to \mathcal{PF}$ defines the process variants to which each link between a PPI and its attributes applies.
- $L_M^V : L_M \to \mathcal{PF}$ defines the process variants to which each link between measures or between a measure and a process element applies.

Functions P^V, L_P^V and L_M^V introduce the modelling of the variability dimensions described in Sect. 4 as follows:

- P^V allows expressing **Dim-1** by providing a mechanism to specify which are the process variants to which a PPI applies.
- L_P^V allows expressing **Dim-2** by providing a mechanism to specify which are the process variants to which the alternative attributes for a PPI apply. This includes target, scope, human resources and measure definition, which are the links included in L_P
- L_M^V allows expressing **Dim-2.M1** and **Dim-2.M2** by providing a mechanism to specify which are the process variants to which the links between measure definitions and process elements (**Dim-2.M1**) or to which a certain structure of a measure definition (**Dim-2.M2**) apply. The former includes *cond* and *data* links, whereas the latter includes *cyclic*, *agg*, *uses* and *der fun* links.

Note that these variability functions can also be defined intensionally, i.e., by defining properties that all process variants to which a certain model element apply must fulfill (e.g., the presence of a certain activity in the variant).

A function that represents the process variants to which each measure applies (M^V) is not necessary because it can be derived from the variability functions of the PPIs (L_P^V) and measures (L_M^V) linked to it as follows:

$$M^V(m) = \bigcup_{(p_i,m)\in mes} L_P^V(p_i, m) \cup \bigcup_{(m_i,m)\in agg} L_M^V(m_i, m) \cup \bigcup_{(d_i,m,x)\in uses} L_M^V(d_i, m, x)$$

Based on these definitions, the concept of a syntactically correct variable performance model can be defined. In short, a syntactically correct variable performance model adds the necessary requirements to PM^V that ensure that each process variant has a syntactically correct performance model.

Definition 6 (Syntactically correct variable performance model). *Let PF be a process family, $\mathcal{PF} = \mathcal{P}(PF) \setminus \emptyset$ the power set of PF, $\mathcal{C}_{PF} = \mathcal{C}_{bp_1} \cup \ldots \cup \mathcal{C}_{bp_n}$ be the set of possible conditions defined over any process in the process family, $PM^V = (P, M, L_P, L_M, P^V, L_P^V, L_M^V)$ is syntactically correct if it fulfills the following requirements:*

(1) There is at least one PPI for each process variant: $\forall bp_i \in PF(\exists p_i \in P(bp_i \in P^V(p_i))$

(2) *Each PPI attribute can only have exactly one single value linked to a PPI p in each variant in which the PPI applies $P^V(p)$, except for the informed attribute: $\forall p \in P, t \in T_P \setminus \{inf\}(\bigcup_{lp \in L_P[p,t]} L_P^V(lp) = P^V(p) \wedge \forall lp_i, lp_j \in L_P[p,t](lp_i \neq lp_j \Rightarrow L_P^V(lp_i) \cap L_P^V(lp_j) = \emptyset)$*

(3) *Measures have at most one link for each possible type of link in L_M except for uses in each variant: $\forall m \in M, t \in T_M \setminus \{uses\}(\forall lm_i, lm_j \in L_M[m,t](lm_i \neq lm_j \Rightarrow L_M^V(lm_i) \cap L_M^V(lm_j) = \emptyset))$*

(4) *Depending on its type, measures require at least one element of their links in each variant:*

- $\forall tm \in TimeM(\bigcup_{lm \in L_M[tm,from]} L_M^V(lm) = M^V(m) \wedge \bigcup_{lm \in L_M[tm,to]} L_M^V(lm) = M^V(m))$
- $\forall cm \in CountM(\bigcup_{lm \in L_M[cm,when]} L_M^V(lm) = M^V(m))$
- $\forall sm \in StateM(\bigcup_{lm \in L_M[sm,meets]} L_M^V(lm) = M^V(m))$
- $\forall dm \in DataM(\bigcup_{lm \in L_M[dm,data]} L_M^V(lm) = M^V(m))$
- $\forall am \in AggM(\bigcup_{lm \in L_M[am,agg]} L_M^V(lm) = M^V(m))$
- $\forall dm \in DerM(\bigcup_{lm \in L_M[dm,derfun]} L_M^V(lm) = M^V(m))$
- $\forall dm \in DerM(\bigcup_{lm \in L_M[dm,uses]} L_M^V(lm) = M^V(m))$

(5) *Measures must not be applied to variants that do not contain the elements of the process they are linked to: $\forall(m,c) \in cond(\forall bp_i \in L_M^V(m,c)(c \in C_{bp_i}))$ and $\forall(m,d,s,a) \in data(\forall bp_i \in L_M^V(m,d,s,a)((d,s) \in C_{bp_i}))$*

(6) *A derived measure cannot be related in each variant to more than one measure with the same identifier, which means that if they have the same identifier, the intersection of their variants must be empty: $\forall(d,m_i,x) \in uses \neg \exists(d,m_j,y) \in uses (x = y \wedge m_i \neq m_j \wedge L_M^V(d,m_i,x) \cap L_M^V(d,m_j,y) \neq \emptyset)$*

(7) *The identifiers used for a derived measure in each variant must be sequential: $\forall(d,m_i,x) \in uses(\forall bp_i \in L_M^V(d,m_i,x)(x \leq |\{u \in L_M[d,uses] \,|\, L_M^V(u) = bp_i\}|)$.*

(8) *For all $(d,fn) \in derfun$, $fn \in F$ must be a function defined over the Cartesian product of the set of all possible values of the set of measures linked to d that apply for each variant bp_i to which (d,fn) applies ($\{m \in M| (d,m,x) \in uses \wedge bp_i \in L_M^V(d,m,x)\}$), ordered according to x.*

Finally, using these definitions, it is easy to obtain a performance model $PM_i = (P_i, M_i, L_{P_i}, L_{M_i})$ for a specific process variant bp_i. For P_i, L_{P_i} and L_{M_i}, it just includes the elements of the variable performance model that apply to the process variant at hand. For M_i, it includes the measures that are used in the links of L_{M_i}. This can be formalised as follows.

Definition 7 (Performance model of a process variant). *Let $PF = \{bp_1, \ldots, bp_n\}$ be a process family, and $PM^V = (P, M, L_P, L_M, P^V, L_P^V, L_M^V)$ be a variable performance model of PF, the performance model of a variant bp_i of the process family is a tuple $PM_i = (P_i, M_i, L_{P_i}, L_{M_i})$, where:*

- $P_i = \{p \in P \,|\, bp_i \in P^V(p)\}$
- $L_{P_i} = \{lp \in L_P \,|\, bp_i \in L_P^V(lp)\}$

- $L_{M_i} = \{lm \in L_M \mid bp_i \in L_M^V(lm)\}$
- $M_i = \{m \in M \mid \exists lm \in L_{M_i}(\Pi_M(lm) = m)\}$

A measure that varies for three PVs was modeled using the formal definition of PPINOT and we have also modeled three PVs of the *Deliver* process to graphically represent the dimensions of change (see http://www.isa.us.es/ppinot/variability-bpm2016/). To represent the elements of the metamodel in a visual way, we have used an extension of the graphical notation of PPINOT to specify the variants of each PPI together with a C-EPC model of the PVs.

7   Conclusions and Future Work

From this paper, we can conclude that the performance perspective of BPs is subject to variation like other perspectives and, as such, it is convenient to develop models and tools that manage this variability, favor reuse and reduce design and maintenance time.

This conclusion is the result of an analysis of several BPV cases and different models to represent PPIs that have allowed us to identify two dimensions of change in the definition of PPIs and another two dimensions of change in the definition of measure definitions. Some of these dimensions (**Dim-2.M1**) are related to variations in other perspectives like control-flow, but other dimensions show that PPIs can also be subject of their own variations regardless of the other perspectives such as changes in the target value of the PPI. Furthermore, the cases that we have analyzed show that the variability of PPIs is quite common, affecting almost half of the PPIs defined in each case.

In addition, based on this analysis, we provide a model to extend the modelling of BPV to the performance perspective of BPs. To this end, we extend the PPINOT metamodel with the concept of variable performance model and formalize the requirements of a syntactically correct variable performance model that ensures that each PV has a syntactically correct performance model.

Our formal extension of the PPINOT metamodel is a first step to develop techniques and tools that facilitate the design and analysis of variability in PPIs, to ensure their correct definition and to reduce errors in the performance measurement.

As a direction for future work, we want to describe in detail and assess the graphical notation for the modelling of PPIs taking into account the BPV and all the PPI variability cases detected. To do this, we also need to develop tools that meet definitions and restrictions defined for PPI variability, and that will facilitate their complete managing until evaluation phase.

References

1. Hallerbach, A., Bauer, T., Reichert, M.: Configuration and management of process variants. In: Handbook on Business Process Management 1. International Handbooks on Information Systems, pp. 237–255. Springer, Berlin Heidelberg (2010)

2. Reichert, M., Hallerbach, A., Bauer, T.: Lifecycle management of business process variants. In: Handbook on Business Process Management 1, pp. 251–278. Springer, Berlin Heidelberg (2015)
3. Hallerbach, A., Bauer, T., Reichert, M.: Guaranteeing soundness of configurable process variants in Provop. In: 2009 IEEE Conference on Commerce and Enterprise Computing, pp. 98–105, July 2009
4. da Mota Silveira Neto, P.A., do Carmo Machado, I., McGregor, J.D., de Almeida, E.S., de Lemos Meira, S.R.: A systematic mapping study of software product linestesting. Inf. Softw. Technol. 53(5), 407–423 (2011)
5. Milani, F., Dumas, M., Ahmed, N., Matuleviius, R.: Modelling families of business process variants: A decomposition driven method. Inf. Syst. 56, 55–72 (2016)
6. Aiello, M., Bulanov, P., Groefsema, H.: Requirements and tools for variability management. In: 2010 IEEE 34th Annual Computer Software and Applications Conference Workshops (COMPSACW), pp. 245–250 (July 2010)
7. Saidani, O., Nurcan, S.: Business process modeling: a multi-perspective approach integrating variability. In: Bider, I., Gaaloul, K., Krogstie, J., Nurcan, S., Proper, H.A., Schmidt, R., Soffer, P. (eds.) BPMDS 2014 and EMMSAD 2014. LNBIP, vol. 175, pp. 169–183. Springer, Heidelberg (2014)
8. Rosa, M.L., Dumas, M., ter Hofstede, A.H., Mendling, J.: Configurable multi-perspective business process models. Inf. Syst. 36(2), 313–340 (2011)
9. La Rosa, M., van der Aalst, W.M.P., Dumas, M., Milani, F.P.: Business process variability modeling: A survey. Report, ACM Digital Library (2013)
10. Torres, V., Zugal, S., Weber, B., Reichert, M., Ayora, C., Pelechano, V.: A qualitative comparison of approaches supporting business process variability. In: La Rosa, M., Soffer, P. (eds.) Business Process Management Workshops. LNBIP, vol. 132, pp. 560–572. Springer, Heidelberg (2012)
11. Lodhi, A., Koppen, V., Wind, S., Saake, G., Turowski, K.: Business process modeling language for performance evaluation. In: 47th Hawaii International Conference on System Sciences (HICSS), pp. 3768–3777 Jan 2014
12. del Río-Ortega, A., Resinas, M., Cabanillas, C., Ruiz-Cortés, A.: On the definition and design-time analysis of process performance indicators. Inf. Syst. 38(4), 470–490 (2013)
13. Milani, F., Dumas, M., Matulevičius, R.: Identifying and classifying variations in business processes. In: Bider, I., Halpin, T., Krogstie, J., Nurcan, S., Proper, E., Schmidt, R., Soffer, P., Wrycza, S. (eds.) EMMSAD 2012 and BPMDS 2012. LNBIP, vol. 113, pp. 136–150. Springer, Heidelberg (2012)
14. Cognini, R., Corradini, F., Polini, A., Re, B.: Extending feature models to express variability in business process models. In: Persson, A., Stirna, J. (eds.) CAiSE 2015 Workshops. LNBIP, vol. 215, pp. 245–256. Springer, Heidelberg (2015)
15. Rolland, C., Nurcan, S.: Business process lines to deal with the variability. In: 43rd Hawaii International Conference on System Sciences (HICSS), pp. 1–10 (Jan 2010)
16. Machado, I., Bonifácio, R., Alves, V., Turnes, L., Machado, G.: Managing variability in business processes: An aspect-oriented approach. In: Proceedings of the 2011 I Workshop on Early Aspects. EA 11, pp. 25–30. ACM, New York, NY, USA (2011)
17. Hallerbach, A., Bauer, T., Reichert, M.: Capturing variability in business process models: the Provop approach. J. Softw. Maintenance Evol. Res. Pract. 22(6–7), 519–546 (2010)
18. Rosemann, M., van der Aalst, W.M.P.: A configurable reference modelling language. Inf. Syst. 32(1), 1–23 (2007)

19. Razavian, M., Khosravi, R.: Modeling variability in business process models using UML. In: Fifth International Conference on Information Technology: New Generations, ITNG 2008, pp. 82–87 (April 2008)
20. del-Río-Ortega, A., Cabanillas, C., Resinas, M., Ruiz-Cortés, A.: PPINOT tool suite: a performance management solution for process-oriented organisations. In: Basu, S., Pautasso, C., Zhang, L., Fu, X. (eds.) ICSOC 2013. LNCS, vol. 8274, pp. 675–678. Springer, Heidelberg (2013)
21. Strecker, S., Frank, U., Heise, D., Kattenstroth, H.: MetricM: a modeling method in support of the reflective design and use of performance measurement systems. Inf. Syst. e-Bus. Manage. **10**(2), 241–276 (2011)
22. Popova, V., Sharpanskykh, A.: Modeling organizational performance indicators. Inf. Syst. **35**(4), 505–527 (2010)
23. Suhartono, D.: Variability model implementation on key performance indicator application. Int. J. Innov. Manage. Technol. **6**(1), 77–80 (2015)
24. Vianden, M., Lichter, H.: Variability model towards a metric specification process. In: Proceedings of the International Conference on Computer Science and Information Technology, pp. 76–79 (2011)
25. Apics, S.C.C.: Supply Chain Operations Reference Model: SCOR Version 11.0. Supply Chain Council APICS, CCOR, CPIM, CSCP, DCOR, SCOR, and SCORmark are all registered trademarks of APICS. All rights reserved (2015)

A Checklist-Based Inspection Technique for Business Process Models

Rafael Maiani de Mello[(⊠)], Rebeca Campos Motta,
and Guilherme Horta Travassos

Federal University of Rio de Janeiro, POBOX 68511, Rio de Janeiro, Brazil
{rmaiani, rmotta, ght}@cos.ufrj.br

Abstract. Business process models support the business process management, being BPMN a widespread used notation for their modeling. However, the lack of consistent correspondence between the business process textual description and its derived models can jeopardize their quality. The technical literature offers diverse approaches for verifying the quality of such models, but there is a lack of supporting detection of semantic defects in BPMN models. Thus, based on our previous experiences on developing and applying inspection techniques for different Software Engineering artifacts, we developed BPCheck, a checklist-based inspection technique for BPMN models. Results from a first observational study conducted with inexperienced reviewers indicate the viability of BPCheck. Most of the subjects were able to detect more defects than false positives, taking from 10 to 20 min to report a defect. Such findings will drive us to evolve BPCheck aiming at to improve its efficiency and effectiveness.

Keywords: Inspection · Checklist · Business process management · Business process modeling · BPMN · Empirical software engineering

1 Introduction

Organizations frequently provide the description of their business processes through textual artifacts in different levels of abstraction. These materials may include artifacts such as general process descriptions, task execution standards, business rules and so on. When up-to-date, such artifacts can support the business analysts on modeling the organization business processes. Through the modeling of such processes, it is expected to get a better understanding of the business workflows, facilitating their management, the communication among customers and technical staff, the identification of improvement opportunities and the delimitation of the automation scope [1, 2]. In this sense, BPMN (Business Process Modeling and Notation) has been widely used to support the modeling of business processes [2].

BPMN (version 2.0), maintained by the Object Management Group (OMG), *"provides a simple means of communicating process information to other business users, process implementers, customers, and suppliers"* [3]. It evolves concepts from other modeling notations such as UML Activity Diagrams and Event-driven Process Chains. Four basic categories divide the BPMN process elements: *flow objects* (events, activities, and gateways), *connection objects* (sequence flow, message flow, and

© Springer International Publishing Switzerland 2016
M. La Rosa et al. (Eds.): BPM Forum 2016, LNBIP 260, pp. 108–123, 2016.
DOI: 10.1007/978-3-319-45468-9_7

associations), *swimlanes* (pools and lanes) and *artifacts* (data objects, groups, and annotations). Although it has been identified some gaps on the comprehensiveness of BPMN for supporting specific workflow patterns and business activities [4–6], it is still one of the fastest spreading process modeling notations spreading worldwide. BPMN models have been created to describe business processes regarding diverse domains, including kidney transplantation [7], crisis management [8] and software processes [9].

Apart from the involved business domains, the quality of business processes models must be assured. The manual effort involved in modeling business processes through diagrams is error-prone and can introduce different syntactic (notation rules) and semantic (meaning of concepts) defects. Semantic defects are dependent on contextual interpretation and human reasoning, unlike the syntactic defects that can be easily detected by modeling tools offering support to models' verification. Thus, semantic defects are hard to be caught by automated tools because of knowledge required to detect this type of defect. For instance, a syntactically correct model can hold issues regarding the omission of activities, wrongly mapped events, and inconsistent deviations in process flows and so on. Thus, the semantic verification of business process models should be performed before their execution.

In the last decades, software inspections, i.e. the visual examination of artifacts [10], have shown an effective technique to detect semantic defects in software artifacts [11]. Inspections can identify defects in the early stages of the software development process, increasing the productivity and reducing the costs to fix them. In this context, different inspection techniques have been proposed to support the identification of defects not just in the source code but also in various high abstraction level software artifacts, such as feature models [12], architectural models [13], design models [14] and software requirements [15]. For instance, ActCheck [16] is a checklist-based inspection technique to support the identification of defects in UML Activity Diagrams.

Different tools can be identified in the technical literature supporting the (semi) automated verification of BPMN models. However, as far as we were able to investigate, we did not identify any inspection technique for BPMN models in which process elements are described in natural language. So, taking into account the structural similarities (control flow, data, and resource patterns) observed between UML Activity Diagrams and BPMN for describing business processes models [4], we identified the opportunity of extending the benefits of checklist-based techniques such as ActCheck [16] to support the inspection of BPMN models. Thus, we used our experience in the development of different inspection techniques [12, 14, 16, 17] to design BPCheck, a checklist-based inspection technique for detecting defects in BPMN models.

The interest in developing an inspection technique for BPMN models arose from the need on verifying more than 400 administrative process models at COPPE/UFRJ. These processes were modeled into the context of an institutional project regarding the introduction of an integrated management system (SGI). To ensure their syntactic and semantic correction was a cornerstone project activity. Evidence obtained through an observational study (*in vitro*) using process models from SGI project with different levels of complexity indicates the feasibility of BPCheck.

This paper introduces BPCheck, and it is organized as follow. Besides this introduction, Sect. 2 presents the research background and related works obtained from a structured literature review. Section 3 describes the methodology used to build

BPCheck, introducing its checklist and using examples. Section 4 presents the observational study conducted for investigating the contributions of BPCheck on identifying defects in BPMN models with different levels of complexity. Conclusions, in Sect. 5, give some perspectives on the evolution of BPCheck.

2   Background and Related Works

In this Section, we briefly introduce inspection and other related concepts. Then, we present the main results of a structured literature review conducted to identify technologies supporting the semantic verification of BPMN models.

2.1   Inspection

Inspection is a type of static analysis technique. It is based on the visual examination (reading) of artifacts to detect inconsistencies, violation of patterns, and other anomalies [10]. In Software Engineering, inspections have been shown useful to identify more than 60 % of existing defects in software artifacts [18]. Laitenberger [19] and de Mello et al. [16] provide an overview of the potential contributions of inspections in the software development process. These authors present different categories of inspections techniques commonly used by practitioners: (a) *ad-hoc*, self-technique highly dependent on the reviewer knowledge and experience; (b) *checklist-based*, when a list of quality characteristics or verification items (questionnaire) makes explicit for the reviewers the perspectives to look for defects; and (c) *reading techniques*, i.e., procedures to guide reviewers on understanding a software artifact and detecting defects. All the three inspections techniques support the finding of defects. *Checklists* are more sophisticated and efficient than *ad-hoc*. However, they require less effort (tailoring and training), and they are less systematic than reading *techniques* [15].

Regardless the adopted inspection technique, reviewers should be aware of the different defect types. Different defect taxonomies can be used [20–22] to better interpret and classify the detected defects. The importance of consistently using defect taxonomy regards the understanding the root causes of each defect, which leads to spot its origin point and facilitates its fixing and avoidance in future modeling. BPCheck adopts the taxonomy [22] presented in Table 1. It is due to its previous use in different software inspection techniques, including ActCheck [16].

Table 1. Defects taxonomy [22] tailored to BPCheck.

Defect category	Description
Omission	The artifact omits necessary information about the business process
Incorrect fact	Information in the artifact contradicts the business process description
Inconsistency	Information in certain part of the artifact is not consistent with information in another part
Ambiguity	Information is not clear, allowing multiple interpretations
Extraneous information	Information in the artifact is out of scope

Inspections are usually individually performed by one or more reviewers that usually report any discrepancy (i.e., a possible defect) identified in the inspected artifact (s), typically attributing a defect category to each one and indicating its location in the artifact (and where the discrepancy repeats if it is the case). Then, other professionals (typically involved in the development of the inspected artifact) evaluate each reported discrepancy, characterizing each one as a defect or false positive. Eventually, they may fix the category attributed to each defect to support better representation and future use. Next, the artifacts' authors can fix the defects.

2.2   Related Work

Aiming at identifying available works that could contribute to our project, we performed a structured literature review, driven by the following question: *"What are the approaches available for identifying semantic defects in BPMN models?"*. Then, we searched for papers indexed by Scopus, a comprehensive and stable database frequently used to undertake systematic literature reviews (SLR) in Software Engineering. Considering the scope of our investigation, we organized the following *search string*:

(TITLE-ABS-KEY (inspect* OR review* OR verif* OR validat* OR check*) AND TITLE-ABS-KEY (BPMN OR "Business Process Modeling Notation" OR "Business Process Model and Notation"))

Some inclusion criteria were established to pre-select the articles retrieved due to the search execution: (i) the article should be written in English; (ii) the complete article should be available for download; (iii) the article abstract should present or cite at least an approach for identifying defects in BPMN models.

The titles and abstracts of the pre-selected articles shall be read, being selected only those presenting or citing some inspection technique for detecting defects in BPMN models, taking into account the IEEE standard [10] definition (visual examination of artifacts). Thus, we had not considered the articles presenting BPMN design rules or heuristics not associated with a verification approach or presenting automated verification tools for BPMN models (typically syntactic model checking).

We executed the initial search in 2014 and then re-executed it in February 2016 to update the results. In total, 410 documents were retrieved from Scopus, including 42 conference proceedings identifications and three duplicated articles (discarded). Among the remaining 365 distinct articles, it was identified by reading their titles and abstracts that most of them (352) frequently report works related with BPMN but out of the scope of our investigation. Such works include diverse approaches regarding automated verification, such as model checking tools. We also discarded works introducing or validating quality metrics (product, process or models) addressed to other notations such as Petri Nets or YAWL, not directly addressing inspections.

Thirteen technical papers apparently concerned with the semantic verification of BPMN models were selected. However, we have identified that most of these papers (ten) do not address the semantic verification of BPMN models, typically introducing model-checking technologies. On the other hand, although we have identified the three other papers address semantic issues, they do not support the verification of BPMN components described in natural language. Weber et al. [23] present a formal algorithm to verify BPMN models and their pre-conditions based on Petri net models established through using ontologies. Börger and Talheim [24] present a framework providing the semantic extension of BMPN models through abstract state machines for support the building of reliable implementations of BPMN models. Dijkman and Van Gorp [25] present a tool to support the inclusion of semantic rules in BPMN models and their verification through a transformed version of the model.

Additionally, throughout this work we also had identified a contemporary work [26] where the authors present a multifaceted approach (using linguistic analysis with semantic similarity measures) to observe the correspondence between the process model and its textual description and check for possible defects of inconsistency and omission. However, the success of such approach is limited to the capacity of the algorithms used for processing natural language. Thus, we did not identify that any previous work is presenting an inspection technique for supporting the detection of semantic defects in BPMN models. We are aware of the possible incompleteness of the string applied to Scopus, which can restrict the search scope. The business processes modeling area is quite extensive and comprehensive both in industry and academia. However, taking into account the widespread use of BPMN and the considerable coverage of Scopus we expect to have identified a representative set of works.

3   BPCheck

To avoid the propagation of BPMN models' defects to the business process execution or even to future software products designed based on these models, it is crucial the early detection of such defects. This section presents the steps followed for developing the first version of BPCheck, a checklist-based inspection technique for supporting the detection of defects in BPMN models. Since many different types of defects can be identified, Subsect. 3.1 presents the set of mapped discrepant cases, i.e., possible generic cases of defect [12]. Subsection 3.2 presents the first version of BPCheck checklist with examples of its use on inspecting business processes concerned with a "material inventory management" macro process (extracted from the observational study presented in Sect. 4).

3.1   Discrepant Cases

Discrepant Cases (DCs) are scenarios characterizing *discrepancies*, i.e. a general situation in which defects can be detected [12]. Based on BPMN 2.0 specification [3], we investigated DCs following the defect taxonomy presented in Table 1. Thus, taking into account all process elements available in BPMN, it was identified 109 DCs addressed to the *consistency* between the model elements, the *clearness* of their description and their *correctness* and *completeness* when compared with the business process textual description. This set of DCs does not intend to cover all possible scenarios of semantic defects addressed to BPMNs. However, all BPMN process elements were included and distributed in the following groups:

1. *Activities (Tasks):* ten DCs addressed to the clearness, completeness and correctness of business process activities and the consistency between them and other process elements;
2. *Events:* 29 DCs addressed to the suitability of the different event types used in the model and its flow. Some of these DCs apply to all event types (eight) while others apply to specific event types: *error/cancelation* (five), *message/signal/time* (nine), *conditional* (six) and *multiple* (one);
3. *Parallel gateways:* nine DCs addressed to the correctness and consistency on using forks and joins in the process model workflow in comparison with the business process description;
4. *Decision gateways:* 13 DCs addressed to the correctness and the consistency on using decisions and merges in the process model workflow in comparison with the business process description. Most of these DCs apply to decision gateways in general (nine) while others apply to specific gateway types: *exclusive* (two), *inclusive* (one) and *complex* (one);
5. *Data Objects:* 19 DCs addressed to anomalies in the data objects description and its association with the business process activities;
6. *Pools/Lanes:* eleven DCs addressed to anomalies in the use of *pools* and *lanes* on distributing the process elements;
7. Annotation: four DCs addressed to the wrong use of *annotations*;
8. *Process, subprocess and groups*: five DCs mainly related to the traceability between process models representing different levels of abstraction of the business process, and;
9. *Loop and ad-hoc subprocess*: nine DCs addressed to the wrong use of such special types of subprocesses.

3.2   The Checklist

One challenge in developing checklists is concerned with its size. Once an excessive amount of items can lead reviewers to fatigue and discourage its use, we tried to group two or more DCs into a single verification item based on their similarities. However, in some few cases, we opted for using two or more specific verification items to cover a single DC. Table 2 exemplifies both cases for DCs identified to events. As a result,

Table 2. Excerpt of DCs identified to events and their respective BPCheck verification items.

BPCheck Id (s)	Discrepant case
26	B01. An event is omitted (Omission)
28	B02. The event type is not characterized, although the business process description allows it. (Omission)
46	B03. An event is positioned wrongly in the model (Incorrect fact)
25	B04. The event description is incorrect (Incorrect fact)
28, 30, 31, 32, 34	B05. The event type used is incorrect (Inconsistence)
25	B06. The event description is not clear (Ambiguity)

we designed a checklist composed by 55 verification items covering all the 109 DCs. However, the BPCheck checklist can also be tailored to a reduced set of verification items.

We propose the following inspection steps to apply BPCheck: First, a valid *base document* (or a set of base documents) needs to be available representing the *Oracle*, i.e., a valid textual description (standardized or not) of the business process. The inspection moderator can tailor the checklist by excluding those BPMN elements not usually used in the organization's business process models to avoid useless work. Then, the inspection moderator distributes the tailored checklist to the reviewers, which can perform their individual reviews. Next, the discrepancy reports generated by the reviewers are sent to the inspection moderator that can compile a complete and not redundant list of discrepancies. Finally, the business analysts can identify the discrepancies representing defects, which will be fixed by the business process model authors. Since a valid base document should be provided to support the inspection activities, the reviewers do not need to have previous knowledge/experience on the business process domain. On the other hand, the reviewers' background can be useful to detect additional discrepancies remained in the textual description.

Another challenge on designing checklists is concerned with the distribution of its verification items. Based on our experience in building different inspection techniques [12, 16, 17], we established the following verification groups: *static, process flow* and *data objects*. By such grouping we intend to reduce the reviewer re-work on examining the entire business process model several times, looking each moment to a different element type or a particular defect category. The static verification group is composed of 12 verification items, covering all DCs addressed to the description of activities, pools, lanes, annotations, sub-process, and groups. Such items do not take into account the process workflow and its deviations. Table 3 presents all the verification items composing the static verification group. The ten first ones were included in the checklist used in the observational study (Sect. 4). For each verification item, the reviewer should answer "Yes," "No" or "N.A." (not applicable to the inspected model).

Figure 1 exemplifies the use of verification item 9 to identify a defect as reported in the observational study presented in Sect. 4. The next examples given in this Section are also from this study. The inspected process model was *sending physical inventory to the rectory*. In this context, the reviewer identified that the role *warehouse administrative assistant* represented in the model was not mentioned in any part of the Oracle, which resulted in *extraneous information*.

Thirty and six items support the process flow verification group. These items cover DCs addressing possible defects in the process workflow, including its control over events and gateways. Table 4 presents the process flow verification group. The nine verification items marked with an asterisk were not included in the observational study checklist.

Figure 2 exemplifies a defect identified through the verification item 19. The model describes the macro-process *material consuming accountability*. However, the textual description (Oracle) indicates that events generated by the sub-process *send* invoice are correlated, different from the representation provided by the model. Thus, this defect can be classified as an *incorrect fact*. Figure 3 gives another example of a defect found by using a verification item from this group in the same process model. Supported by

Table 3. Static verification group.

Id	Description
1	Are all activities clearly described? Are they easy to understand?
2	Is there any activity which the description should provide more information?
3	Does each activity exclusively provide the sufficient and necessary information to be correctly understood? Is there any unnecessary information, although eventually correct?
4	Does any activity describe operational details out of the business process modeling context, such as software algorithms or tasks performed and managed by third-parties?
5	Does any activity in the model represent, indeed, a process event?
6	Should any activity be dismembered into two or more activities (or even into a new process) to be in compliance with the abstraction level followed by the model?
7	Does any activity refer to a nonexistent process/subprocess?
8	Should any activity be represented as a process/subprocess call?
9	Are the model pools and lanes clearly described and free from unnecessary information? Is it possible to identify each one in the business process description?
10	Is there any activity associated with an incorrect pool/lane?
11	Does each annotation is clearly and correctly described, containing only relevant information regarding the business process?
12	Is there any annotation in the model that should be represented as an event or even as an activity?

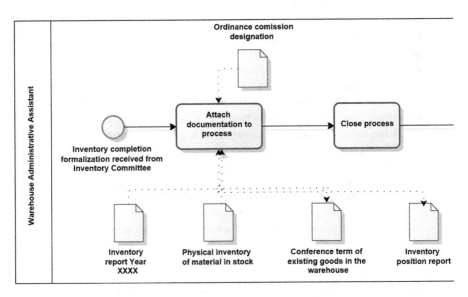

Fig. 1. Excerpt of the *sending physical inventory to the rectory* process.

Table 4. Process flow verification group.

Id	Description
13	Does each sequence composed of two activities can be clearly interpreted, allowing the understanding of the whole business process described in the model? Is there no confusing or incomplete sequence of activities?
14	Is each sequence of activities in compliance with the business process?
15	Is there any activity in the model out of the process scope?
16	Is there any activity relevant to the business process omitted from the model?
17	Should any *decision gateway* (exclusive, inclusive or complex) in the model be in fact represented as a *parallel gateway* or vice versa?
18	Is there any *fork, join* or *merge* between two or more activity flows that should not be synchronized (controlled)? Is there any *fork, join* or *merge* in the model that should be synchronized?
19	Are all *gates* (conditions) required in the *decision gateways* correctly provided (clearly described and free of unnecessary information)? Are all these conditions feasible from the business process' point of view?
20	Is there any redundant *default gate* in the model, since the other *gates* from the same gateway can cover all possible alternatives?
21	Is there any *exclusive gateway* composed by a non-exclusive set of gates?
22	Is there any *exclusive event-based* gateway in which one or more event-based gates are in fact simple data-based gates?
23	Is there any *exclusive event-based gateway* composed of a single event-based gate?
24	Are there concurrent activities also represented as non-concurrent ones in the model?
25	Are all *conditional, error, cancellation, timer, message, link and* signal *events* clearly and correctly described in the model?
26	Is there any *event* of the business process omitted from the model?
27	Should any *catching event* be characterized as a *throwing event* (or vice versa)?
28	Are all events in the model associated with a suitable event type?
29	Is it possible to identify the source of each *signal event* and *link* received by all activities in the model?
30	Is there any *signal event* that should be better characterized as a *message event*?
31*	Is there any *error event* that should be better characterized as a *cancellation event*?
32*	Do all *error events* adequately represent errors in the business process execution?
33	Are all technology for sending-receiving messages correctly described in the model *events*?
34	Is there any *timer event* not effectively based on a temporal condition? Is there any *timer event* based on *cyclic temporal condition* although the business process had specified a specific date/time to it happens (or vice-versa)?
35	Is there any *multiple events* in the model not connected to two or more distinct process events?
36	Should be any *conditional event* in the model implemented as a *decision gateway* or vice versa?
37*	Are all *compensation events* associated with the right compensation activities?

(Continued)

Table 4. (*Continued*)

Id	Description
38	Is there any *pool/lane* neglected in the model, omitting (for instance) a department, role or area described in the business process?
39	Are there similar/identical activities in the model performed by different pools/lanes?
40*	Do all model transactions support all BPMN conditions to be characterized as that?
41*	Does each *loop sub-process* present only the tasks that should be repeated under the conditions given?
42*	Are all *loop sub-processes conditions* correctly provided (clearly described and free of unnecessary information)? Are all these conditions feasible from the business process?
43*	Is there any *serial loop sub-process* that should be implemented as *parallel* or vice versa?
44*	Is there any incomplete *ad hoc activity* or even incorrectly classified as *ad-hoc*?
45*	Does each group highlighted in the model is composed of elements from the same category, helping to understand the business process better?
46	Taking into account all combinations of events and gates presented in the model, can we ensure that all possible scenarios of the process execution are correct?
47	Is there any inconsistency among the model elements? For instance, does any subsequence of activities contradict another subsequence or even does any gateway from the model gateway contradict another one?
48	Is there a clear correlation between the process model element in a lower level of abstraction and another model describing the same process in a higher level of abstraction?

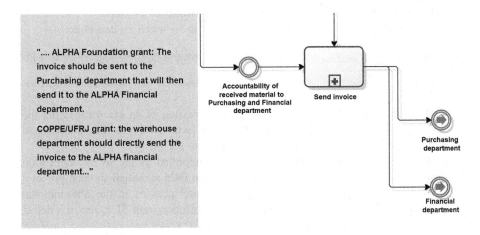

Fig. 2. An excerpt of the process *material consuming accountability* and an excerpt of the Oracle.

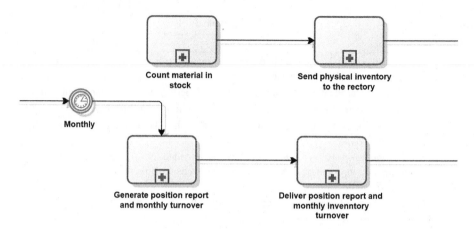

Fig. 3. Another excerpt of the process *material consuming accountability.*

Table 5. Data objects verification group.

Id	Description
49	Are all data objects in the model part of the business process? Are they clearly described without unnecessary/redundant information?
50	Is there any missing data object in the model?
51	Are all data objects represented in the model generated, consulted or modified by the activities associated with them? Do the directions of the arrows in such associations correctly represent such behaviors?
52	Is it possible to clearly understand each data object *property/state*? Is there no unnecessary or redundant information in such descriptions?
53	Is there any relevant data object *property/state* omitted from the model?
54	Is there two similar sub-flows (or more) in the model in which the data object *properties/states* diverge?
55	Do the possible model execution scenarios suggest any divergence with a data object state/property?

the verification item 26, a reviewer reported the *omission* of an event regarding the *physical inventory generation* in the same model. In fact, such event should have been inserted before the activity *send physical inventory to the rectory.*

Finally, the *data objects* verification group is supported by the seven verification items presented in Table 5, exclusively covering the DCs identified to such process' elements. Only the three first verification items were included in the observational study checklist. Figure 4 exemplifies the use of verification item 51 to report a defect found by a reviewer. The inspected business process model was *delivering material* previously required to the warehouse. In this context, the reviewer identified that *material* is not a *data object* in the context of the business process while the *control record* generated while storing the material is. Thus, such defect indicates an *inconsistency.*

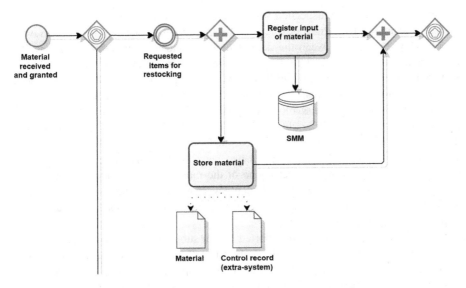

Fig. 4. Excerpt of the process *delivering material.*

4 Observational Study

We planned an *observational study* to investigate the use of BPCheck. Through using GQM we established the following research goal:

To analyze the anomalies (discrepancies or defects) reported through applying BPCheck

In order to characterize

With respect to its capability of providing *efficiency (defects/time)* and *effectiveness (defects/discrepancies)* to the inspection activities

From the point of view of SE researchers

In the context of evaluating the discrepancies reported by BPCheck users inspecting business processes related to *inventory management.*

The following three business processes were selected from a real business process modeling project conducted at COPPE/UFRJ (SGI). They were selected based on the structural complexity analysis of 15 business process models describing the *inventory management macro-process*:

- *Sending physical inventory to the rectory (SPI): lower* complexity, composed of five activities and a single exclusive gateway but involving two swimlanes and seven data objects;
- *Delivering material (DM): intermediary* complexity, consisting of six activities, two gateways, two events, two swimlanes and six data objects;
- *Material consuming accountability (MCA):* considered the most complex model from the macro-process, composed of seven subprocesses, two gateways, seven events and two swimlanes.

The *efficiency* of each inspection was calculated as the ratio between the number of defects detected and the time devoted to the inspection, while its *effectiveness* was calculated as the ratio between the defects detected and the total amount of discrepancies reported. We invited all the 12 graduate students from the 2014' Object-Oriented Software Engineering course (COPPE/UFRJ) to take part in the observational study. The subjects were equally distributed among three groups. None of them had participated in the business process modeling tasks of the project. All subjects signed a consent form and attended the classes introducing BPMN and inspections before the study execution. Since each group was assigned to individually inspecting a different model, it was expected that each model had been individually inspected four times. However, two subjects that inspected one of the models (MCA model) did not complete their tasks. Since some BPMN elements were not used in the modeling activities from the SGI project, 15 BPCheck verification items were not included in the inspection checklist (Subsect. 3.2).

In total, 56 discrepancies were reported by ten subjects, distributed as presented in Table 6. Two researchers individually analyzed each reported discrepancy, classifying each one as a *defect* or *false positive*. Then, they compared their analyses and reviewed together with the divergences, resulting in 37 defects and 19 false positives. One can see from Table 6 that most of the reviewers reported more defects than false positives while two reviewers did not match any discrepancy reported to SPI model. One possible explanation for such result relies on the simplicity of the inspected model, which could have led such reviewers to perform cursory inspections, although they had devoted a considerable time to perform their tasks. On the other hand, among the inspections in which any defect was detected, it was observed a trend of detecting one defect by each 10–20 min. Through applying Spearman correlation test (the distribution of effectiveness was not normal, Shapiro-Wilk test), we could not observe a correlation between efficiency and effectiveness of the analyzed inspections (0.5986, Spearman Rho, p-value = 0.0517).

Table 6. Distribution of time, false positives, and defects by subject and their own effectiveness and efficiency.

Id	Model	Time (min.)	#False positives	#Defects	Effectiveness	Efficiency
A	SPI	55	0	4	1.00	0.07
B	SPI	50	1	1	0.50	0.02
C	SPI	68	2	0	0	0
D	SPI	90	2	0	0	0
E	DM	72	7	6	0.46	0.08
F	DM	85	4	5	0.56	0.06
G	DM	90	1	7	0.88	0.08
H	DM	30	0	3	1.00	0.10
I	MCA	80	0	4	1.00	0.05
J	MCA	94	2	7	0.78	0.07
Total		714	19	37	0.66	0.05

Table 7. The incidence of distinct false positives and defects reported by model.

Model	Total time	#Distinct false positives	#Distinct defects	#Repeated defects
SPI	263	5	5	0
DM	277	9	20	1
MCA	174	2	9	2
Total	714	16	34	3

Table 7 presents the amount of distinct false positives and defects reported for each process model. Although the inspections performed in the DM and MCA process models present favorable values to BPCheck, one can see that the incidence of repeated defects is small, especially regarding the DM process model in which all four subjects reported defects but only one defect in common. Although the low incidence of repeated defects is expected in checklist-based inspection techniques due to the little systematization involved, it is important to point out that subjects' previous inexperience with both software inspections/business process modeling activities could also be contributed to such results. Also, each artifact was individually inspected by few subjects.

Regarding the distribution by defects' categorization, it was observed the predominance of omissions (15/34). However, we had observed the omissions reported were highly concentrated in the DM model. Since we did not have seeded defects in the original models, such results provide valuable feedback for the business analysts on improving the quality of models in future business process modeling activities.

4.1   Threats to Validity

As an *external threat* to validity, the inspected three models came from the same project. However, we introduced some diversity in the inspection tasks through analyzing the structural complexity of the 15 available models and then selecting three of them with different levels of complexity. Another external threat regards the small sample size available, which had been established by convenience. However, we claim that such experimental arrangement could be considered suitable for a first observational study. However, due to the available sample size, we decided to do not use a control group and therefore we were not able to perform comparisons with *ad-hoc* inspections.

Although we conducted the study in a controlled environment (classroom), the time and resources available could have influenced in the subjects' performance. First, it was scheduled only one hour and a half to the inspection activities. Second, subjects seated in a typical classroom desk had to handle with printed copies of the Oracle, models and the checklist attached to the discrepancies' report.

5   Conclusion

To support business process modeling activities, BPMN has been widely used for diagrammatically representing this type of model. However, the expected contributions of such practices can be hampered whether the correspondence between the business process' textual description and its derived models are not assured. One can observe a similar concern in the Software Engineering field, in which inspections have been supporting the quality of different artifacts. In this sense, this paper introduced BPCheck, a checklist-based inspection technique to support the detection of defects in BPMN models.

The results of an observational study provided initial evidence on the feasibility of using BPCheck. From all 10 participants - with only theoretical knowledge about inspection/business process modeling - 8 were able to detect defects and 6 of them reported more defects than false positives. The time needed by these eight subjects to report a defect varied from 10 to 20 min. However, the use of more/less time to report a defect was not related to their effectiveness. The lessons learned with this study are supporting the evolution of the BPCheck checklist on providing more systematic support to the reviewers and, consequently, driving them to individually detecting a more comprehensive set of defects. Next step will be the conduction of a controlled experiment to compare the results of ad-hoc inspections with BPCheck.

Acknowledgments. We thank the students of the 2014' Object-Oriented Software Engineering course (COPPE/UFRJ) to their collaborations. Guilherme Travassos is a CNPq researcher (grant 305929/2014-3).

References

1. Aguilar-Saven, R.S.: Business process modeling: review and framework. Int. J. Prod. Econ. **90**(2), 129–149 (2004)
2. Harmon, P., Wolf, C.: Business process modeling survey. Business process trends. http://www.bptrends.com
3. Object management group: Business process model and notation. http://www.bpmn.org
4. Wohed, P., van der Aalst, W.M., Dumas, M., ter Hofstede, A.H., Russell, N.: On the suitability of BPMN for business process modelling. In: Dustdar, S., Fiadeiro, J.L., Sheth, A. P. (eds.) BPM 2006. LNCS, vol. 4102, pp. 161–176. Springer, Heidelberg (2006)
5. Börger, E.: Approaches to modeling business processes: a critical analysis of BPMN, workflow patterns, and YAWL. Softw. Syst. Model. **11**(3), 305–318 (2012)
6. Schultz, M., Radloff, M.: Modeling concepts for internal controls in business processes – an empirically grounded extension of BPMN. In: Sadiq, S., Soffer, P., Völzer, H. (eds.) BPM 2014. LNCS, vol. 8659, pp. 184–199. Springer, Heidelberg (2014)
7. Penteado, A.P., et al.: Kidney transplantation process in Brazil represented in business process modeling notation. Transplant. Proc. **47**(4), 963–966 (2015)
8. Thanh Le, N.T., Hanachi, C., Stinckwich, S., Ho, T.V.: Mapping BPMN processes to organization centered multi-agent systems to help assess crisis models. In: Núñez, M., Nguyen, N.T., Camacho, D., Trawinski, B. (eds.) ICCCI 2015. LNCS, vol. 9329, pp. 77–88. Springer, Heidelberg (2015). doi:10.1007/978-3-319-24069-5_8
9. Campos, A.L., Oliveira, T.: Software processes with BPMN: an empirical analysis. In: Heidrich, J., Oivo, M., Jedlitschka, A., Baldassarre, M.T. (eds.) PROFES 2013. LNCS, vol. 7983, pp. 338–341. Springer, Heidelberg (2013)
10. IEEE: IEEE standard glossary of software engineering terminology, standard 610.12. IEEE Press (1990)

11. Shull, F., Seaman, C.: Inspecting the history of inspections: an example of evidence-based technology diffusion. IEEE Softw. **25**(1), 88 (2008)
12. de Mello, R.M., Nogueira, E., Schots, M., Werner, C.M.L., Travassos, G.H.: Verification of software product line artefacts: a checklist to support feature model inspections. J. UCS **20** (5), 720–745 (2014)
13. Vasconcelos, A., Werner, C.: Architecture recovery and evaluation aiming at program understanding and reuse. In: Overhage, S., Ren, X.-M., Reussner, R., Stafford, J.A. (eds.) QoSA 2007. LNCS, vol. 4880, pp. 72–89. Springer, Heidelberg (2008)
14. Travassos, G., Shull, F., Fredericks, M., Basili, V.R.: Detecting defects in object-oriented designs: using reading techniques to increase software quality. In: ACM Sigplan Notices, vol. 34, no. 10, pp. 47-56. ACM (1999)
15. Shull, F., Rus, I., Basili, V.: How perspective-based reading can improve requirements inspections. Computer **33**(7), 73–79 (2000)
16. de Mello, R.M., Pereira, W.M., Travassos, G.H.: Activity diagram inspection on requirements specification. In: 2010 Brazilian Symposium on Software Engineering, pp. 168–177. IEEE (2010)
17. Teixeira, E.N., de Mello, R.M., Motta, R.C., Werner, C.M.L., Vasconcelos, A.: Verification of software process line models: a checklist-based inspection approach. In Proceedings of XVIII Ibero-American Conference on Software Engineering, Peru, Lima (2015)
18. Denger, C., Shull, F.: A practical approach for quality-driven inspections. IEEE Softw. **24** (2), 79–86 (2007)
19. Laitenberger, O.: A survey of software inspection technologies (2002)
20. Basili, V.R., Selby, R.W.: Comparing the effectiveness of software testing strategies. IEEE Trans. Softw. Eng. **12**, 1278–1296 (1987)
21. Parnas, D., Weiss, D.: Active design reviews: principles and practice. In: Proceedings of the 8th International Conference on Software Engineering, pp. 132–136. IEEE Computer Society Press (1985)
22. Travassos, G.H. apud Rocha, A.R.C., Maldonado, J.C., Weber, K.C.: Qualidade de Software. Prentice Hall, São Paulo (2001)
23. Weber, I., Hoffmann, J., Mendling, J.: Semantic business process validation. In: Proceedings of the 3rd International Workshop on Semantic Business Process Management, vol. 472 (2008)
24. Börger, E., Thalheim, B.: A method for verifiable and validatable business process modeling. In: Börger, E., Cisternino, A. (eds.) Advances in Software Engineering. LNCS, vol. 5316, pp. 59–115. Springer, Heidelberg (2008)
25. Dijkman, R., Van Gorp, P.: BPMN 2.0 execution semantics formalized as graph rewrite rules. In: Mendling, J., Weidlich, M., Weske, M. (eds.) BPMN 2010. LNBIP, vol. 67, pp. 16–30. Springer, Heidelberg (2010)
26. van der Aa, H., Leopold, H., Reijers, H.A.: Detecting inconsistencies between process models and textual descriptions. In: Motahari-Nezhad, H.R., Recker, J., Weidlich, M. (eds.) BPMN 2010. LNCS, vol. 9253, pp. 90–105. Springer, Heidelberg (2015)

Activity Matching with Human Intelligence

Carlos Rodríguez[1]([⊠]), Christopher Klinkmüller[2,3], Ingo Weber[3,4],
Florian Daniel[5], and Fabio Casati[1]

[1] University of Trento, Via Sommarive 9, 38123 Povo, TN, Italy
{crodriguez,casati}@disi.unitn.it
[2] Department of Computing, Macquarie University, Sydney, Australia
[3] Data61, CSIRO, Sydney, Australia
{christopher.klinkmuller,ingo.weber}@data61.csiro.au
[4] University of New South Wales, Sydney, Australia
[5] Politecnico di Milano, Via Ponzio 34/5, 20133 Milano, Italy
florian.daniel@polimi.it

Abstract. Effective matching of activities is the first step toward successful process model matching and search. The problem is nontrivial and has led to a variety of computational similarity metrics and matching approaches, however all still with low performance in terms of precision and recall. In this paper, instead, we study how to leverage on human intelligence to identify matches among activities and show that the problem is not as straightforward as most computational approaches assume. We access human intelligence (i) by crowdsourcing the activity matching problem to generic workers and (ii) by eliciting ground truth matches from experts. The precision and recall we achieve and the qualitative analysis of the results testify huge potential for a human-based activity matching that contemplates disagreement and interpretation.

Keywords: Activity matching · Label matching · Crowdsourcing

1 Introduction

Organizations with sizable process model collections encounter several use cases where matching activities of process models (deciding which of the activities of the process models are similar or even the same) is important, including search over the collection [9,15,19,21] or identifying cloned models or fragments in models [10]. This problem has been addressed with a multitude of automated approaches over the last decade [3,7,17,20,23–25]. However, the success of fully automated, one-size-fits-all approaches is very limited when applied to heterogeneous process model collections, as observed in the Process Model Matching Contest of 2013 and 2015 [2,5]. In some earlier work of ours we thus pursued a semi-automated approach, where user feedback was collected and the matching was improved based on corrections provided by the users [16]. Based on this input, the f-measure could be increased by around 40–50 % in comparison to earlier works. The limiting factor of the approach is however the low availability of users with the necessary skills and time to invest.

© Springer International Publishing Switzerland 2016
M. La Rosa et al. (Eds.): BPM Forum 2016, LNBIP 260, pp. 124–140, 2016.
DOI: 10.1007/978-3-319-45468-9_8

In this paper, we start from the observation that deciding if two activities are similar or even the same is nontrivial, that purely computational approaches are not always able to correctly interpret the activities' textual labels, and that *human intelligence* (like in the case of user feedback [16]) can indeed make a difference. One of the reasons for the low performance of automated techniques is that often process models are not correctly formalized and, at best, come in the form of semiformal process models that, for instance, lack proper definitions of actors (e.g., no pools or swim lanes in the model), don't explicitly model data objects, use different activity labeling conventions (e.g., with or without mentioning the actor, the data object or the actual action to be performed), and so on. As a consequence, matching activities requires interpretation, an interpretation we claim needs to comprise also the context of the activities to be matched (e.g., the surrounding activities and the respective control flow structure). In line with the approach pushed forward in [16], we further believe this interpretation requires human intelligence, while the specific challenge we approach in this paper is to match activities by relaxing the assumption that this human intelligence necessarily comes from experts. We thus show how to match activities with the help of the crowd by crowdsourcing and studying different task designs oriented to generic, non-expert workers (the members of the crowd).

Crowdsourcing in fact provides convenient access to human intelligence via the Web, thanks to dedicated crowdsourcing platforms connecting workers with requesters who offer work. While there is a multitude of platforms supporting different crowdsourcing models, such as marketplaces [14], contests [4] and auctions [22], we specifically concentrate on marketplace platforms for *micro-tasks* with fixed rewards, as assessing the similarity of two activities is fine-grained enough to be formulated as a micro-task. Other examples of typical micro-tasks are annotating images, translating text or performing search activities on the Web. Prominent platforms supporting micro-tasks are Amazon Mechanical Turk (https://www.mturk.com) or CrowdFlower (http://crowdflower.com).

Designing effective crowdsourcing micro-tasks is however known to be challenging [1]. For instance, if too little information is given on a task, workers may not be able to complete the task; if too much information is given, they may abort the task or give arbitrary answers. Understanding if and how crowdsourcing can be leveraged to match activities in a way that indeed allows workers to bring in their human intelligence, as well as understanding if and how matching decisions by the crowd differ from those computed by algorithms or, instead, from those provided by process modeling experts, has therefore no immediate answer. We answer these questions by making the following contributions:

- A *conceptual model* of how the activity matching problem can be mapped to micro-tasks with basic, built-in quality controls;
- The design and implementation of a *ground truth elicitation experiment* with process modeling experts to study expert agreement inside a given domain;
- The design and implementation of *three crowdsourcing experiments* to study the performance (precision and recall) of the crowd compared to automated algorithms and the experts;

– A discussion of the *effect of human intelligence* and of the *effect of context visibility* on the quality of matches.

Next, we discuss the difference between machine- and human-based matching and review related works. In Sect. 3, we introduce crowdsourcing and a conceptual framework for task design, which we use in Sect. 4 to implement three tasks, along with an exercise to elicit ground truth mappings. In Sect. 5, we report on the outputs by experts, two automated matchers, and the crowd and discuss the results and findings in Sect. 6.

2   Activity Matching: Background

An *activity* is commonly interpreted as an action performed by an actor on some data object and represented by a textual label that describes the activity, $a = \langle act, role, obj, lab \rangle$. For example, an activity "Submit online form" may express a student submitting an online application form through some admission system. Typical *actions* are "create", "read", "update" and "delete" for documents, "send" and "receive" for messages, and "decide" for decisions. The *roles* depend very much on the domain of the process; for instance, a university admission process may involve a student, an admin and an examiner. The *data object* varies too, depending on the documents/artifacts worked on during the process; typical data objects are virtual/physical documents or entries in a database.

2.1   Machine- vs. Human-Based Activity Matching

Given two business processes models BP_1 and BP_2 and two activities $a^1 \in BP_1$ and $a^2 \in BP_2$, the purpose of *activity matching* is to decide whether the two activities match, that is, if they have the same or similar actor, role and data object, respectively (note that, for conciseness, *prop* is used to iterate over properties, and *pmatch* matches properties):

$$match(a^1, a^2) \iff \bigwedge_{prop \in \{act, role, obj\}} pmatch(prop^1, prop^2)$$

The basic problem is that of identifying 1:1 matches of activities of type $match(a^1, a^2)$. In general, however, matching activities is a 1:n or even an m:n problem: $match(a^1, \{a_j^2\})$ or $match(\{a_i^1\}, \{a_j^2\})$. For example, while one process may use an activity "Send documents," another one may split the group of documents into the individual documents to be sent and use the activities "Send form" and "Send ID" to represent the same activity. This would correspond to a $match($"Send documents", {"Send form", "Send ID"}$)$. In practical settings that ask for the matching of process models that stem from different organizations and/or different modelers, 1:n and m:n correspondences are unavoidable.

The presence of 1:n and m:n correspondences, in turn, implies for activities that actions may have sub-actions, roles may have sub-roles, and documents may have sub-documents. Thus there may also exist $partof(a^1, a_j^2)$ relationships between two activities that, for instance, qualify $a_j^2 \in \{a_j^2\}$ as part of a^1, starting from a $ppartof$ relationship among the individual properties of the activities (we assume $ppartof(a, b) = true \iff a = b$ or $b = subelement(a)$):

$$partof(a^1, a_j^2) \iff \bigwedge_{prop \in \{act, role, obj\}} ppartof(prop^1, prop_j^2)$$

A 1:n activity match can thus be defined as a match of an activity a^1 with a set of activities $\{a_j^2\}$ that perform parts of a^1:

$$match(a^1, \{a_j^2\}) \iff \bigwedge_{j \in |\{a_j^2\}|} partof(a^1, a_j^2)$$

Merging the activity matches and part-of relationships from BP_1 to BP_2 with those from BP_2 to BP_1 identifies the m:n matches between the processes.

Now, asserting an exact match both among activities and their individual properties is generally hard, and the use of *similarity metrics* that assess a degree of matching is common practice [8]. In the case of automated matching algorithms, similarity is typically based on objective, syntactic or semantic features of the *labels* describing the activities (t^a is a threshold value) [17,20]:

$$match^a(a^1, a^2) \iff sim^a(lab^1, lab^2) > t^a$$

If instead of by machines, activity matches are to be identified by human actors, such as process modelers or domain experts, subjective similarity metrics are applied. The respective criteria are based on the personal experience and expertise of the human actor, and typically don't consider only the labels of activities in an isolated fashion, but also interpret parts of or the full process models containing the activities to be matched. That is, humans don't simply assert similarity based on labels, but naturally also take into account the context of the activities, i.e., other surrounding model constructs (activities, data objects, control flow constructs, etc.). Activity labels are the starting point of the analysis, while the objective is the identification of the real meaning of activities in the process models, that is, the actual action, role and data object an activity refers to. Two activities therefore match if the perceived similarity of these properties exceeds some subjective threshold:

$$match^h(a^1, a^2) \iff \sum_{prop \in \{act, role, obj\}} \alpha_{prop} * sim^h(prop^1, prop^2) > t^h$$

The exact values of t^h and of the weights $\alpha_{prop} \in [0, 1]$ are subjective, and only the expert himself/herself can judge how and when he/she wants to assert a match or not. The expert might–depending on his view–consider also other properties, e.g., resources, process context, dependencies, or similar that help him/her in the decision process. Analogous considerations hold also for the *partof* relationship that allows the identification of 1:n and m:n matches if assessed by human actors. To the best of our knowledge, computational approaches do not focus so far on *partof* relationships with the meaning defined above; existing matching techniques are not limited to 1:1 matches only, but identified 1:n or m:n matches are the result of label similarity not of a reasoning on the actual meaning of activities.

In this paper, we are particularly interested in eliciting the interpretation represented by the $match^h$ function (including possible *partof* relations) and less in that of the $match^a$ function. The intuition is that humans reason on the essence of the problem, while machines do so only on a proxy of it (the labels).

2.2   Related Work

The identification of correspondences between models has been studied in the field of ontology and schema matching [11]. However, the applicability of such approaches to process model matching is limited as process models depict actions and their execution order instead of concepts and their relations. Accordingly, a poor performance was observed when applying schema and ontology matchers to process models [2,7]. Furthermore, process similarity search techniques [8] which measure the overall similarity of process models provide basic concepts for comparing process models on a fine-grain level. Such techniques rely on textual [18], structural [6,12], and behavioral information [19,26].

Based on these approaches, a variety of process model matching techniques has been proposed [3,7,17,20,23,25]. Essentially, all these techniques determine correspondences based on the comparison of activity labels, i.e., they try to estimate the functional overlap of activities based on their textual description. Additionally, some approaches integrate structural and behavioral information to decide whether activities correspond or not [3,7,20,23]. However, comparative evaluations based on different data sets revealed that the quality of these approaches is too low to be applicable in practice [2,5].

Human intervention has been recognized as a source for improving the performance of matchers [16,24]. In [24] experts are required to provide correspondences for a subset of the model pairs in a model collection. With regard to these correspondences the quality of different matchers is determined. Then, a prediction model that correlates process characteristics to the quality of the matchers is trained and used to select matchers for the remaining model pairs. Similarly, an approach that exploits expert feedback to learn the domain specific vocabulary used in a model collection is introduced in [16]. Correspondences that were automatically determined and manually corrected by experts are analyzed and the textual similarity assessment is adopted. This way improvements with regard to the f-measure of up to 53 % compared to the state-of-the-art were achieved. We pursue the idea of relying on human intelligence, in particular utilizing the crowd, to reduce the workload for experts and speed up the matching process.

3   Crowdsourcing the Activity Matching Problem

Crowdsourcing (CS) is the outsourcing of a unit of work to a crowd of people via an open call for contributions [13]. A *worker* is a member of the crowd (a human) that performs work, and a *requester* is the organization, company or individual that crowdsources work. For the purpose of this paper, we specifically leverage on work expressed as *micro-tasks*, where crowdsourcing a micro-task (simply "task" in the following) involves the following steps: The requester publishes a description of the task to be performed in a crowdsourcing platform. The crowd inspects and possibly expresses interest for tasks. The requester also defines the reward workers will get for performing the task and how many answers (task instances) should be collected (instantiated) per task. Not everybody of the crowd may, however, be eligible to perform a given task, either because the task requires specific capabilities (e.g., language skills) or because the workers should satisfy given properties (e.g., only female workers). Deciding which workers are allowed to perform a task is called pre-selection, is optional, and may be done either by the requester manually or by the platform automatically (e.g., via gold data). Once workers are enabled to perform a task, the platform creates as many task instances as necessary to collect the expected number of answers. Upon completion of a task instance (or a set thereof), the requester may inspect the collected answers and validate the respective quality. Work that is not of sufficient quality is not useful, and the requester may not reward it.

The major challenge in designing a crowd task is to ensure that the requester can rely on the results. That means the results obtained from the crowd have to be of a high quality and should only contain a small portion of imprecise or incorrect answers. To achieve this goal, the task designer has to bring together both worlds, that of the requester and that of the crowd. On the one hand, it is therefore necessary to design tasks in such a way that (i) workers obtain sufficient insights into the context, (ii) they can conveniently express their decisions, and (iii) quality is adequate in order to leverage the potential of the crowd. On the other hand, requirements imposed by the requester, like time or cost constraints as well as the confidentiality of information, need to be taken into account.

In this paper, we are specifically interested in studying opportunities to crowdsource the task of activity matching as an instance of the more general problem of correspondence identification. We thus started this study by structuring the problem space, in order to be able to discuss task design alternatives and guide our research. As a result, we developed a *conceptual crowdsourcing design framework for activity matching*, which decomposes the overall task into several fine-grained aspects that need to be considered. The framework is the result of a discussion on how to relate, combine or slice the aspects.

As shown in Table 1, on an abstract level the framework is concerned with (i) how *questions* are posed to workers, (ii) which options workers have when *answering*, and (iii) how *answer quality* is controlled. In the following, we discuss the complete framework with all of its dimensions in more detail.

Table 1. The conceptual crowdsourcing design framework for activity matching

Groups	Dimensions	Options		
Question	Task description	Correspondence identification	Activity cluster identification	Activity annotation
	Representation	Whole process	Process fragment	Activity label
	Documentation	Additional		None
Answer	Modality	Fixed	Free	Combination
	Range	Binary	Numeric	Semantic
	Direction	Unidirectional		Bidirectional
Quality	Audience	External	Internal	Team
	Timing	Before	During	After
	Test nature	Gold questions		Ad-hoc questions

Question group: This group defines what specific tasks the contributors are asked to perform, in order to enable the matching of activities from different process models, and which information is provided.

Task description—It is important to describe well the task and its purpose to clarify what the requester wants to obtain from the workers. *Correspondence identification* asks for feedback on the relations between activities or sets thereof to separate corresponding from non-corresponding activities. *Activity cluster identification* addresses relations of activities within the same model to identify activities that relate to a same higher-level activity. *Activity annotation* solicits feedback regarding a single activity to enable an indirect alignment of activities, e.g., by mapping them to a taxonomy that could be a set of harmonized labels, a set of semantic annotations or a reference process.

Representation—As process models show the internals of how an organization operates, there may exist privacy concerns in showing them to public workers. Instead of showing the *whole process model*, only a *process fragment* may be shown, or even only *activity labels* without any further information. This dimension is also characterized by a tradeoff between complexity and quality: showing large models at full may overwhelm workers, while it might be necessary for workers to have sufficient information to take decisions.

Documentation—*Additional* documentation, such as a short explanation or even process handbooks or glossaries, might be presented to workers to provide help and instructions on how to perform the task. Yet, it could be a choice to provide *no* documentation, if the task is self-explaining or the documentation might again overwhelm the worker.

Answer group: While the question group refers to the presentation of the task, this group defines how workers can answer questions.

Modality—This concerns the degree of freedom a worker has in answering. The workers might be asked to select from a *fixed* set of options or to enter a *free* text answer. Furthermore, *combined* versions where workers can select from a set of options or enter a new answer are conceivable.

Range—Requesters might be interested in different aspects of relations between two activities or one activity and a taxonomy element. In the most simple case, workers are expected to give a *binary* value indicating whether a relation holds or not. Alternatively, the degree to which a relation holds can be measured on a *numeric* scale, e.g., 0–100 %. Relations might also be assigned to a *semantic* class, such as "unrelated", "A subsumes B", or "equal".

Direction—This dimension specifies if relations among activities expressed by a worker by relating one activity to another are *unidirectional* or *bidirectional*. The use of bidirectional relations may reduce the effort needed to match activities.

Quality group. This group characterizes the methods adopted to ensure that the answers by the crowd are reliable and useful to the requester.

Audience—In general, tasks may be crowdsourced to different audiences. If the requester is an organization with own employees, *internal* workforce might be considered, while *external* crowds can be involved by any kind of requester. The involvement of *teams* of workers, which have proven to promise better results (e.g., experts that work together on the alignment of processes), is harder.

Timing—Quality control methods can be applied *before* (e.g., by excluding workers based on skill tests), *during* (e.g., by incorporating test questions to validate the experts answers) or *after* (e.g., by removing inconsistent and unreliable answers) feedback collection. Several methods can be used in an experiment.

Test nature—Tests can come in the form of so-called *gold questions*, that is, questions that workers are asked to answer but for which the answers are already known, or in the form of *ad-hoc questions*, which are added to the task only for testing purposes (e.g., skills test or CAPTCHA-like tests to tell workers and robots apart) without any real use for the requester.

Jointly, these dimensions span a space of potential task designs. A particular crowdsourcing experiment can be understood as a point in this space. Without considering that selected options can be implemented in different ways or that certain combinations might be impractical, the space has $2^3 \times 3^6 = 5832$ points. Yet, the framework can still be extended with additional dimensions, e.g., we do not specifically study the effect of different rewards in this paper. Nevertheless, the framework serves as a useful tool for taking informed decisions about task designs and for comparing them. In the next section, we will use the framework to describe the three task designs we adopt in our study.

4   Study Design

4.1   Dataset

The *dataset* we use for the experiments in this paper is a subset of that introduced in [20], which consists of nine models (36 different model pairs) of the study admission processes at different German universities. The models were created by graduate students from Humboldt-Universität zu Berlin within a research seminar on process modeling in three semesters. We use the respective BPMN models with 10 to 44 activities and an average of 21 activities per model.

The *subset* of process models we selected for the study described in this paper consists of four models (Frankfurt (F), TU Munich (M), Cologne (C), FU Berlin (B)) and three model pairs. Models were paired to represent different levels of syntactical label similarity, so as to enable a representative comparison of the crowd with automated algorithms: F/M has 10 activities with exactly the same activity labels, C/F only 6, and C/B 0 (none). Limiting the study to three model pairs was necessary to contain the cost of the crowd and expert experiments.

All process models express semi-formal, high-level views on the processes and are not executable without further refinement. For instance, the models do not make use of pools and swim lanes, follow different activity naming conventions (they stem from different modelers), are characterized by ambiguity (for instance, it is very hard to assess what action and/or role the activities "Keep in Applicant pool" or "document" refer to), and gateways partly lack conditions. Yet, this is the typical situation of process repositories that contain models whose purpose is documentation rather than execution. The dataset has already been used for a comparative evaluation of matching approaches in [5] as well as for the evaluation of a matching approach based on expert feedback in [16] and represents a convenient choice for the comparison with prior works.

Since in this study we are particularly interested in understanding the effect of the human interpretation of models by both the crowd and experts, we opted not to reuse the *ground truth* mappings proposed in [20]. On the one hand, these mappings turned out to be too restrictive in our initial trials and mostly focused on exact matches (no separation of the *match* and *partof* relationships); on the other hand, without insight into the individual researchers' mappings prior to the consolidation it is not possible to assess inter-expert agreement. The creation of a new ground truth is thus part of the experiment described next.

4.2 Expert-Based Activity Matching Exercise

In order to (i) be able to study the agreement among experts about activity matchings and (ii) have a ground truth for the comparison of the crowd with automated algorithms, we set up an activity matching exercise that involved five process modeling experts (one PhD candidate, three PhDs and one assistant professor, all with BPMN expertise). The exercise aimed to produce four *individual mappings* for each of the three model pairs, plus one *consolidated mapping* that integrates the other four according to the judgement by the most senior participant. All participants were provided with the BPMN models of the four chosen processes and asked to identify all possible *match* and *partof* relationships for each of the three process pairs (F/M, C/F, C/B–see Sect. 4.1). Data were collected using a Google Spreadsheet (https://goo.gl/N3xNgb), and activities and relationships could be selected from suitable dropdown lists; the spreadsheets also contained links to the graphical BPMN models and allowed the experts to express a similarity degree for identified matches using a 7-point Likert scale ranging from "somehow similar" to "the same" as well as to provide informal feedback. All experts concluded the exercise within 30–60 min and were rewarded with a free lunch for their effort.

4.3   Machine-Based Matching Algorithms

As a baseline for the assessment of the crowd's performance we use two automated matching techniques. First, we consider the *bag-of-words technique* (BOT) [17]. For a given pair of process models, BOT iterates over the set of all activity pairs where each pair contains one activity from each model being matched. It computes a similarity score based on the activity labels, and retains all activity pairs with a score higher than a predefined threshold. To compute the similarity score, the labels are split into sets of words, and each word in one set is compared to each word in the other set using a word similarity function. The final similarity score is the average of the maximum similarity scores for each word. If the two sets of words are of a different size, the larger set is reduced to the size of the smaller set by removing the words with the lowest maximum word similarity. In this study, we specifically use the configuration we submitted to the first Process Model Matching Contest and that yielded the best results on the university admission dataset in this contest [5].

The second technique is the *order preserving bag-of-words technique* (OPBOT) which contains different BOT configurations that it applies to a model collection separately. For each configuration it predicts the quality by investigating structural relations between the proposed correspondences. OPBOT then selects the most promising configuration and proposes its results. Similar to BOT, we utilized the configuration that participated in the second contest and was named as one of two outstanding matching techniques [2].

4.4   Crowd-Based Micro-Tasks

Crowdsourcing platforms have different built-in options that support the aspects of the design framework in Table 1 to different degrees. We use Crowdflower (www.crowdflower.com) and propose three different task designs that vary in terms of the contextual information provided (none vs. process fragments) and the freedom given to workers in choosing matches (none vs. free definition of matches). The intuition behind these design options is that (i) contextual information (surrounding activities) helps making better judgements about the similarity of tasks and (ii) freedom of choice allows us to match activities more cost-effectively. All task designs ask workers to (i) decide if one or more pairs of activities are similar (*yes/no* answer) and to provide, for each identified match, (ii) the type of relationship (*match/partof*), (iii) a similarity score using a 7-point Likert scale (1-Not similar at all–7-Very similar or identical); and (iv) a free-text explanation of the judgment. The specific designs are (see design sketches in Fig. 1):

- *LabelOnly* is the most simple task design. It applies the computational approach to the crowd: workers are only presented with two activity labels.

- *ContextOne* shows two fragments with 3–5 activities from two process models and highlights the activities to be matched (1 per fragment).
- *ContextSet* shows the same process fragments as *ContextOne*, without however highlighting any pair of activities. If the workers spot a similarity, they can freely choose the respective activities from dropdown lists; the design allows the identification of up to 10 matches. No explanations are required.

For *LabelOnly* and *ContextOne* we have a total of 989 activity pairs to be compared; for *ContexSet* we have 63 process fragment pairs, given how we split the models. For all three task designs, we collect 3 judgements per pair (to improve quality), which leads us to a total number of 6123 units of work to crowdsource. We also use Crowdflower's built-in quality control based on gold questions (with known answers). For *LabelOnly* and *ContextOne*, the gold question asks whether or not the activities are similar; for *ContextSet* the gold question asks if there are similar activities in process fragments. As reward for *LabelOnly* and *ContextOne* we pay US\$ 0.01 for each unit of work, while for *ContextSet* we pay US\$ 0.05 as it requires more effort.

In terms of the design framework introduced in Sect. 3, all designs ask workers to identify *correspondences*, *without* providing additional documentation beyond an example. *LabelOnly* shows only *activity labels*, the other two designs use *process fragments*. All designs, except *ContextSet* (only *selections*) allow workers to input a *combination* of selections and free text in the form of *binary*, *numerical* and *semantic* inputs. Matchings are *bidirectional*, part-of relations *unidirectional*. The crowd is *external* (indep. of the authors), and quality control is done *during* task execution and *afterwards* with the help of *gold questions*.

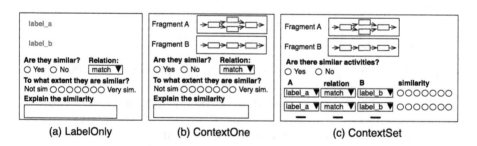

(a) LabelOnly   (b) ContextOne   (c) ContextSet

Fig. 1. Micro-task designs for activity matching. Actual screenshots of the tasks deployed in Crowdflower can be found in https://goo.gl/xjCHmv

4.5   Evaluation Metrics

For the evaluation of the agreement between the experts in the creation of the ground truth and with the consolidated set of matchings, we use the *Jaccard similarity coefficient*, which expresses the similarity/diversity of sample sets:

$$J(M_i, M_j) = \frac{|M_i \cap M_j|}{|M_i \cup M_j|} \tag{1}$$

where M_i and M_j are the sets of correspondences identified by experts i and j. If the experts agree on each match, $J(M_i, M_j) = 1$, otherwise $J(M_i, M_j) < 1$.

Now, given a ground truth, each correspondence identified by an activity matching approach can be classified as true positive (TP), false positive (FP) or false-negative (FN). This allows the computation of the common *precision*, *recall* and *f-measure*, as defined by the following formulas:

$$P = \frac{TP}{TP + FP} \quad (2) \qquad R = \frac{TP}{TP + FN} \quad (3) \qquad F = \frac{2 \times P \times R}{P + R} \quad (4)$$

Since in this study we explicitly distinguish between *match* and *partof* relationships among activities, we compute P, R and F for exact matches and part-of relationships individually, as well as for the union of both relationships. This allows us to study the strengths and weaknesses of the approaches.

5   Experiment

5.1   Expert-Based Activity Matching

The activity matching exercise with the experts produced a rich set of activity matchings, as reported in Table 2. Overall, the five experts identified 252 correspondences, 95 exact matches and 157 part-of relationships, with an average of 6.33 matches and 10.47 part-of relations per process model pair. The consolidation of the four individual results yielded 14 matches and 45 part-of relationships. Part-of relationships among activities are therefore so frequent that they cannot be neglected in practical activity matching exercises.

Table 3 analyzes the correspondences by the five experts in more detail with a cross-analysis of the respective Jaccard similarities, in order to understand the level of agreement or disagreement among the experts. We immediately note that there is no clear agreement among any of the experts. We also note that the consolidated mapping generally represents well the output by the four individual experts, especially if we compute similarity by merging both (b) matches and part-of relations; only expert 1 seems to have more affinity with expert 2 than with the consolidated mapping. This qualifies the consolidated mapping as the best choice for the evaluation of the performance of the crowd and the algorithms.

5.2   Machine-Based Activity Matching

Table 4 presents the performance of the automated matchers with regard to the consolidated ground truth. The f-measures vary from 0.276 to 0.538 for BOT and from 0.276 to 0.621 for OPBOT across all three model pairs. OPBOT performs slightly better than BOT (0.481 > 0.448) with a better precision and a similar recall. Overall, it is interesting to note that the precision of the identified matches is generally high, while the recall is instead rather low. That is, if activity labels are similar, both algorithms are able to spot the similarity; if instead labels of

Table 2. Number of *match* (m) and *partof* (p) relations identified by the experts.

	Expert 1		Expert 2		Expert 3		Expert 4		Consolidated	
	m	p	m	p	m	p	m	p	m	p
F/M	6	5	9	12	8	5	18	5	7	12
C/F	5	9	6	8	6	3	7	8	4	12
C/B	3	14	4	19	4	6	5	18	3	21
total	14	28	19	39	18	14	30	31	14	45

Table 3. Jaccard similarity among experts of *match* (m), *partof* (p) and both together (b), averaged over the three process pairs; in bold the biggest similarities.

	Expert 1			Expert 2			Expert 3			Expert 4		
	m	p	b	m	p	b	m	p	b	m	p	b
Expert 1	–			.435	.340	.515	.391	.077	.345	.333	.311	.431
Expert 2	**.435**	**.340**	**.515**	–			.609	.205	.452	.441	.400	.566
Expert 3	.391	.077	.345	.609	.205	.452	–			**.500**	.286	.431
Expert 4	.333	.311	.431	.441	.400	.566	.500	**.286**	.431	–		
Consolidated	.400	.304	.464	**.650**	**.615**	**.746**	**.684**	.229	**.468**	.467	**.551**	**.667**

similar activities are not similar enough, the algorithms fail. Also, computing recall over matches (R_m) and part-of relations (R_p) independently unveils that the algorithms are better in identifying exact matches than part-of relations.

Table 4. Average precision (P), recall (R, R_m, R_p) and f-measure (F) of BOT and OPBOT for the three process pairs separated by matching relation.

BOT					OPBOT				
P	R	R_m	R_p	F	P	R	R_m	R_p	F
.700	.359	.536	.258	.448	.900	.338	.536	.230	.481

5.3   Crowd-Based Activity Matching

Table 5 reports on P, R and F for the crowdsourcing experiments, distinguishing between different levels of worker agreement on correspondences (recall that each activity pair was assessed 3 times). We consider two activities to be similar if either a *partof* or *match* relation was indicated by the crowd. For *LabelOnly* and *ContextOne*, the precision is lower than that of the algorithms, while the recall is higher. Interestingly, *ContextSet* shows a very good precision, up to 0.861 for 3/3 votes, however with a lower recall; the freedom given to workers seems to intrinsically favor precision, e.g., because workers only propose matches they are highly confident with. If we split R into R_m (matches only) and R_p (part-of relations only), we see that the crowd is particularly good at recalling exact

Table 5. Average P, R, R_m, R_p, and F values for LabelOnly, ContextOne and ContextSet as a function of worker agreement (x out of 3 votes); best averages in bold.

	LabelOnly					ContextOne					ContextSet				
	P	R	R_m	R_p	F	P	R	R_m	R_p	F	P	R	R_m	R_p	F
1/3 votes	.194	**.791**	.758	**.393**	.207	.207	.781	**.917**	.349	.320	.548	.512	.758	.123	**.530**
2/3 votes	.410	.558	.758	.274	.453	.467	.600	.869	.222	.509	.635	.321	.647	.059	.417
3/3 votes	.582	.491	.758	.190	.515	.631	.460	.758	.147	.515	**.861**	.192	.516	.016	.310

matches ($R_m \in [.758, .917]$ for *ContextOne*). Of course, the higher the agreement among workers, the higher the precision and the lower the recall.

Table 6 analyzes in more detail the correctness of the *TPs* by model pair using the agreement level with the highest f-measure in Table 5. For instance, for F/M all matches proposed by the workers are correct, while only 30 % of their part-of relations are correct. Overall, the proposed matches are very precise; the part-of relations less so.

Table 6. Correctness of workers' *match* and *partof* relations (true positives only).

	LabelOnly (3/3 votes)		ContextOne (3/3 votes)		ContextSet (1/3 votes)	
	m	p	m	p	m	p
F/M	1.00	.300	.947	.400	1.00	.333
C/F	1.00	.480	.900	.364	1.00	.100
C/B	.571	.552	.875	.615	.500	.471
Avg	.912	.459	.919	.471	.926	.333

A qualitative analysis of the *FNs* (31) confirms the difficulties with the part-of relations, e.g., with the similarity between "Apply Online" and "add certificate of bachelor degree," as well as with modeling ambiguity, e.g., with "Evaluate" (activity) vs. "less than 16 cp in mathematics" (condition). An analysis of the *FPs* (15) reveals that the crowd may actually be right in some cases, e.g., "certificate received" vs. "documents received" (synonyms) or "Acceptance" vs. "accepted provisionally" (part-of), if the domain of the study was different. That is, most *FPs* actually are plausible ground truth candidates.

The cost of the experiments was US\$40.56, US\$40.80 and US\$28.32 for *LabelOnly*, *ContextOne* and *ContextSet*, respectively, including platform fees.

6   Discussion

We summarize the findings of this study as follows: (i) Process models can be *intrinsically ambiguous*, underspecified and even contradicting. Matching activities under these conditions requires an interpretation that goes beyond the scope of individual activity labels. (ii) Given this ambiguity, even *experts may not agree* on how to match activities. In fact, the disagreements we encountered in our experiments are both consistent and high among all experts. (iii) On the newly created ground truth data, the performance of the tested computational matchers was characterized by *high precision and low recall*, with a particular weakness in discovering part-of relationships among activities. (iv) Crowd-based activity matching outperformed the automated matchers by a margin of about 10 %. Depending on the logic used for combining crowd worker answers, however, *high recall can be achieved when sacrificing precision*. The crowd was also able to elicit non-obvious part-of relationships by reasoning on activities like experts do, that is, trying to figure out the essence of activities (action, role, object). (v) The design of the micro-tasks for activity matching has a *strong effect on the quality* of the produced matchings. The three task designs we tested showed significant performance differences, depending on the level of insight into the context of activities as well as on the level of freedom (responsibility) given to workers. Asking the crowd to reactively judge a given activity pair tends to favor recall (*ContextOne*); asking it to proactively identify similar pairs tends to favor precision (*ContextSet*). (vi) Given the low agreement among the experts, the *P/R values reported here must however be handled and interpreted with care*. The less formal and complete models are, the more ambiguous they are, and the harder it is also to define a reliable ground truth and, hence, to reliably test approaches. The variance and disagreement in human feedback leads to the larger question: *is the assumption that an objective ground truth or "gold" standard exists valid?*

These findings advance the state of the art of activity and process matching with an original perspective on the problem compared to prior works on the topic, i.e., that of the human. To the best of our knowledge, this is the first study that proposes a crowd-based activity matching approach and compares it with state-of-the-art computational approaches. It is also one of the first studies that critically analyzes the (lack of) agreement among experts and that shows that performance tests based on ground truth data elicited from experts must be interpreted with care, perhaps more care than devoted to this aspect so far.

A consideration regarding the "noise" (spectrum and variety of matchings) produced by the crowd: while false positives (compared to the ground truth) by algorithms may not present useful information, the "false positives" by the crowd may even represent an *added value* in the context of process model matching. In fact, these matches may represent similarities the experts did not consider when creating the ground truth, e.g., because they simply were focused on a specific domain while the crowd was not. Especially in the context of exploratory search over process repositories (to search for similar practices, to understand how a given organization approaches typical problems, to identify processes that could be merged and consolidated, etc.) the different viewpoints and interpretations provided by the crowd may allow the discovery of unexpected models that indeed present semantic similarities not considered before. This kind of knowledge is hard if not impossible to elicit without the contribution of human intelligence.

Of course, the study described in this paper also comes with its very own limitations: The dataset we used contains processes that are very similar; results might change for more heterogeneous datasets. The micro-task designs we used represent a reasoned best effort, and we did not yet try to optimize results, for example by varying the reward of workers. Our experiments exemplarily analyzed three process model pairs, and obtaining statistical relevance of the results would require more data; due to resource restrictions, we opted for a more qualitative analysis. Finally, even though the results are promising, given the crowd costs reported in our study and the efforts in setting up an experiment like this, there is a trade-off that needs to be considered before opting for a crowd-based approach.

In our future work, we intend to extend the presented work in several directions. Different approaches from crowd workers and algorithms have different strengths: while some approaches have a high recall, others achieve high precision. We thus plan to investigate how we can combine approaches into novel matching workflows that combine the benefits of several approaches. For instance, we could use a crowd task design that yields high recall values at the expense of precision, and use an automated matcher to filter the crowd results. We also see as highly interesting understanding the human perception of similarity better. Such research would likely benefit from an interdisciplinary approach, in collaboration with psychologists, linguists, or sociologists.

Acknowledgement. We would like to thank M. Vitali, G. Meroni, P. Plebani (Politecnico di Milano) and S. Tranquillini and J. Stevovic (Chino, Trento) for their help with the creation of the ground truth matchings for the experiments.

References

1. Allahbakhsh, M., Benatallah, B., Ignjatovic, A., Motahari-Nezhad, H., Bertino, E., Dustdar, S.: Quality control in crowdsourcing systems: issues and directions. IEEE Internet Comput. **17**(2), 76–81 (2013)
2. Antunes, G., et al.: The process model matching contest 2015. In: EMISA (2015)
3. Castelo Branco, M., Troya, J., Czarnecki, K., Küster, J., Völzer, H.: Matching business process workflows across abstraction levels. In: France, R.B., Kazmeier, J., Breu, R., Atkinson, C. (eds.) MODELS 2012. LNCS, vol. 7590, pp. 626–641. Springer, Heidelberg (2012)
4. Cavallo, R., Jain, S.: Efficient crowdsourcing contests. Proc. AAMAS **2**, 677–686 (2012)
5. Cayoglu, U. et al.: The process model matching contest 2013. In: PMC-MR (2013)
6. Dijkman, R., Dumas, M., García-Bañuelos, L.: Graph matching algorithms for business process model similarity search. In: Dayal, U., Eder, J., Koehler, J., Reijers, H.A. (eds.) BPM 2009. LNCS, vol. 5701, pp. 48–63. Springer, Heidelberg (2009)
7. Dijkman, R., Dumas, M., Garcia-Banuelos, L., Kaarik, R.: Aligning business process models. In: EDOC 2009, pp. 45–53 (2009)
8. Dijkman, R., Dumas, M., van Dongen, B., Käärik, R., Mendling, J.: Similarity of business process models: metrics and evaluation. Inf. Syst. **36**(2), 498–516 (2011)
9. Dumas, M., García-Bañuelos, L., Dijkman, R.M.: Similarity search of business process models. IEEE Data Eng. Bull. **32**(3), 23–28 (2009)
10. Ekanayake, C.C., Dumas, M., García-Bañuelos, L., La Rosa, M., ter Hofstede, A.H.M.: Approximate clone detection in repositories of business process models. In: Barros, A., Gal, A., Kindler, E. (eds.) BPM 2012. LNCS, vol. 7481, pp. 302–318. Springer, Heidelberg (2012)
11. Euzenat, J., Shvaiko, P.: Ontology Matching. Springer, Secaucus (2007)
12. Grigori, D., Corrales, J.C., Bouzeghoub, M.: Behavioral matchmaking for service retrieval. In: IEEE ICWS, pp. 145–152 (2006)

13. Howe, J.: Crowdsourcing: Why the Power of the Crowd Is Driving the Future of Business, 1st edn. Crown Publishing Group, New York (2008)
14. Ipeirotis, P.G.: Analyzing the amazon mechanical turk marketplace. XRDS **17**(2), 16–21 (2010)
15. Jin, T., Wang, J., Rosa, M.L., ter Hofstede, A.H., Wen, L.: Efficient querying of large process model repositories. Comput. Ind. **64**(1), 41–49 (2013)
16. Klinkmüller, C., Leopold, H., Weber, I., Mendling, J., Ludwig, A.: Listen to me: improving process model matching through user feedback. In: Sadiq, S., Soffer, P., Völzer, H. (eds.) BPM 2014. LNCS, vol. 8659, pp. 84–100. Springer, Heidelberg (2014)
17. Klinkmüller, C., Weber, I., Mendling, J., Leopold, H., Ludwig, A.: Increasing recall of process model matching by improved activity label matching. In: Daniel, F., Wang, J., Weber, B. (eds.) BPM 2013. LNCS, vol. 8094, pp. 211–218. Springer, Heidelberg (2013)
18. Koschmider, A., Blanchard, E.: User assistance for business process model decomposition. In: IEEE RCIS, pp. 445–454 (2007)
19. Kunze, M., Weidlich, M., Weske, M.: Behavioral similarity – a proper metric. In: Rinderle-Ma, S., Toumani, F., Wolf, K. (eds.) BPM 2011. LNCS, vol. 6896, pp. 166–181. Springer, Heidelberg (2011)
20. Leopold, H., Niepert, M., Weidlich, M., Mendling, J., Dijkman, R., Stuckenschmidt, H.: Probabilistic optimization of semantic process model matching. In: Barros, A., Gal, A., Kindler, E. (eds.) BPM 2012. LNCS, vol. 7481, pp. 319–334. Springer, Heidelberg (2012)
21. Sakr, S., Awad, A., Kunze, M.: Querying process models repositories by aggregated graph search. In: Rosa, M., Soffer, P. (eds.) BPM Workshops 2012. LNBIP, vol. 132, pp. 573–585. Springer, Heidelberg (2013)
22. Satzger, B., Psaier, H., Schall, D., Dustdar, S.: Auction-based crowdsourcing supporting skill management. Inf. Syst. **38**(4), 547–560 (2013)
23. Weidlich, M., Dijkman, R., Mendling, J.: The ICoP framework: identification of correspondences between process models. In: Pernici, B. (ed.) CAiSE 2010. LNCS, vol. 6051, pp. 483–498. Springer, Heidelberg (2010)
24. Weidlich, M., Sagi, T., Leopold, H., Gal, A., Mendling, J.: Predicting the quality of process model matching. In: Daniel, F., Wang, J., Weber, B. (eds.) BPM 2013. LNCS, vol. 8094, pp. 203–210. Springer, Heidelberg (2013)
25. Weidlich, M., Sheetrit, E., Branco, M.C., Gal, A.: Matching business process models using positional passage-based language models. In: ER 2013, pp. 130–137 (2013)
26. Zha, H., Wang, J., Wen, L., Wang, C., Sun, J.: A workflow net similarity measure based on transition adjacency relations. Comput. Ind. **61**(5), 463–471 (2010)

Process Model Comparison Based on Cophenetic Distance

David Sánchez-Charles[1]([✉]), Victor Muntés-Mulero[1],
Josep Carmona[2], and Marc Solé[1]

[1] CA Strategic Research Labs, CA Technologies, Barcelona, Spain
{David.Sanchez,Victor.Muntes,Marc.SoleSimo}@ca.com
[2] Universitat Politècnica de Catalunya, Barcelona, Spain
jcarmona@cs.upc.edu

Abstract. The automated comparison of process models has received increasing attention in the last decade, due to the growing existence of process models and repositories, and the consequent need to assess similarities between the underlying processes. Current techniques for process model comparison are either structural (based on graph edit distances), or behavioural (through activity profiles or the analysis of the execution semantics). Accordingly, there is a gap between the quality of the information provided by these two families, i.e., structural techniques may be fast but inaccurate, whilst behavioural are accurate but complex. In this paper we present a novel technique, that is based on a well-known technique to compare labeled trees through the notion of *Cophenetic distance*. The technique lays between the two families of methods for comparing a process model: it has an structural nature, but can provide accurate information on the differences/similarities of two process models. The experimental evaluation on various benchmarks sets are reported, that position the proposed technique as a valuable tool for process model comparison.

1 Introduction

Nowadays process models are ubiquitous objects in companies and organizations. They are becoming precious for representing unambiguous and detailed descriptions of real processes. On the one hand, *BPMS* platforms, which allow designing, deploying and managing the processes in organizations, are based on process models. On the other hand, evidence-based process models (i.e., process models with a high alignment with respect to the underlying real process) can be used to analyze the process formally, e.g., detecting inconsistencies or performance problems that may hamper the correct and optimal execution of the process. Furthermore, the existence of environments for creating, managing and querying *process model collections* enable the hierarchical and cross-organizational analysis, with process models as atomic objects.

A core technique necessary in many of the aforementioned situations is the automated comparison of process models. Due to its importance, this problem has received significant attention in the BPM field, which can be split into

© Springer International Publishing Switzerland 2016
M. La Rosa et al. (Eds.): BPM Forum 2016, LNBIP 260, pp. 141–158, 2016.
DOI: 10.1007/978-3-319-45468-9_9

structural techniques based on graph-edit distance [8–10,18], and *behavioural techniques* that focus on the execution semantics or behavioural relations of the corresponding models [1,7,13,16,17]. Intuitively, structural techniques are fast but inaccurate (in terms of the differences found), whereas pure behavioural techniques are complex (both in computation time and memory usage) but accurate.

In this paper we propose a novel method to compare process models[1]. The technique is based on a recent algorithm [5] from the field of *computational phylogenetics*, where the objects to compare are labeled trees showing the inferred evolutionary relationships among various biological species. We adapt the algorithm to the BPM context, thus using *process trees* [4] as notation. Our proposed similarity metric sits halfway between pure structural similarity methods (inheriting their low complexity features), and behavioural similarity metrics (capable of providing similar behavioural information). Moreover, the performance of our approach allow us to consider this metric for large process models.

The paper is organized as follows: next section provides an intuition of the metric over a realistic example. In Sect. 3 the necessary preliminaries are provided. Then in Sect. 4 we present the main contribution of the paper: a similarity metric for deterministic process trees. The deterministic restriction is dropped in Sect. 5, giving rise to a heuristic technique that relies on an approximate matching algorithm. The techniques of the paper are evaluated thoroughly in Sect. 6. Finally, Sect. 7 concludes the paper and provides pointers for future investigations.

2   Motivating Example

Let us use a real-life example to motivate the contributions of this paper. A product manager decides to monitor all accesses to an SVN repository. Those accesses are done through HTTP/S, as specified in the WebDAV/DeltaV protocol. It turns out that those read and write requests over HTTP/S can be translated to human-friendly SVN commands such as *svn update* or *svn commit*. Continuing the work done by Li Sun et al. [15], the product manager plans to model the developer's behaviour based on the SVN commands they execute daily. Our goal is to measure the differences between those models, inducing a behavioural distance between individuals. This way, intruder attacks to the repository can be detected globally by analyzing process behaviour that is clearly separated from the rest.

Figure 1 depicts the access behaviour of two users to the same repository, using a block-structured process discovery algorithm[2]. In our preliminary study,

---

[1] We assume the problem of dealing with real activity labels, e.g., when the name of an activity in the models does not perfectly match, is resolved prior to the techniques of this paper.

[2] We used *Discover a Process Tree using Inductive Miner (ProM 6.5)* and then converted them to Petri Nets.

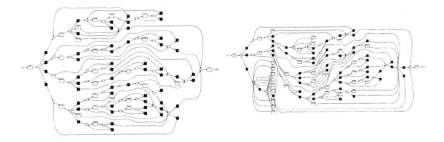

Fig. 1. Two process models describing how two users access an SVN repository.

the process model of an average user shows lots of concurrency, duplicate activities and iterative behaviour[3]. Existing behavioural comparison techniques struggle when dealing with such models. Either they fall short in describing duplicate activities and loops [16], or the underlying technique does not scale in the presence of concurrent process branches [1].

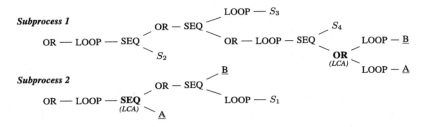

Fig. 2. Extract of the tree representation of the two processes in Fig. 1. Only the subtrees related to two common activities A and B are represented, and their least common ancestors are depicted in bold. Activities S_i are unrelated to A and B.

The approach presented in this paper evaluates the difference of the two minimum subtrees containing a selected pair of activities, and extends the comparison to all possible pairs. Analysis over such subtrees is expected to be more simple and efficient, while still capable of comparing both the structure and behaviour of the two processes. See Fig. 2 for an example, which focuses on activities A and B in both models. One can check that the difference between the depth of the two activities is an approximation to the graph distance between those two models. For instance, in Fig. 2, depths of A are 11 in the first subprocess and 4 in the second subprocess, whilst depths of B are 11 and 6. The difference of their depths sum 12, implying that 8 nodes must be removed and 2 extra edges are needed in order to transform one model into the other. Besides, and more

---

[3] The most common sequence of commands in the dataset is *svn-options, svn update, svn -options* indicating they use an IDE that overwrites the SVN options just to perform an update and then returns to its previous status.

importantly, one can see that the common ancestors of activities A and B in Fig. 2 model two different behaviours: On the first subprocess, activities A and B are mutually exclusive; On the second, A is executed after activity B. Notice that the depth of this common ancestor also highlights how long it takes to make the *behavioural decision* of how activities A and B relate to each other. Therefore, by incorporating these notions into the distance function, we would be able to not only measure structural differences but also highlight differences in the behaviour of two process models. For instance, one could obtain the sentence: *Activities A and B in Fig. 2 are mutually exclusive in the first subprocess, but activity A always occurs after B in the second subprocess. Besides, the behavioural decision in the first subprocess is done 6 steps after the decision is taken in the second subprocess.*

3   Background

3.1   Process Trees: A Tree-Like Representation of Business Processes

A **rooted tree** is a directed graph with a distinguished node, called the root, from which every node can be reached with exactly one path. A **weighted rooted tree** is a pair (T, ω) consisting of a rooted tree T and a weight function $\omega : E \rightarrow \mathbb{R}_{>0}$ that associates every arc $e \in E$ a non-negative real number $\omega(e) > 0$. A **labeled rooted tree** is a rooted tree T such that there exists a mapping between a subset of the nodes of the tree and a set of labels S.

Let $T = (V, E)$ be a rooted tree. Whenever $(u, v) \in E$, we say that v is a child of u and that u is the parent of v. The nodes without children are the leaves of the tree, and the other nodes are called internal. Whenever there exists a path from a node u to a node v, we say that v is a descendant of u and also that u is an ancestor of v. An internal node is **elementary** if it only has one child. The **depth** of a node u in a tree T, denoted by $\delta_T(u)$, is the sum of the weights of the arcs in the path from the root to u. Weights are usually set to 1, but we will later see that we can encode behavioural information from the process by modifying these weights.

Definition 1 ([4]). *A **process tree** is a labeled rooted tree T in which activities are represented as leaves of the tree and internal nodes describe the control-flow of the process.*

We say that a process tree is **deterministic** if there is a one-to-one mapping between activity labels and leaves of T. For the sake of simplicity, we will label internal labels as OR^4, AND, SEQ and $LOOP$ to represent the usual behavioural structures in a process model. We will also denote these internal nodes by **gateways**, following the BPMN nomenclature. We allow silent activities by labeling them as $\emptyset$.

---

[4] Following the semantics of block-structured models in [4], only exclusive ORs are modeled.

Definition 2. *A process tree is **reducible** if there are elementary nodes, silent transitions hanging over a gateway other than OR, or there exist a pair of internal nodes u and v such that (u, v) is an edge in the graph and both model the same type of gateway.*

Any *reducible* process tree can be converted into an *irreducible* tree by merging all conflicting nodes. We will suppose that all process trees are given in its irreducible form. Figure 3 depicts an example of a reducible process tree and its irreducible counterpart.

Fig. 3. Two process trees modeling exactly the same behaviour. The left model is reducible, and the right model is its irreducible representation. The silent transition ∅ is removed because it is not part of an OR structure. The OR elementary node does not provide behavioural information.

3.2   Cophenetic Vectors

The **least common ancestor** (LCA) of a pair of nodes u and v of a rooted tree T, denoted by $[u, v]_T$, is the unique common ancestor of them that is a descendant of every other common ancestor. The definition of the Cophenetic vector is based on the discrepancies on the depth of the LCA of every pair of activities.

Definition 3 ([14]). *Let S be the set of labels of a weighted labeled rooted tree T. For every pair of different labels i, j, their Cophenetic value is*

$$\varphi_T(i, j) = \delta_T([u, v]_T) \qquad u, v \text{ have labels } i, j$$

To simplify notation, we denote the depth of a node with label i by $\varphi_T(i, i)$, and $\varphi_T(i, j) = 0$ if either i or j are not activities of the process tree T.

Definition 4. *Let T be a weighted rooted tree, and S the set of activity labels of the tree T, its **Cophenetic vector** is*

$$\varphi(T) = (\varphi_T(i, j))_{i,j \in S}$$

In an already fifty years old paper [14], Sokal and Rohlf proposed the use of the cophenetic values to compare dendrograms. Authors in [5] show that cophenetic values can also be applied to uniquely project labelled trees into a multidimensional vector space, allowing them to define a distance on labelled trees as Theorem 1 states.

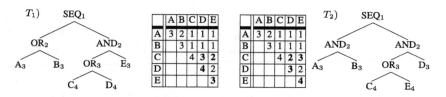

Fig. 4. Example of process trees and their Cophenetic vector (in matrix representation), assuming the depth of the root is 1. For simplicity, we included node's depth as a subscript of the label. For instance, the LCA of activities C and E in T_1 is the AND gateway that is one children of the root and, hence, its Cophenetic value is 2.

Theorem 1 ([5]). *Two weighted labeled trees without elementary nodes, unlabeled leaves nor repeated labels are equal if, and only if, they share the same Cophenetic vector.*

Cophenetic vectors are not enough for determining process tree similarity: for instance, in Fig. 4 if the OR and AND labels of the left tree are interchanged, the Cophenetic vectors of both trees are equal whilst the behaviour represented is different. Besides, constraints in Theorem 1 do not allow models with multiple silent transitions. Next section shows how to transform process trees in order to overcome this limitation.

4   Distance Between Deterministic Process Trees

4.1   Cophenetic Distance Definition

As we have seen, Cophenetic values unequivocally represents weighted labeled rooted trees. As it is well known, this allows to induce distance metrics in the set of labeled trees. Let $dist$ be any distance between two points in a vectorial space, we define

$$d(T, T') = dist(\varphi(T), \varphi(T'))$$

as the distance between two trees. For instance, by using the L^1-norm we get

$$d_1(T, T') = \sum_{i,j \in S} |\varphi_T(i, j) - \varphi_{T'}(i, j)|$$

The Cophenetic values were originally conceived to measure structural differences between the leaves of two dendograms, but we can extend its use to deterministic process trees thanks to Theorem 1. This result allow us to modify the depth of each node in order to model the path of gateways we are tracing from the root to activities (the leaves of the tree). In Definition 5 we propose a depth function to overcome the following weaknesses of the original Cophenetic distance over labelled trees: (1) ensures that non-common activities increases the distance between two models; (2) depth of activities in a sequential order increase in the same sequential order, modeling the complexity of the blocks already seen by the process; (3) allows for silent transitions; and (4) differentiates two processes with the same structure but modeling different gateways at the root.

Definition 5. *Let T be a deterministic process tree. We define the depth function δ'_T as follows:*

1. *Root node has depth 1.*
2. *Iterate over all nodes in a pre-order traversal.*
3. *The depth of all nodes is 1 plus the depth of its parent, except*
   (a) *If the parent is an OR clause, increase 0.5 instead of 1.*
   (b) *If the activity is silent, increase 0.25 the depth of the parent and any other sibling. Afterwards, remove the silent activity.*
   (c) *If the parent is the start of a LOOP, increase also by the maximum depth of the underlying tree.*
   (d) *If the parent is a SEQ gateway, consider the depth of deepest visited children of the node's siblings instead of the parent.*
4. *Any remaining elementary node will be removed, and its parent and children will be directly connected.*

For the sake of simplicity, $trf(T)$ will denote the combination of the tree T with the aforementioned depth function δ_T.

Figure 5 depicts the transformation of the two processes in Fig. 4. With the aforementioned depth function, Cophenetic values now highlight, for example, differences in the two activities A and B due to the behavioural change of their parent node. This transformation allow us to overcome the limitations of Theorem 1, since silent transitions are allowed, but also by ordering children of sequential gateways. As we state in Theorem 2, this transformation uniquely represents deterministic process trees.

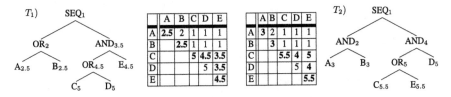

Fig. 5. Transformation of the process trees in Fig. 4. For the sake of simplicity, we included node's depth as a subscript of the label. For instance, depth of the *AND* gateway in T_1 is 3.5 because its parent represents a sequence and the maximum depth of the previous processed branch is 2.5

Theorem 2. *Let T and T' be two deterministic process trees. If $trf(T)$ and $trf(T')$ share the same Cophenetic vector, then T and T' are the same process tree.*

This theorem shows that Theorem 1 is also applicable to the new depth definition, and therefore useful for checking equality of two process trees and measuring differences between the models. The proof of this theorem is based on the observation that the Cophenetic values of any subtree are highly related to the Cophenetic values of the complete tree, as Lemma 1 shows. Details of the proof of this lemma are omitted, but it is a direct consequence of the pre-order traversal approach of Definition 5.

Lemma 1. *Let T be a weighted rooted tree, and S a subtree of T. Then the Cophenetic vector of S satisfies that*

$$\varphi_S(i,j) = \varphi_T(i,j) - \delta'_T(root\,of\,S) + 1$$

Proof (Theorem 2). Let's proof this by induction.

- For processes with 1 or 2 activities, one can list all possible deterministic process trees and check that no two processes share the same transformed tree.
- For processes with $n > 2$ activities, we will show that every strict subtree[5] of T is equal to another subtree of T'. Let VT be a strict subtree of T. Suppose A and B are two activities such that $[A, B]_T$ is the root of VT. Activities A and B are also included in the deterministic process tree T', and $[A, B]_{T'}$ is the root of a certain subtree VT'.

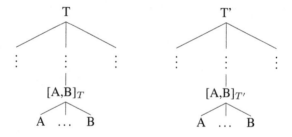

Lemma 1 ensures that

$$\varphi_{VT}(i,j) = \varphi_T(i,j) - \delta'_T([A, B]_T) + 1$$
$$= \varphi_{T'}(i,j) - \delta'_T([A, B]_{T'}) + 1 = \varphi_{VT'}(i,j)$$

where the second equality holds since $trf(T) = trf(T')$ and Theorem 1. And therefore, VT and VT' share the same Cophenetic vector and its size is smaller than T and T'. By induction, we can say that both process trees are equal. There is one case where there are no two activities A and B such that $[A, B]_T$ is the root of VT: The root of VT is an OR-clause, and one children is a silent transition. In this particular case, we can work with the non-silent children

---

[5] Here a strict subtree of T is any subtree that does not contain the root of T.

VT_{ns}. The combination of two consecutive OR conditions is not possible in a valid deterministic process tree, and therefore VT_{ns} falls under the proved assumption. Hence, there is a subtree VT'_{ns} of T' that is equal to VT_{ns}.

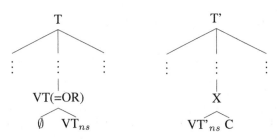

VT_{ns} and VT'_{ns} share the same activities, and VT_{ns} is a strict subtree of T. Therefore, VT'_{ns} is also a strict subtree of T'. Let X be its parent node. We will show that X is in fact an OR condition, and it only has another silent branch. Let's assume there exists an activity C under X but not included in VT'_{ns}. There are two options:

- X is the root of T'. In that case, we can replace the subtrees VT_{ns} and VT'_{ns} by a mock activity C'. We reduced the problem to the 2 activities case, already solved. In that case, we share the same Cophenetic value but the two process trees are different (T' does not have a silent transition). We arrived to this contradiction by assuming that C exists.
- X is not the root of T'. In that case, the subtree VX induced by the node X is a strict subtree of T' and X is not and OR condition. By applying the previous reasoning, there is a subtree W of T that is equal to VX and includes VT_{ns}. Notice that, in that case, the only possibility is that C is a silent transition.

This shows that any subtree of T is equal to a certain subtree of T'. By applying this result to all the direct children of the root of T one can see that T and T' are indeed equal.   □

4.2   Behavioural Information Captured by Cophenetic Values

The syntax of process trees allow us to easily check the **direct causality** of two activities in the model: one simply needs to check the behaviour explained by their LCA. Co-occurrence of activities is described by an AND gateway, whilst OR internal nodes induce conflict between their underlying activities. Notice that this causal relation is a property for the minimum subtree containing the pair of activities. For instance, if the two activities are inside a bigger loop structure, we would not be able to retrieve this information due to the loop gateway being some levels above the LCA.

To provide a more global information than the local direct causality, depths given by Definition 5 can be used. They summarize the behavioural situation of the given node. See, for instance, the processes of Fig. 5. Depth of activity D could be seen as the sum of the *blocks* found from the root to the node.

$$\delta_{T_1}(D) = 1(root) + 2.5(Seq) + 1(And) + 0.5(Or)$$
$$\delta_{T_2}(D) = 1(root) + 3(Seq) + 1(And)$$
$$\delta_{T_1}(D) - \delta_{T_2}(D) = (1 - 1)(root) + (2.5 - 3)(Seq) + (1 - 1)(And) + (0.5)(Or)$$
$$= -0.5(Seq) + 0.5(Or) \tag{1}$$

Notice that by considering the difference of the two depths, i.e. the value considered by the Cophenetic distance, we start highlighting where are the differences, and the type of changes committed, of the behaviour up to activity D.

When comparing pairs of activities, the cophenetic distance does not only consider the depth of the two activities but also the LCA. Following the previous example, let's compare activity D with C:

$$\delta_{T_1}(C) - \delta_{T_2}(C) = (1 - 1)(root) + (2.5 - 3)(Seq)$$
$$+ (1 - 1)(And) + (0.5 - 0.5)(Or) \tag{2}$$
$$= -0.5(Seq) \tag{3}$$
$$\delta_{T_1}([C, D]_{T_1}) - \delta_{T_2}([C, D]_{T_2}) = (1 - 1)(root) + (2.5 - 3)(Seq) + (1 - 0)(And)$$
$$= -0.5(Seq) + 1(And) \tag{4}$$

The Cophenetic value of C stores the differences on the previous block in the sequence, as it did with Activity D. Besides, the Cophenetic value of activities C and D captures again the difference in the sequence and also an AND gateway. Hence, the pair of activities C and D are a step closer to the end in one of the two process models. But more interesting properties could be extracted by measuring the difference of such Cophenetic values: Whilst the cophenetic value $\delta_{T_1}([C, D]) - \delta_{T_2}([C, D])$ gives an idea of the difference of the two processes up to the LCA $[C, D]$, these two new values provides the same differential analysis on the paths from the ancestor to the activities. In this example, $(2) - (3) = 1$ indicates that the position of C with respect to their common ancestor differ in the insertion of an AND gateway; whilst in the case of activity D, $(1) - (2) = 0.5$ recognizes that an OR gateway has been added, or replaced by an AND, in one of the models.

This example shows the potential of the LCA, and the Cophenetic values, to generate more understandable and user-friendly comparison tools between process trees. Definition 6 shows two possible sentences we could build thanks to this information.

Definition 6. *A set of human-readable differences can be generated using the Cophenetic values.*

- *Given a pair of activities A and B such that they differ in the behaviour explained by their LCA. We could say that*

"In the first model, Activities A and B are (in sequential
order/co-occurrent/conflict). Whilst they are (in sequential
order/co-occurrent/conflict) in the second model. Besides, the position of
this behavioural decision differ in $\delta_{T_1}([A, B]) - \delta_{T_2}([A, B])$ units."

– Given a pair of activities A and B showing the same causality but
$\delta_{T_1}([A, B]) - \delta_{T_2}([A, B]) \neq 0$. We could say that

"Activities A and B show the same causality, but the position of this
behavioural decision differ in $\delta_{T_1}([A, B]) - \delta_{T_2}([A, B])$ units."

In this section a formal guarantee for process tree equality based on Cophenetic distance has been presented, which restricts process trees to be deterministic. Next section lifts this restriction deriving an approximate metric based on the existence of a matching between the two process trees.

5   Distance Between Indeterministic Process Trees

Only a small fraction of the process models generated from the human interaction with the source code repository are deterministic Process Trees. In the general case, each SVN command is executed several times during a developer day of work, and usually in different contexts producing processes with several duplicated activities. Unfortunately, the Cophenetic distance definition does not easily extend to such a kind of process. Figure 6 depicts an example of two indeterministic process trees where one activity, A, is duplicated. The Cophenetic distance cannot be used as it is was previously defined. First, the left model has two options for the depth of activity A. And more importantly, when computing the LCA of A and C, the results depend on which copy of activity A we chose. For instance, the LCA of A^3 and C is the root, but the AND gateway w.r.t. A^4. Nevertheless, we can still approximate an upper bound similarity metric between indeterministic process trees. In this section we present a technique that can still be applicable when (some of) the input process trees are indeterministic.

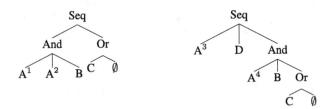

Fig. 6. Example of two indeterministic process trees. Activities A are indexed for the sake of simplicity, but all of them are indistinguishable.

Notice that two process trees T_1 and T_2 are equal if there exists a relabeling of both process trees such that each new label replaces the same label in both models, the resulting process trees are deterministic and their cophenetic distance is zero. Such a relabeling could also be seen as a matching between the activity nodes of both process trees. We could tackle the challenge of extending the Cophenetic distance by making use of such a matching: instead of considering pairs of activities (uniquely represented in a deterministic process tree), this similarity metric compares two pairs of matched nodes. The aforementioned ambiguities among repetitions of an activity are removed by considering these matches.

Definition 7. *Let ω be a matching between the nodes of T_1 and the nodes of T_2, we define their **matching Cophenetic distance** over ω as*

$$d\omega_\varphi = \sum_{(i_1,i_2)\,\in\,\omega} \sum_{(j_1,j_2)\,\in\,\omega} |\varphi_{T_1}(i_1,j_1) - \varphi_{T_2}(i_2,j_2)|$$

Notice that the nodes i_1, i_2, j_1, j_2 in Definition 7 are not necessarily representing activities in the model. Such a distance considers all nodes as labeled. The quality of such a similarity metric depends on the quality of the matching ω. On top of that, the utility of the measurement decreases if activity labels are not preserved by the matching.

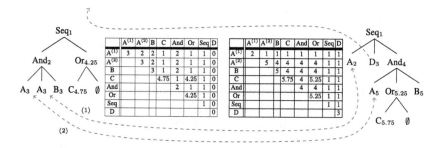

Fig. 7. Example of two indeterministic process trees and a matching Cophenetic distance (represented as a matrix) with respect to a certain node matching. All nodes are matched to their respective nodes with the same label, except activities A (discontinued lines (1) and (2) depict how they are paired) and activity D that does not have a representative node in the first tree. Subscripts depict the depth of the nodes.

Figure 7 depicts an example of such a matching Cophenetic distance of the models of Fig. 6. From the set of all the possible matching, we choose to pair activities with the same label and, for activities A and D, we considered the pairs depicted by discontinued lines. Notice that activity D does not have a matched node in the first tree. In the middle of the Figure, one can find the Cophenetic vectors of both process trees. When considering Activity D, we treat this case as is if the activity does not exist in the first model. This example shows how the matching Cophenetic distance is computed for a specific node matching, but we could iterate over all matchings and get the minimum value possible.

Definition 8. *We define the **minimum matching Cophenetic distance** as*

$$d_{\min \varphi}(T_1, T_2) = \min_{\omega} d\omega_{\varphi}(T_1, T_2)$$

where the matching ω preserves activity's labels.

Although the matching Cophenetic distance is a quadratic-time algorithm [5], once we have chosen a particular matching ω, it is still computationally infeasible to compute this distance for each candidate ω in the *minimum matching Cophenetic distance*. In a practical scenario in which the size of the process trees made it impossible to test all possible matchings, one would be able to bound this ideal distance with an approximate node matching. Although current matching algorithms [2,11,12] focus on preserving the structure of the graph, they could be used to approximate this matching due to the structural approach of the Cophenetic distance.

We have chosen the Flexible Tree Matching algorithm (FTM) [11] for estimating the minimum matching Cophenetic distance with indeterministic process trees. The FTM finds the minimum-cost matching that takes into account the cost of relabeling a node, removing or adding a node, and breaking structural relations between nodes (such as direct descendants and siblings). Notice the resemblance to the definition of the Graph Edit Distance (GED): The cost of the matching resulting from FTM is an approximation of the GED, but assessing also the cost of not having the same neighbors. Tuning these costs allows us to focus on mapping nodes with the same activity (we set to 1, the maximum value, the cost of relabeling) and diminishes the relevance of structural differences. The following proposition establishes also a complexity bound:

Proposition 1. *The FTM needs at least $O(M \cdot N^3 \log N^2)$ operations to approximate the matching between two process trees T_1 and T_2. Where M is the number of iterations needed by the algorithm (i.e. the expected quality of the results) and N is the total number of nodes in T_1 and T_2.*

Proof. The Flexible Tree Matching iterates M times over a randomly generated matching, to retrieve the find the best possible matching. In each iteration, the algorithm needs to recompute the N pair of matches. A weighted bipartite N^2 graph is considered, where weights represent the cost of adding such a pair to the matching. To get the best outcomes from this choice, the algorithm sort all the edges and randomly chooses one of the costless edges. Hence, each iteration of the Flexible Tree Marching needs $O(N^3 \log N^2)$ operations, plus the complexity of computing the cost of each pair of nodes (which may involve traversing the whole matching depending on the implementation). □

In summary, extending the technique of this paper to indeterministic process trees requires to first compute a matching and then compute the Cophenetic distance over this matching. This comes with an increase of the complexity due to the need to compute a matching, a step that dominates the complexity of the whole approach. In the next section we evaluate the proposed method on various types of benchmarks.

6   Evaluation

We divided the evaluation of our similarity metric in three experiments: First we consider a small set of synthetic process models to position our metric with respect to already established comparison tools. Secondly we check that the results given by our approach are consistent with two other metrics in a set of real process models. Finally, we stress the Cophenetic distance with large process models to assess its scalability.

Qualitative Comparison. Figure 8 depicts eight models extracted from [3]. These models were used in [3] to evaluate different similarity metrics. All models are deterministic, and share the same activity set except process model V_3. Table 1 depicts the similarity given by the Cophenetic distance and state-of-the-art process models distances. In order to compute the Cophenetic distance, all models have been represented as process trees. Notice that the inclusive gateway of model V_3 cannot be translated to a deterministic process tree (because only exclusive ORs are accepted), but it was translated to an AND gateway with all internal branches being completely optional. The Cophenetic distance differentiates models V_0 and V_2, but considers V_0 more similar to V_5 than V_4. Discrepancies shown in Table 1 highlights the lack of a clear definition of *similarity*. Overall, the Cophenetic distance offers a different view for the comparison with respect to the other metrics.

Correlation with Two Other Metrics. We gathered 700 pairs of deterministic process models from the SAP Reference Book [6] to compare our approach to two other established process model similarity metrics in a real scenario. We have chosen the traditional graph edit distance as a representative of a structural comparison tool; and, for the behavioural part, we have chosen the Event Structures technique [1]. Figure 9 depicts the comparison of the three metrics:

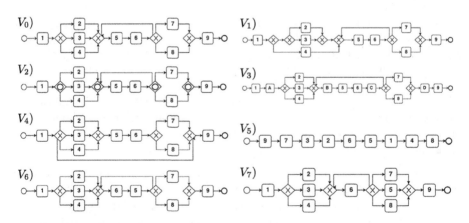

Fig. 8. 8 process models extracted from [3]. Process models $V_1, \ldots, V_7$ are variants from the same process model V_0.

Table 1. Similarity of model V_0 to the rest of models from Fig. 8 with respect to several similarity metrics. Similar models are depicted by darker cells. Values were extracted from [3], except for the Cophenetic and Event Structures [1].

V_0 compared to	V_1	V_2	V_3	V_4	V_5	V_6	V_7
Cophenetic Distance							
Percentage of Common Nodes and Edges							
Node- and Link-Based Similarity							
Graph Edit Distance							
Label Similarity and Graph Edit Distance							
Number of High-Level Change Operations							
Comparing PMs Represented as Trees							
Comparing Dependency Graphs							
Causal Behavioural Profiles							
Event Structures							
Longest Common Subsequence of Traces							
Similarity Based on Traces							

The X and Y coordinates of a point depicts the distance given by two comparison tools, and the color represents the density of pairs in such a situation. I.e., the less dark blue a point is, the more pairs of models satisfying this relation. One can check, for instance, that most of the models differ at 10 units by the behavioural technique and the graph edit distance. Histograms show that the measurements given by the three metrics are correlated[6]. It is not clear that the same factual differences are measured by the three metrics, but the scores obtained are aligned with the two other established metrics.

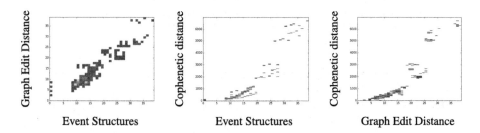

Event Structures   Event Structures   Graph Edit Distance

Fig. 9. A set of two-dimensional histograms comparing the results of the three comparison tools in the SAP dataset. (Color figure online)

Scalability of the Cophenetic Distance. We also study the differences in performance over large process models. We considered 7 additional pairs of process

---

[6] In all three cases, the Pearson correlation coefficient is above 0.85 with a p-value, for testing non-correlation, below 10^{-12}.

models and run the three comparison tools on each pair. The size of the processes, presence of concurrent blocks and loops varies among the models to test the applicability of the three tools. Table 2 depicts the size of such models, and the time needed to measure the differences. The Graph Edit Distance wins all the tests, the tree structure made this algorithm work way faster than usual. The complexity of the other two tools increases significantly with respect the number of activities, although the growth rate in the Cophenetic distance is considerably smaller. Notice the second pair of models, in which concurrency is present, make the behavioural tool run out of memory. Besides, we decided to stop the behavioural tool after 12 hours in all tested process models with more than 100 activities, even with deterministic process models in which the cophenetic distance showed significantly smaller times. This analysis allow us to recommend the Cophenetic distance over other behavioural approaches to analyze big process models [7].

Table 2. Time spend in computing the distance between a few selected process models. The table shows the number of activities in each process model, the distance given by the Cophenetic metric and the other two selected comparison tools, and the time used.

Size	Deterministic	Concurrency	Realistic	d_φ	Time	d_{ES}	Time (Event Structures)	d_{GED}	Time (GED)
25	No	No	No	0	1.71 s	0	1.63 s	0	0.03 s
30	Yes	Yes	No	7250	0.005 s	Run out of memory		40	0.009 s
50	No	No	No	3713	54.37 s	9	90.54 s	93	0.12 s
60	No	No	Yes[8]	190	322.48 s	> 12 h		167	0.19 s
100	No	No	No	16615	467.23 s	> 12 h		184	0.42 s
100	Yes	No	No	452299	0.57 s	> 12 h		189	0.14 s
200	Yes	No	No	2441571	2.28 s	> 12 h		371	0.53 s

[8] We discover these processes by analyzing the accesses of two developers to an internal source code repository. Figure 1 depicts an example of a pair of such type of processes.

7 Conclusions and Future Work

In this paper we have adapted Cophenetic vectors from computational phylogenetics area to be able to automatically compare process models. Previous techniques were binary classified as structural and behavioural techniques, but we have shown that such a classification is indeed fuzzy. Albeit behavioural techniques are computationally demanding, the structural-but-behavioural intermediate approach we presented will allow BPM experts to efficiently asses behavioural comparison between models.

Next steps would focus on extending behavioural differences from the difference of Cophenetic values. There is also room to improve the utility and efficiency of the comparison of indeterministic process trees. The presented approximated

---

[7] Remember that the scale of metrics d_φ, d_{ES} and d_{GED} is different, a fact that explains the differences on the absolute values provided in each one.

matching is computed without taking into account the Cophenetic distance itself, but there might be a better matching algorithm that exploits the properties of the Cophenetic values.

Acknowledgements. This work is funded by Secretaria de Universitats i Recerca of Generalitat de Catalunya, under the Industrial Doctorate Program 2013DI062, and European Commission's 7th Framework Programme project LeanBigData (Agreement 619606), and the Spanish Ministry for Economy and Competitiveness, the European Union (FEDER funds) under grant COMMAS (ref. TIN2013-46181-C2-1-R).

References

1. Armas-Cervantes, A., Baldan, P., Dumas, M., García-Bañuelos, L.: Behavioral comparison of process models based on canonically reduced event structures. In: Sadiq, S., Soffer, P., Völzer, H. (eds.) BPM 2014. LNCS, vol. 8659, pp. 267–282. Springer, Heidelberg (2014)
2. Arvind, V., Köbler, J., Kuhnert, S., Vasudev, Y.: Approximate graph isomorphism. In: Rovan, B., Sassone, V., Widmayer, P. (eds.) MFCS 2012. LNCS, vol. 7464, pp. 100–111. Springer, Heidelberg (2012)
3. Becker, M., Laue, R.: A comparative survey of business process similarity measures. Comput. Ind. **63**(2), 148–167 (2012)
4. Buijs, J., van Dongen, B.F., van der Aalst, W.M.P.: A genetic algorithm for discovering process trees. In: 2012 IEEE Congress on Evolutionary Computation (2012)
5. Cardona, G., Mir, A., Rosselló, F., Rotger, L., Sánchez, D.: Cophenetic metrics for phylogenetic trees, after Sokal and Rohlf. BMC Bioinform. **14**(1), 1–13 (2013)
6. Curran, T., Keller, G., Ladd, A.: SAP R/3 business blueprint: understanding the business process reference model. Prentice-Hall Inc., Upper Saddle River (1997)
7. Dijkman, R.: Diagnosing differences between business process models. In: Dumas, M., Reichert, M., Shan, M.-C. (eds.) BPM 2008. LNCS, vol. 5240, pp. 261–277. Springer, Heidelberg (2008)
8. Dijkman, R., Dumas, M., García-Bañuelos, L.: Graph matching algorithms for business process model similarity search. In: Dayal, U., Eder, J., Koehler, J., Reijers, H.A. (eds.) BPM 2009. LNCS, vol. 5701, pp. 48–63. Springer, Heidelberg (2009)
9. Dijkman, R.M., Dumas, M., García-Bañuelos, L., Käärik, R.: Aligning business process models. In: EDOC 2009, Auckland, New Zealand, 1–4 September 2009, pp. 45–53 (2009)
10. Dijkman, R.M., Dumas, M., van Dongen, B.F., Käärik, R., Mendling, J.: Similarity of business process models: metrics and evaluation. Inf. Syst. **36**(2), 498–516 (2011)
11. Kumar, R., Talton, J.O., Ahmad, S., Roughgarden, T., Klemmer, S.R.: Flexible tree matching. In: Twenty-Second International Joint Conference on Artificial Intelligence (IJCAI 2011) (2011)
12. Mena, A.A., Rosselló, F.: Ternary graph isomorphism in polynomial time, after luks. CoRR, abs/1209.0871 (2012)
13. Polyvyanyy, A., Weidlich, M., Conforti, R., La Rosa, M., ter Hofstede, A.H.M.: The 4C spectrum of fundamental behavioral relations for concurrent systems. In: Ciardo, G., Kindler, E. (eds.) PETRI NETS 2014. LNCS, vol. 8489, pp. 210–232. Springer, Heidelberg (2014)

14. Sokal, R.R., Rohlf, F.J.: The comparison of dendrograms by objective methods. Taxon **11**(2), 33–40 (1962)
15. Sun, L., Boztas, S., Horadam, K., Rao, A., Versteeg, S.: Analysis of user behaviour in accessing a source code repository. Technical report, RMIT University and CA Technologies (2013)
16. Weidlich, M., Mendling, J., Weske, M.: Efficient consistency measurement based on behavioral profiles of process models. IEEE Trans. Soft. Eng. **37**(3), 410–429 (2011)
17. Weidlich, M., Polyvyanyy, A., Mendling, J., Weske, M.: Causal behavioural profiles - efficient computation, applications, and evaluation. Fundam. Inform. **113**(3–4), 399–435 (2011)
18. Yan, Z., Dijkman, R.M., Grefen, W.P.W.J.: Fast business process similarity search. Distrib. Parallel Databases **30**(2), 105–144 (2012)

Management

Unlocking the Potential of the Process Perspective in Business Transformation

Greet Bontinck[1]([⊠]), Öykü Isik[1], Joachim Van den Bergh[1],
and Stijn Viaene[1,2]

[1] Vlerick Business School, Ghent, Belgium
{Greet.Bontinck,Oyku.Isik,Joachim.vandenbergh,
Stijn.Viaene}@vlerick.com
[2] KU Leuven, Louvain, Belgium

Abstract. The purpose of this research is to gain insights in the positioning and role of the business process support function and, more generally, process-oriented thinking in a business transformation context. The main promise that has been associated with the discipline of Business Process Management (BPM) and process orientation is providing critical support for making business transformation successful. Thus, intuitively, we can expect process support functions in organizations which apply the BPM principles in day-to-day business activities, to take a prominent role in realizing their organization's current transformation agenda. But is this the case? Through an interview-based qualitative research approach, the question is raised whether business process support function today, in what is claimed to be a more turbulent business environment than before, is actually a co-driver for business transformation. From this research, key takeaways are distilled on the elements shaping the context for process support functions to co-drive business transformation.

Keywords: Business transformation · Process Management · Change management · Qualitative research

1 Introduction

Today's business environment is changing faster and faster. Entire industries are confronted with disruptive powers, and 'digital', 'social', 'global' and 'mobile' are not just a list of buzzwords, but have become an integral part of daily life. We are unmistakably entering a new age where emerging technologies are overhauling the business models of established organizations, as well as their current ways of operating. In order to turn these challenges into opportunities, the transformation initiatives require support from management as well as from dedicated transformation teams.

Since its inception in the 90s by Hammer and Davenport, the concept of business process reengineering (BPR) has been seen as an enabler for business transformation and a way to achieve radical performance improvements and competitive advantage through the analysis and design of work flows and processes within and between organizations [1, 2]. Since then, business process management (BPM) has been established as a discipline capable of radically improving performance through a focus

© Springer International Publishing Switzerland 2016
M. La Rosa et al. (Eds.): BPM Forum 2016, LNBIP 260, pp. 161–176, 2016.
DOI: 10.1007/978-3-319-45468-9_10

on measurement and redesign of business processes [3–5], as well as to play an essential enabling role in organizational change [6]. Today, BPM is more relevant than ever; as emphasized by a recent Gartner report [7], successful business transformation requires the redesign of existing operations through business processes, and promotes process thinking as a way of identifying and driving improved customer experience. Gartner predicts that 30 % of large organizations will improve customer experience in the following years by integrating customer journey maps with business process models. This evidence makes a case for BPM as a management discipline providing critical support in business transformation. One would expect BPM to play a prominent role in the current business environment, which is characterized by turbulence and change. However, it is signaled that this is not the case. As frequently observed in literature, many organizations are facing difficulties with regard to the implementation of BPM practices throughout the organization [8, 9], resulting in high failure rates for BPM initiatives [8, 10]. Moreover, we see that the uptake of BPM in the business has not reached its expected level [11]. Although many organizations have established support units taking on a process perspective, the tasks and responsibilities of such units do not typically have an enterprise-wide scope, and have a limited impact [12, 13]. Thus, the belief has emerged that BPM has become a commodity, and does not offer a significant competitive advantage anymore [14]. In addition, research shows that an enterprise-wide acceptance of a process-oriented mind-set is a long-term process which demands significant time and effort [15], which also seems to discourage organizations from investing in BPM initiatives.

Addressing this contrast between the potential and actual uptake of BPM in a business transformation context, the purpose of this research is to gain insights in whether business process support units, regardless of their formation (virtual or formal) or their actual label ("Business Process Office", "Business Transformation Group", etc.), are co-drivers for their organization's business transformation, thus having both the formal and moral authority to co-steer the transformation. This research-in-progress paper reports on the first phase of the research, which focuses specifically on the current role and positioning of the business process support function (BPO)[1] in the context of a business transformation. In a second phase of the research, the insights from the first phase will be complemented with the insights from perspective of those taking up a leading function or role with regard to the transformation, being the "transformation leads".

The paper is structured as follows: Sect. 2 reports on the background of our research, providing an overview of the literature and the framework in which we examine the role of the BPO in the context of an enterprise-wide transformation. In Sect. 3, we present the research methodology, while Sect. 4 provides an overview of the research findings and distilled key takeaways. Section 5 of the paper concludes and provides an outlook on the next research phase.

---

[1] Due to the wide variety of business process support functions names/titles observed in organizations, this paper refers to these units as 'business process offices' (BPOs).

2 Background

The underlying assumption of this research is that BPM is a critical enabler for business transformation [6]. However, in accordance with Fiedler's contingency theory, this research takes the position that there is no "best way" for organizations to organize themselves, and that, while a specific organizational style may be efficient in one organization, it may not necessarily be preferable in another organization [16]. In accordance with the principle of context awareness, this research approaches the role of the BPO as rooted into its specific organizational setting [12, 17]. As such, this research does not aim to define a set of one-size-fits-all best practices as to which role the BPO should assume in a business transformation context; instead, it aims to detect meaningful patterns with regard to the role of the BPO in a business transformation context by mapping its role on a framework of context elements. This approach allows us to explore whether the presence of these context elements are an indication for the ability of the BPO to co-drive their organization's business transformation.

Although the optimal organizational setting to leverage the potential of the process perspective in a business transformation is contingent upon both internal and external constraints, this research only focuses on intra-organizational context elements, as the most frequently cited obstacles to transformation initiatives in literature are internal factors [6, 20]. In order to identify the intra-organizational context elements which are expected to impact the role and positioning of the BPO, a literature review on context awareness was conducted [8, 12, 17]. Consequently, we reviewed literature to identify the critical success factors (CSFs) for BPM/BPR [8, 12, 18] and Business Transformation [19–21]. From these lists of established CSFs, we selected the common factors which were strictly intra-organizational, being Portfolio, Positioning, Alignment and Maturity. As argued further in Sect. 2.5, this four-element framework was complemented with the element of focus, which was identified as a fifth element.

2.1 Portfolio

The portfolio of the BPO encompasses the tasks and responsibilities in which the team is involved, and it is determined in accordance with the BPO's main objectives. Literature has recently been emphasizing two different BPM practices: (1) exploitation-oriented BPM, aimed at the leveraging of the organization's current competences; and (2) exploration-oriented BPM, aimed at the enabling of innovation and growth by using new emerging technologies and/or techniques [12, 17, 21, 22]. In line with this distinction, the BPO's portfolio either:

1. exclusively encompasses exploitation ("exploitative portfolio"). This is for example the case for BPOs leading a process improvement initiative using methodologies such as lean or six sigma;
2. exclusively encompasses exploration ("explorative portfolio"). This is for example the case for BPOs involved in development of new products and services; or
3. encompasses both exploration and exploitation ("ambidextrous portfolio").

Given the turbulent environment of a business transformation, literature has described ambidexterity as a competitive advantage in coping with revolutionary and evolutionary change in the organization [23]. As such, the BPO's portfolio was selected to be assessed as a context element for the BPO's role in business transformation [12, 17, 21, 22].

2.2   Positioning

The discipline of BPM advocates the shift from considering organizations simply as a collection of departments to viewing them as systems of interdependent processes overarching different departments and silos. In accordance with Harmon's framework [2], the "level of concern" of the tasks and responsibilities entrusted to the BPO is distinguished as a potential influential element when assessing the role of the BPO. Positioning of the BPO at process-level implies a role mainly encompassing improvement of specific processes. BPO positioning at enterprise-level, on the other hand, implies that its tasks and responsibilities also relate to the development of enterprise-wide business process architectures, defining organization-wide process governance, and aligning these processes with strategies [13]. Previous research has shown that, as organizations become more process-oriented, they move away from operating within silos, and enterprise-wide, end-to-end thinking becomes imminent [24]. Thus, the context in which the BPO is operating is shaped by its positioning at either process-level or enterprise-level.

2.3   Alignment

Alignment of the core transformation team with the business is considered as a pre-requisite for successful business transformation [19], thus being a key element to include in the framework. Inspired by business-IT alignment literature [25], the following cumulative elements were considered to be critical in the BPO-business alignment: (1) regular interactions and discussions between the business, represented by the transformation lead, and the BPO; (2) the BPO is considered as a strategic partner of the business, and there is established trust between both parties; and (3) perceived value: the BPO does not have to defend its existence regularly and the business sees the value brought by the BPO.

2.4   Maturity

The discipline of BPM is an established enabler for business transformation [5, 20]. Moreover, BPOs in organizations with higher business process maturity are expected to have gained experience in applying the principles of BPM, which enable these offices to co-drive the business transformation, while BPOs in organizations with lower maturity levels will have gained less experience in applying these principles. Thus, the BPM maturity level is an important element which shapes the context in which the BPO operates, as it is a measure that provides valuable insights in an organization's BPM capabilities. As a BPM maturity model, the Capability Maturity Model Integration (CMMI) framework was used. This assessment tool provides a process management standard, classifying organizations in different levels, depending on the maturity of their processes. This framework was chosen because it integrates multiple maturity models into one, it is user-friendly [26], and enables organizations to conduct a swift assessment of their organization's status, based on the 5 maturity levels. This contrasts with other BPM maturity models such as the Process Enterprise Maturity Model (PEMM), which requires a more detailed level of analysis of the organization [3].

2.5   Focus

The BPO is a centralized repository of knowledge which sources the support and execution efforts for the business transformation. This is similar to the concept of a Project Management Office (PMO), where the PMO mainly focuses on providing ownership and accountability of IT project management initiatives [27]. Inspired by research conducted on PMOs, we also included the element of 'focus' as a part of our framework: BPOs specifically established for the transformation have been established as a separate corporate function with an exclusive focus on the transformation, whereas the focus of BPOs which were operational before goes beyond the transformation initiative. In the latter case, the BPO is either a corporate support function operating independently from such a dedicated Business Transformation Group, or the BPO has merged into a Business Transformation Group [28].

Considering the wide variety and level of activities the BPO may be involved in, a critical factor for understanding the value generated by the BPO is 'establishing the background' [29], whereby we gain insights in the trigger that led to the establishment of the BPO and whether the BPO is being established to provide a focal point for a strategic program such as an enterprise-wide transformation. As such, the BPO's focus, which represents the reason of existence and the main set of responsibilities the BPO is accountable for, indicates whether the BPO is solely focused on the business transformation or also has other responsibilities.

3   Research Methodology

An interview-based qualitative approach was chosen for this research, as this approach is particularly useful when gauging retrospective and anticipatory elements, such as expected future evolutions, and to assess underlying opinions or beliefs as to the role and positioning of the BPO [29]. Using convenience sampling, a list of middle- and large-sized organizations from multiple sectors was compiled. Following the initial contact, 25 organizations consented to collaborate, all of which were going through (or recently have gone through) an enterprise-wide transformation. Next, preliminary interviews were conducted with representatives of these organizations, during which the following inclusion criteria were assessed:

1. (current or recent) involvement of the organization in an enterprise-wide transformation, which was defined as "the orchestrated redesign of the genetic architecture of the corporation" [30]. This term 'enterprise-wide' is to be interpreted in a broad

sense, including transformations with regard to a specific business unit of a certain size; and

2. the existence of a support unit, in any shape or form, that takes on a process perspective. No distinction was made with regard to the specific name of this support organization (E.g. Business Process Office, Enterprise Architecture Group, Business Transformation Group). Closely related with this inclusion criterion, only organizations with a minimum process maturity level were included in the research.

During these preliminary interviews, 11 organizations were eliminated due to practical constraints (such as schedule constraints) or because they did not meet the research inclusion criteria. Next, we conducted in-depth interviews with the heads of the business process support functions in 14 organizations (five Belgian organizations and nine international organizations).

3.1   Data Collection

The data were collected through face-to-face, in-depth interviews by two researchers. A semi-structured list of open-ended questions was used to guide the interviews, which took 1,5 h on average. This gave the researchers the opportunity to dive into the specific characteristics of each organization and its transformation, as well as to search for generalizable evolutions, across organizations and industries [29]. Where face-to-face interviews were not feasible, the interviews were conducted via video-conferencing tools, as these technologies also provide synchronous interaction without losing visual and interpersonal aspects of the interaction [31]. All interviews were recorded with prior permission by the interviewees. The data were transcribed and analyzed by the two researchers. Next, the transcriptions were analyzed by two additional researchers. By using this method of investigator triangulation, subjective views of individual researchers were levelled out [32]. Table 1 provides the interview guide,

Table 1. Interview protocol

INTERVIEW PROTOCOL				
Main Sections	Topics addressed in each section			
Research introduction	Introductory briefing			
Interviewee introduction	Function	Role		Responsibilities
Business transformation	Nature of trans-formation	Timeline	Involved departments/ employees	(Expected) results
Role of BPM in practice	Main use of BPM	Exploration/Exploitation		Maturity assessment
Role of the BPO	Specific respon-sibilities	Positioning of the BPO	Current and past challenges	Business alignment	Role in the transforma-tion

consisting of two blocks; (1) introductory questions about the interviewee and the transformation, and (2) specific questions with regard to the role and positioning of the BPO and the context elements.

4 Qualitative Insights and Key Takeaways

This section provides an overview of the organizations included in the sample and presents our observations with regard to the role of the BPO in a business trans-formation context, taking into account the 5 elements impacting the role of the BPO, as identified in Sect. 2.

4.1 Sample Overview

Table 2 provides an overview of the organizations included in the research sample. While most of our organizations included in the sample had more than 2000 employees, and half of them had over 1 million euro turnover in 2014, the transfor-mation drivers are rather universal; most of the organizations were in the midst of some type of digital transformation (enterprise system or emerging technology implemen-tation) or the transformation was motivated by changing customer needs.

Table 2. Sample overview: industry and transformation drivers

	INDUSTRY	TRANSFORMATION DRIVERS
1	Health care	Changing customer needs, emergence of new technologies and ERP implementation
2	Health care	Series of acquisitions, implementation of ERP system
3	Health Care	Shift in leadership, becoming more customer-centric
4	Banking & insurance	Changing customer behaviour and digitisation
5	Banking & insurance	Rapid growth, high employee turnover and increasing regulatory requirements
6	Services	ERP implementation, becoming more customer-centric
7	Services	Changing customer behaviour, increasing prices of raw material and energy
8	Technology	Emergence of new technologies
9	Technology	Rising costs and implementation of an ERP system
10	Energy	Becoming more customer-centric and improving efficiencies
11	Energy	New technologies
12	Retail	Competitive pressures, becoming more customer-centric and maintain-ing current efficiencies
13	Manufacturing	Rapid growth and changing customer needs
14	Food production	Becoming more customer-centric

4.2   Role of the BPO in a Business Transformation Context

The interview-based research revealed a high variety of structural forms and perspectives taken on the business process support function. While some BPOs are virtual teams, others are formally established departments, and whereas some BPOs operate from within a specific business function (IT, Quality Control), other BPOs operate as independent units. This variety is also reflected in the labels attributed to the BPOs, as listed in Table 3.

Table 3. Overview of business process offices

#	BUSINESS PROCESS SUPPORT FUNCTION
1	Reporting, Tools and Processes
2	Information Management/Information Technology team
3	Project & Process Excellence Team
4	Business Plan Implementation Team
5	Project Management Office
6	Business Process Management Office
7	Quality Team
8	Business Process Office
9	Information Management Team
10	Continuous Improvement Office
11	Continuous Improvement and Transformation
12	Organization Management Office
13	Information, BPM and Quality Team
14	Virtual support organization, embedded in business units

During the interview analysis, the organizations were classified into two groups, based on the role of the BPO in the business transformation: (1) organizations where BPO is a co-driver for business transformation, hereafter referred to as organizations where the BPO is a '*Transformation Protagonist*'; and (2) organizations where BPO is not a co-driver for business transformation, but merely works in the margins of the transformation, hereafter referred to as organizations where the BPO is a '*Transformation Peripheral*'.

The BPO is identified as a co-driver of the transformation if (1) the BPO's involvement in the transformation is not left to the support unit's own initiative, but has received a mandate by the transformation lead to play a co-directing role, delivering input for strategic decisions on a regular basis (Formal Authority); and (2) the BPO is recognized and trusted by the organization, including the leadership team, as having expertise on how to approach an enterprise-wide transformation (Moral Authority). In summary, Transformation Peripherals either have only formal or moral authority, or no authority, whereas Transformation Protagonists have both. A BPO with only moral authority would correspond to a 'shadow organization' operating via informal connections; this shadow unit supplements the enterprise transformation by autonomously developed systems and processes, which are generally not known, accepted or supported by the formal business transformation support unit [33].

Out of the 14 BPOs included in the research, nine were identified as BPOs with only formal authority (*Transformation Peripherals*) and five as BPOs with formal and moral authority (*Transformation Protagonists*). Next, the context element framework (cf. Section 2) was used to assess patterns in the specific contexts in which Transformation Peripherals on one hand, and Transformation Protagonists on the other hand, are operating. This mapping is illustrated in Table 4.

Table 4. Context element framework mapping

	Transformation Protagonists				Transformation Peripherals		
Portfolio	Exploita-tion 2	Explo-ration 0	Both 2	Not assess-able 1	Exploitation 9	Exploration 0	Both 0
Position-ing	Process-level 1	Enterprise-level 4			Process-level 6	Enterprise-level 3	
Align-ment	No close business alignment 0	Close business alignment 5			No close business alignment 5	Close business alignment 4	
Process maturity	Low – medium 2	High 3			Low –medium 4	High 5	
Focus	General 2	Transformation only 3			General 8	Transformation only 1	

Portfolio. The portfolio of BPOs included in the research was observed to either include exploitation only, or both exploitation and exploration (ambidextrous portfolio). A clear discrepancy is noticed when comparing the portfolio of the Transformation Peripherals and the Transformation Protagonists. While all Peripheral BPOs have a portfolio focused on exploitation, the number of Protagonist BPOs with a portfolio encompassing exploitation only, and with a portfolio encompassing both exploitation and exploration is equally distributed.

Within the group of Peripherals, where BPM is not a co-driver of the transformation, the majority of interviewees representing the BPO indicate not to see opportunities for BPM to contribute to exploration. As one interviewee states: "BPM is a rigid discipline, which sharply contrasts with the creativity required in exploration". However, other BPO representatives within the Peripherals group do see the added value of BPM in exploration, but report that they are not invited by the business to participate here. Amongst the representatives of Peripheral BPOs, there is a general sense of not being perceived as a strategic partner of the business, but rather as a service center, engaged in optimizing existing processes, and signaling potential for improvement to business. A BPM manager clarifies: "We are not asked by the business to participate in exploration, which is mainly a responsibility of the Strategy Department. Nevertheless, I think the BPO is able to make contribution to our company's exploration activities by thinking along with the business about innovation and anticipate future needs." Another interviewee highlights the BPO's ambition to be involved in exploration as follows: "I believe the involvement of our team in exploration is essential, as we can make the link between future goals and processes. Unfortunately, our team is not doing this today."

In organizations where the BPO was identified to be a Protagonist, two BPOs exclusively engage in exploitation for similar reasons, while two other BPOs do play a role in exploration. In those organizations, process analysis and process design are used for new product development. One interviewee explains: "We consider BPM as a fantastic enabler for innovation, as it creates more focus on adding value and transparency, and faster communication about problems, and the business supports us in that vision."

The views and information with regard to the BPO's portfolio, which was gathered from the BPO representatives, was cross-checked during an additional and brief interview with the 'transformation lead', i.e. the person from the business side taking up a leading role in the transformation. In two cases, the transformation leads clarified that, although the BPO was currently not expressing the ambition to engage in exploration, this would have a huge added value and help the organization to take the next step in the transformation. This is illustrated by a transformation director: "In a large organization as ours, it is hard to be truly innovative and fast-paced. I believe the process perspective can be an important lever for faster decision-making, and I would encourage a more proactive attitude from the BPO with regard to exploring new opportunities than they are currently doing." As such, we encountered organizations where the transformation lead reaches out to the BPO to co-drive the transformation. Yet, this call for collaboration remains unanswered and is a lost opportunity for the BPO to make the transition from being a *Peripheral* to *Protagonist*, as there is more to BPM than exploitation only.

Key takeaway 1: Adding both exploration and exploitation to the BPO's portfolio is a crucial context element for BPOs to co-drive business transformation. This implies that, next to traditional process improvement tasks, BPOs are also to be engaged in innovation in order to be co-drivers for the transformation.

Positioning. The framework in Table 4 demonstrates a clear contrast between the BPOs identified as Transformation Protagonists and those identified as Transformation Peripherals. The activities of all Protagonists, except one, are mainly positioned at enterprise-level, whereas two thirds of the Peripherals' activities indicated to be exclusively positioned at process-level. One representative of a Protagonist BPO explains why this enterprise-level concern is a determining factor for their BPO to co-drive the transformation: "The BPO translates management decisions on the transformation into day-to-day business processes. In order to achieve this, our team has to transcend the process-level, as an enterprise-wide transformation requires a view on transversal processes with often no clear owner guarding the end-to-end perspective."

The tasks and responsibilities of BPOs exclusively involved at process-level, are profoundly different. Here, BPOs are working on isolated projects, failing to bring in end-to-end thinking. One BPO lead explains the scope of the projects in which his team is involved: "In our company, there's no central BPM unit, but each team has its own process experts. My team is currently working on a specific project for one business unit, while also doing some process improvements for that unit." Within this group of 'process-level BPOs', a mandate from senior management to play a more extensive role in the transformation is missing. As one interviewee of a BPO positioned at the process-level puts it: "BPO involvement in the transformation is limited as there is no broad support for it among senior management. The process perspective remains a bottom-up initiative whereby the BPO group supports various individual initiatives. If we had more management buy-in, our involvement could go beyond this limited scope." This reduced senior management support in the BPOs positioned at process-level sharply contrasts with the finding that all BPOs positioned at enterprise-level had received a prior mandate from senior management.

Although the number of organizations included in this exploratory research is limited, these contrasting results suggest that the role of the BPO in enterprise-wide transformation is closely correlated with the BPO's level of concern. The results indicate that BPOs mainly active at the process-level are unlikely to be a co-driver for enterprise-wide transformation, as only one out of seven BPOs positioned at the process-level was identified to be a Protagonist. On the other hand, the results suggest that the enterprise-level concern is closely associated with being a co-driver of the transformation, as four out of five Protagonists had an enterprise-level positioning.

These exploratory research results indicate that positioning at enterprise-level is an enabler for changing the business' impression that BPOs are only involved in commodity business. Therefore, re-positioning from process-level to enterprise-level may help BPOs that aim to co-drive their organization's business transformation to make the shift from involvement in projects in the margins of the transformation to involvement in projects directly impacting the transformation strategy.

Key takeaway 2: In order for BPOs to co-drive business transformation, it is critical to target projects that cut across organizational silos, embrace end-to-end thinking, and proactively position the BPOs as enterprise-wide partners to the business. Senior management support is indispensable in order to achieve this.

Business Alignment. In order to assess the alignment between the BPO and the business, we cross-checked the BPO interview findings with the transformation leads from the business side. In these additional interviews, we assessed (1) whether regular interactions are taking place between the BPO and the business, (2) whether the business perceives the BPO as a strategic partner, and (3) how they perceive the value of the input delivered by the BPO. Interestingly, all BPOs identified as Transformation Protagonists demonstrate close alignment with the business, delivering valuable input to the business on how to approach certain challenges. One interviewee heading the BPO explains that achieving this alignment has been a long-term process: "Until a few years ago, the business perceived us as a 'helpdesk', providing the tools to support processes throughout the organization. Our team worked hard to change this perception. Today, the business looks at our team as a partner: they understand that our team is helping them to gain insights in how to improve the organization of various aspects of the business in the future, while they can keep focusing on business as usual." When asking transformation leads about their relationship with BPOs which were identified as Transformation Protagonists we received similar responses: "The transformation we are currently going through is a shining example of how the business strategy is implemented: the (virtual) BPO is setting up a framework, together with the business, in support of that transformation strategy by rethinking our company's processes and structures. Together, they form a dedicated group driving the transformation together, whereas in the past, senior management defined a strategy on how to transform, while it was unclear how to effectuate that transformation."

This consistency in close alignment among Transformation Protagonists sharply contrasts with the finding that less than 50% of the Transformation Peripherals is closely aligned with the business. The head of one of these Transformation Peripherals comments: "We regularly have to defend the reason for our existence, and continuously have to prove that, by involving the process-oriented view in the transformation, the results will be achieved better, faster and at a lower cost. There is definitely a feeling amongst our colleagues from the business that the process-oriented approach is heavy-handed and overly complex." A transformation lead collaborating with a Transformation Peripheral BPO comments similarly: "We sometimes feel that the approach of our business process experts is too administrative, and that they are simply guarding our company's processes for the sake of them."

Remarkably, four BPOs were identified as Transformation Peripherals despite their close alignment with the business. In these cases, less tension was felt between the business and BPO representative, as both groups did not see how the BPO could co-steer the organization's transformation.

Key takeaway 3: In order to co-drive business transformation, BPOs must invest in direct communication lines with the business, as well as in the creation of a common vision where they do not need to defend their existence.

Maturity. The BPM maturity level of each organization included in the research was measured through self-assessment of the CMMI framework. Each BPO representative was presented with the different maturity levels of the framework, and was consequently asked to assess their organization's maturity level. As the existence of a business process support unit and existence of minimal process-oriented thinking were among the research inclusion criteria, none of the organizations were assessed at level 1 of the CMMI framework ('Initial'). Overall, interviewees indicate their organizations to have a medium (level 2-3) to high (level 4-5) process maturity, with an average level of 3 ('Defined'), implying that the organization's basic processes are defined, with a certain degree of control over process performance. In organizations with a higher level of BPM maturity, getting the right measures in place to monitor process performance is consistently reported to be an important barrier to making progress in their maturity level. It is striking that a large majority of the interviewees reports a high variance in the level of process maturity throughout the organization, where one silo might have a higher process maturity than the other, as indicated in the following quote: "There is no 'one view on BPM' in our organization; the different heads of the functional organizations independently decide on the level of priority for BPM." Also, none of the organizations indicates to have reached level 5 of the CMMI. As such, none of the researched organizations has a continuous organizational focus on innovation and improvement, despite on-going BPM practice for several years. This observation is in line with earlier research findings that organizations are struggling to evolve and expand BPM practices across the organization [8, 9].

The specific tasks and responsibilities of the BPO are impacted by the level of process maturity: where medium mature organizations report to mainly focus their BPM efforts on documenting and (re)designing end-to-end processes, BPM initiatives in organizations with a higher level of maturity are mainly focused on continuous improvement and monitoring process performance. Nevertheless, no significant differences are observed between organizations where the BPO is identified as a Protagonist and organizations where the BPO is a Peripheral. Despite the limited number of organizations observed, it is clear that low to medium process maturity does not influence the infusion of the process perspective in the transformation.

Key takeaway 4: Even though process maturity is an indication of how well the process-oriented thinking is infused in the organization, it is not indicative of the extent to which BPOs can co-drive business transformation. Thus, an enterprise-wide business transformation can benefit from an experienced BPO and an already established process-oriented mindset in the organization. A transformation initiative can be a good excuse to start infusing process-oriented thinking into the organization.

Focus. Out of the 14 BPOs included in the research, four BPOs were specifically established for their organization's transformation initiative, thus having the transformation as their exclusive focus. The fact that a large majority of the BPOs in the research has been established independently from the transformation initiative is expected; one of the research inclusion criteria (Appendix 1) required at least a minimum level of process maturity, thus most organizations included in the research already had a BPO before the transformation working on several initiatives, which may have been driving their process maturity level.

However, the research results show a contrast between organizations where the BPO is a Transformation Protagonist, and those where the BPO is a Transformation Peripheral. Out of four dedicated 'transformation offices' included in the research, three are Transformation Protagonists. On the other hand, eight out of ten BPOs which were not specifically established for the transformation face difficulties to become a partner of the business with regard to successfully transforming the organization. The latter group of BPOs seems to struggle with positioning themselves in the changing business environment and to push the process perspective to the forefront in the transformation. Nevertheless, it is important to note that a BPO which is responsible for several different initiatives does not indicate a bad practice; it is merely an organizational choice. The fact that the majority of Protagonists are BPOs specifically established for the transformation demonstrates that the identification of the transformation as a mandate is a way of characterizing the BPO [34]. It is also suggested that role diversification, or having multiple responsibilities, may lead to bureaucracy and political lack of transparency [35].

Nevertheless, two BPOs in our research demonstrate that being established along with the transformation initiative is not always a prerequisite for BPOs to become a co-driver of the transformation. These BPOs with a general focus actually take up a co-steering role in that context, mainly due to close alignment with the business, as well as a clear mandate from senior management. A manager of one of these BPOs states that: "Our management understands that business processes are key to achieve a sustainable and consistent transformation, however, always combined with a mindset open to challenge the status quo, and willingness of the BPO to adjust processes when needed." This emphasizes the importance of recognizing the diversity in BPO roles; while certain BPOs are mainly established for serving the rest of the organization with process improvement initiatives, many organizations set up BPOs as strategic partners and give them responsibility for leading new initiatives, providing oversight, as well as guiding knowledge transfers within the organization [35]. BPOs acting as the interface between business and IT/operations are not only there to answer the specific needs of business, but also to lead the initiatives.

Key takeaway 5: A business transformation is an opportunity to identify and recognize the role of the BPO based on their interaction with the stakeholders. Whether the BPO has a more subordinate or a coequal role profile is indicative of its capability as a transformation co-driver.

5   Conclusions, Limitations and Future Research

This paper provides qualitative insights in the role and positioning of the business process support function in a business transformation context. This paper contributes academically by identifying meaningful patterns with regard to the role of the business process support function through the assessment of a set of context elements, established in literature as common critical success factors for BPM and Business Transformation. Thus, this research enhances the understanding of the elements indicating the ability of the BPO to co-drive their organization's business transformation. Besides this academic contribution, this paper contains key-takeaways for practitioners, inspiring them to further involve the process perspective in their enterprise transformation.

A first limitation of this research is the small number of organizations included in the research interviews, which may affect the generalizability of the results. However, the aim of this research is mainly exploratory, and allows to derive preliminary insights on the role and positioning of the BPO. In the second phase of the research, we aim to complement the current research findings with the insights from in-depth interviews conducted with employees overseeing and leading the transformation, thus further triangulating the information gathered from the interviews with the BPO representatives, while also seeking confirmation of the exploratory research findings in phase 1. A second limitation of this research is the time frame. The data from the interviews provide us with information from a single point in time. However, we did not observe the evolution of the BPO's role in a longitudinal study. Also, as the research mainly covered ongoing transformation initiatives, it was not possible to assess the impact of BPO involvement on the outcome of the transformation. A further study could assess the effects of BPOs co-driving business transformation on the success of the transformation initiative.

Given the importance attached to digital business transformation today, we hope that our research contributes to bringing BPM back into the heart of transformation and to emphasize its potential as an enabling discipline.

Acknowledgements. We thank all organizations that have contributed by investing their time to inform this research. We also thank Eddy Helsen and Annelies Helsen of ViCre for the funding of this research.

References

1. Hung, R.Y.: Business process management as competitive advantage: a review and empirical study. Total Qual. Manag. Bus. Excellence **17**(1), 21–40 (2006)
2. Harmon, P.: Business Process Change A Business Process Management Guide for Managers and Process Professionals, 3rd edn. Elsevier, Waltham (2014)
3. Hammer, M.: What is business process management? In: vom Brocke, J., Rosemann; M. (ed.) Handbook on Business Process Management 1: Introduction, Methods and Information Systems. pp. 3–16. Springer-Verlag, Berlin (2010)
4. Hammer, M.: The process audit. Harvard Bus. Rev. **85**(4), 111–123 (2007)
5. Kohlbacher, M., Reijers, H.: The effects of process-oriented organizational design on firm performance. Bus. Process Manage. J. **19**(2), 245–262 (2013)
6. Hammer, M., Stanton, S.: How process enterprises really work. Harvard Bus. Rev. **77**, 108–120 (1999)
7. Gartner, Inc. Predicts 2016: Business Transformation and Process Management Bridge the Strategy-to-Execution Gap. Gartner, Inc (2015)
8. Trkman, P.: The critical success factors of business process management. Int. J. Inf. Manage. **30**, 125–134 (2010)
9. Malinova, M., Mendling, J.: A qualitative research perspective on BPM adoption. In: La Rosa, M., Soffer, P. (eds.) BPM Workshops, pp. 77–88. Springer-Verlag, Berlin (2012)
10. Karim, J., Somers, T.M., Bhattacherjee, A.: The impact of ERP implementation on business process outcomes: A factor-based study. J. Manage. Inf. Syst. **24**(1), 101–134 (2007)
11. Rosemann, M.: Proposals for future BPM research directions. In: Ouyang, C., Jung, J.-Y. (eds.) AP-BPM 2014. LNBIP, vol. 181, pp. 1–15. Springer, Heidelberg (2014)
12. vom Brocke, J., Zelt, S., Schmiedel, T.: On the role of context in business process management. Int. J. Inf. Manage. (2015). http://dx.doi.org/10.1016/j.ijinfomgt.2015.10.002
13. Harmon, P.: The scope and evolution of business process management. In: vom Brocke, J., Rosemann, M. (eds.), Handbook on Business Process Management 1: Introduction, Methods and Information Systems. pp. 37–82. Springer-Verlag, Berlin (2010)
14. Davenport, T.: The coming commoditization of processes. Harvard Bus. Rev. **83**(6), 101–108 (2005)
15. De Boer, F., Müller, C., Schwengber ten Caten, C.: Assessment model for organizational business process maturity with a focus on BPM governance practices. Bus. Process Manage. J. **21**(4), 908–927 (2015)
16. Fiedler, F.: A contingency model of leadership effectiveness. In: Berkowitz, L. (ed.) Advances in experimental social psychology, vol. 1, pp. 149–190. Academic Press, New York (1964)

17. vom Brocke, J., Schmiedel, T., Recker, J., Trkman, P., Mertens, W., Viaene, S.: Ten principles of good business process management. Bus. Process Manage. J. **20**(4), 530–548 (2014)

18. Ahadi, H.R.: An examination of the role of organizational enablers in business process reengineering and the impact of information technology. Inf. Resour. Manage. J. **17**(4), 1–19 (2004)

19. Paper, D., Chang, R.-D., Rodger, J.: Managing radical transformation at Fannie Mae: A holistic paradigm. Total Qual. Manage. Bus. Excellence **14**(4), 475–489 (2003)

20. Franklin, M.: 3 lessons for successful transformational change. Ind. Commercial Training, **46**(7), 364–370

21. Jansen, J., George, G., Van den Bosch, F., Volberda, H.: Senior team attributes and organizational ambidexterity: the moderating role of transformational leadership. J. Manage. Stud. **45**(5), 982–1007 (2008)

22. Benner, M.J., Tushman, M.L.: Exploitation, exploration, and process management: The productivity dilemma revisited. Acade. Manage. Rev. **28**(2), 238–256 (2003)

23. O'Reilly, C., Tushman, M.: The ambidextrous organization. Harvard Bus. Rev. **82**(4), 74–81 (2004)

24. Fisher, D.M.: The Business Process Maturity Model: A Practical Approach for Identifying Opportunities for Optimization. BPTrends (2004)

25. Luftman, J.N., Bullen, C.V.: Managing the Information Technology Resource: Leadership in the Information Age. Pearson Prentice Hall, New Jersey (2004)

26. Turk, D., Butler, C., Muldoon, K.: A case study on the challenges and tasks of moving to a higher CMMI level. J. Inf. Technol. Manage. **26**(2), 20–40 (2015)

27. Desouza, K., Evaristo, J.: Project management offices: A case of knowledge-based archetypes. Int. J. Inf. Manage. **26**(5), 414–423 (2006)

28. Van den Bergh, J., Işik, Ö., Viaene, S., Helsen, E.: Re-positioning Business Process Management: Exploring Key Capabilities for Successful Business Transformation, 17p. (2016)

29. Darlington, Y., Scott, D.: Qualitative Research in Practice: Stories from the Field. Open University Press, Buckingham (2002)

30. Kurian, G.T.: The AMA Dictionary of Business and Management. AMACOM, New York (2013)

31. Redlich-Amirav, D., Higginbottom, G.: New emerging technologies in qualitative research. Qual. Rep. **19**(12), 1–14 (2014)

32. Flick, U.: Triangulation in Qualitative Research. In: Flick, U., Kardoff, E., Steinke, I. (eds.) A Companion to Qualitative Research, pp. 178–183. Sage, London (2004)

33. Rentrop, C., Zimmermann, S.: Shadow IT evaluation model. In: Proceedings of the Federated Conference on Computer Science and Information Systems, pp. 1023–1027 (2012)

34. Hobbs, B., Aubry, M.: An empirically grounded search for a typology of project management offices. Proj. Manage. J. **39**(S1), 69–82 (2008)

35. Müller, R., Glückler, J., Aubry, M.: A relational typology of project management offices. Proj. Manage. J. **44**(S1), 59–76 (2013)

Focusing Business Improvements Using Process Mining Based Influence Analysis

Teemu Lehto[1,2($\boxtimes$)], Markku Hinkka[1,2], and Jaakko Hollmén[2]

[1] QPR Software Plc, Helsinki, Finland
teemu.s.lehto@gmail.com
[2] Department of Computer Science, School of Science,
Aalto University, Espoo, Finland

Abstract. Business processes are traditionally regarded as generalized abstractions describing the activities and common behaviour of a large group of process instances. However, the recent developments in process mining and data analysis show that individual process instances may behave very different from each other. In this paper we present a generic methodology called influence analysis for finding business improvement areas related to business processes. Influence analysis is based on process mining, root cause analysis and classification rule mining. We present three generic target levels for business improvements and define corresponding probability-based interestingness measures. We then define measures for reporting the contribution results to business people and show how these measures can be used to focus improvements. Real-life case study is also included to show the methodology in action.

Keywords: Process analysis · Process improvement · Process mining · Classification rule mining · Root cause analysis · Data mining · Influence analysis · Contribution

1   Introduction

Many organizations have major problems in their business operations. These problems include too long lead times, delayed customer deliveries, bad product quality, operational inefficiencies causing high operational costs, failure to comply with regulations and bottlenecks in sales processes limiting growth. Problem is that with current methodologies it is difficult, expensive and time-consuming to identify the causes for these business problems. One reason for difficulty is that causality itself is a difficult concept in dynamic business systems [10]. In addition the theory of constraints highlights the importance of finding the most relevant constraints which limit any system in achieving more of its goals [5].

Inability to identify root causes for business problems means that business improvements are not targeted to right issues. This further leads to (1) increased costs when the inefficient operations are not improved and resources are spent on improving things providing only small benefits, (2) decreased sales when the

M. La Rosa et al. (Eds.): BPM Forum 2016, LNBIP 260, pp. 177–192, 2016.
DOI: 10.1007/978-3-319-45468-9_11

Table 1. Benefit vs. effort matrix

| | | Potential benefit | |
		Small	Large
Effort: Resources and time needed to implement change	Small	Good if small improvements are enough	BEST CASE: small investment and large benefits
	Large	WORST CASE: large investment and small benefits	Good if large improvements are needed

constraints for making more sales are not removed and (3) continuing regulatory problems when issues keep on repeating. If we identify wrong reasons, then our development efforts are inefficient.

Business improvements can be achieved by developing a better process design and deploying that design to all businesses (business process re-engineering). Alternatively improvements can be achieved by discovering the current problematic areas where the actual operations deviates from the intended design (fixing operative issues like giving training for individual employees). All identified improvement ideas should be prioritized based on the benefit potential and implementation effort needed as shown in Table 1.

Traditionally the improvement areas are identified based on the discussions with people participating in the execution of these processes. In this paper we present an influence analysis methodology that provides a data-driven approach to finding these areas. Influence analysis contains two main ideas: a technique for identifying as many as possible dimensions for categorizing the process instances and a technique for ranking the areas based on business process improvement potential and effort. In practice we can easily identify about 1.000 dimensions each having an average 100 distinct categories for a dataset of 1 million cases. Then the task is to rank the 100.000 individual categories so that the worst and best performing categories are identified and shown to business people so that they can make decisions for focusing the development efforts.

For ranking the individual categories we adapt an idea that it is easier to conduct business improvements when they are limited to certain subset of cases rather than the whole set of cases. This means that the effort is proportional to the amount of cases while the benefit is proportional to the amount of problematic cases. This means that we should focus the improvements to those subsets that have the highest density of problematic cases. On the other hand it is easy to find segments that only have one case and that is a problematic case, so that the density of problematic cases is 100 %. So we need to take into account also the absolute size of the potential benefit which means that we want to find those segments that have the highest density and largest absolute size.

Influence analysis methodology presented in this paper includes the following steps: 1. Identify the relevant business process and define the case, 2. collect event and case attribute information, 3. create new categorization dimensions, 4. form a binary classification of cases such that each case is either problematic or successful, 5. select a corresponding interestingness measure based on the desired level of business process improvement effect, 6. find the best categorization rules, and 7. present the results to business people.

The rest of this paper is organized as follows: Sect. 2 introduces relevant background in process mining and data analysis. Section 3 presents our influence analysis methodology for focusing business improvements. We have also included some actual project experiences and advice to the corresponding steps. Section 4 presents experiments of using our analysis with sample data and Sect. 5 shows a real-life example. Summary and conclusions are presented in Sect. 6.

2   Related Work

The idea of root cause analysis is well known and studied. It includes steps like problem understanding, problem cause brainstorming, data collection, analysis, cause identification, cause elimination and solution implementation [1]. Process mining based contribution analysis methodology presented in this paper supports all these steps and makes root cause analysis itself much more efficient.

Over the past 20 years organizations have been building data warehouses and business intelligence systems to store operational data created during business operations [7]. In 2012 the amount of available data had grown so much that the term Big Data was introduced to highlight new possibilities of data analysis [9]. There are many data mining and statistical analysis techniques that can be used to turn this data into knowledge [11,13]. There has also been more work in detection of differences between groups [19] and finding contrast sets [2].

Recent studies in the field of process mining have highlighted the usage of process mining for business process analysis [16]. Decision tree learning has been used to explain why certain activity path is chosen within the process [14] discovering decisions made during the process flow. Causal nets have been further studied as a tool and notation for process discovery [17]. Our work is partly based on enriching and transforming process-based logs for the purpose of root cause analysis [15]. We also adapt ideas from the framework for correlating business process characteristics [3]. So far these process mining techniques have been focusing on discovering processes, making findings and creating predictions based on the models. In this paper we extend the current process mining framework with easy-to-use presentation metrics which allow the business users to identify root causes for business problems interactively. Our method can also be regarded as an example of abductive reasoning that starts from an observation and tries to find a hypothesis that accounts for the observation [8].

Probability-based interestingness measures are functions of a 2×2 contingency table. Table 2 shows the generic representation of a contingency table for a rule $A \rightarrow B$, where $n(AB)$ denotes the amount of cases satisfying both A and

Table 2. 2×2 Contingency table for rule $A \rightarrow B$

	B	$\bar{B}$	
A	$n(AB)$	$n(A\bar{B})$	$n(A)$
$\bar{A}$	$n(\bar{A}B)$	$n(\bar{A}\bar{B})$	$n(\bar{A})$
	$n(B)$	$n(\bar{B})$	N

Table 3. Contingency table for rule $product = hats \rightarrow durationdays \geq 20$

	B	$\bar{B}$	
A	1	3	4
$\bar{A}$	2	4	6
	3	7	10

B, and N denotes total amount of cases. An example contingency table for a rule $product = hats \rightarrow durationdays \geq 20$ in a database that contains a total of 10 cases such that 3 cases take long time, 4 cases belong to category $hats$, and one case meets both conditions i.e. the product delivered is $hats$ and it took a long time is shown in Table 3.

Probability-based objective measures have been introduced by Piatetsky-Shapiro [11] and well studied by many researchers. Geng shows a summary of 37 different measures all having a clear theoretical background and characteristics [4]. However a typical business person is not familiar with the measures and has difficulties in understanding the business meaning for each measure. In this paper we will present three probability-based objective measures that are derived from a business process improvement levels. Business people can decide the level of improvement they are planning to achieve and select a measure based on that level.

3   Influence Analysis Methodology

3.1   Identify the Relevant Business Process and Define the Case

First task is to identify a high level problem in the operations. If there is no problems, then the potential for business improvements is zero and our method gives no results. After identifying the high level problem we continue by identifying the business process whose instances will be classified as successful or problematic based on whether they experienced the problem or not. If all cases are problematic then again our approach gives no results since improving every area in the organization would be similarly beneficial.

3.2   Collect Event and Case Attribute Information

Scope of our analysis depends on the amount of data available for the analysis in event and case logs. Since our goal is to create new insight for business people we encourage to use all possible event and case attribute data that is available, even though that typically introduces a lot of noise and data that is not relevant regarding the analysed problems. Generation of suitable log files with extended attributes is well studied area [3]. There also exists methods for enriching and aggregating event logs to case logs [15]. Here are some key steps for constructing event and case logs:

- Starting point is to identify the relational database table whose rows correspond to cases C.
- Identify for each case c_i in C, a set of objects O_i such that every object o_{ij} in O_i is linked to c_i directly. Then add recursively all objects linked to o_{ij} as long as the objects seem to be relevant concerning the analysis objectives. Note that since all tables in relational databases are typically somehow linked to each other this may lead to thousands of linked objects for each case.
- Form event log for c_i by including one event for every timestamp attribute of the case c_i and any linked object o_{ij}.
- Form case log for c_i by aggregating all attribute values of c_i and every object o_{ij} in O_i, thus creating potentially thousands of case attributes for each case. Suitable aggregation functions include *count, sum, max, min, average, median, concatenate, first* and *last*.
- Further augment every case c_i by adding external events that have occurred during the lifetime of the case. Example of external events include *machinebreak-started, machinebreak-completed, weekend, strike, queuetoolong* and *badweather*.

3.3 Create New Categorization Dimensions

The purpose of this step is to create new categorization dimensions for the cases. All these dimensions will then be used when finding the best improvement focus areas, so the more dimensions we have the larger the coverage of our analysis will be. Table 4 shows examples of dimensions that can be created for every event log based on the log itself.

3.4 Form a Binary Classification of Cases Such that Each Case Is Either Problematic or Successful

Purpose of this step is to express any discovery related to a business process as an attribute value for each process instance. This binary classification attribute specifies whether the case is problematic or successful. In practice a wide range of process mining methods can be used to make process discoveries [16].

Table 5 shows some example business problems that have been discovered using process mining methods and the corresponding illustrative functions for creating binary classification.

3.5 Select a Corresponding Interestingness Measure Based on the Desired Level of Business Process Improvement Effect

In this step we select an interestingness measure that will be used for finding the best business improvement areas. We propose the following requirements for the interestingness measure:

1. *Easy-to-understand by business people.* Business people are supposed to make actual decisions based on the analysis results so they must understand the

Table 4. Illustrative category dimensions

New category dimensions	Business rationale for including the dimension
Amount of Events per case, amount of Unique Events per case	Cases with very large or small amount of events often behave differently than the others
Start and end timestamp of the whole case	Exact calendar date, month or week is used to detect process changes over the time. Day of the week and Month of the year are useful for discovering periodic and seasonal behaviour
Start and end time of an individual event type	Same rationale as the case level attribute above, this will create at least one new dimension for each event type
One new dimension for specifying the amount of event occurrences separately for each event type	Often the fact that a particular event is executed several times for a case is a root cause for business problems

Table 5. Illustrative binary classifications for discovered business problems

Business problem discovered using process mining methods	Illustrative function for creating the binary classification
Some cases are not completed within the agreed service level agreement	$c.totalduration() > ServiceLevelAgreement$
Cases should not include multiple AddressChanged activities	$c.activitycount('AddressChange') > 2$
Suspiciously many cases have started in March 2015	$c.startmonth() =' 2015 - 03'$
First AddressChanged event should not be recorded by John	$c.getActivity('AddressChanged').first().recordedBy() =' John'$
Size of produced product have bigger than agreed variance	$c.product().size() - mean(product.size()) > \sigma$

results. It is thus important to minimize magic in our analysis and give as simple to understand business meaning for the results as possible.

2. *Big Benefits.* Selected interestingness measure should identify areas that include as many problematic cases as possible. This requirement corresponds to the benefit dimension of Table 1.

3. *Small Effort.* Implementing the change should require as small effort as possible. This requirement corresponds to the effort dimension of Table 1.

Regarding the first requirement *easy-to-understand by business people* we have identified three corresponding target levels for operational business improvements that business people are familiar with:

1. *ideal.* Improvement project will be ideal, all problems will be removed and after the project every future case will be completed without any problems.
2. *other average.* Focus area can be improved so that it reaches the current average performance of other areas. After the improvement project the share of problematic cases in the focus area will be equal to the average share of problematic cases in the other business areas before the improvements.
3. *as-is average.* Focus area can be improved so that it reaches the current average performance of all areas. After the improvement project the share of problematic cases in the focus area will be equal to the average share of problematic cases in the whole business before the improvements.

Regarding the second requirement *Big benefits* we calculate the overall density of problematic cases after the improvement. Table 6 shows these overall density measures calculated for the three identified change types when A is the set of cases selected as a target for business process improvement, B is the set of problematic cases before improvement and B' is the set of problematic cases after improvement.

Table 6. Change types

Change type	To-Be density of problematic cases for the selected segment A after the change $P(B'\|A)$	Overall to-be density of problematic cases after the change $P(B') = P(B'\|A)P(A) + P(B\|\bar{A})P(\bar{A})$	Change in overall density of problematic cases $P(B') - P(B)$
ideal	Zero density $= 0$	$0 P(A) + P(B\|\bar{A})P(\bar{A}) = P(B) - P(AB)$	$-P(AB)$
other average	Average of current cases excluding this segment $= P(B\|\bar{A})$	$P(B\|\bar{A})P(A) + P(B\|\bar{A})P(\bar{A}) = P(B\|\bar{A})$	$P(B\|\bar{A}) - P(B)$
as-is average	Average of current cases including this segment $= P(B)$	$P(B)P(A) + P(B\|\bar{A})P(\bar{A}) = P(A)P(B) + P(B) - P(AB)$	$P(A)P(B) - P(AB)$

Regarding the third requirement *Small Effort* we say that the effort needed to improve a segment is relational to the size of the segment $P(A)$, i.e. the bigger the segment is the bigger the effort needed to make improvement.

Table 7 summarizes the identified change types according to the three requirements. Change type *ideal* sorts the results by the amount of problematic cases thus maximizing benefits. Since it does not take into account the size of the segment at all it performs poorly against the small effort requirement. Change type *other average* performs well regarding the benefits but it fails to make a difference between different sized segments including all problematic cases. It is also a bit difficult for business people to understand since the benefit potential of each segment is related to the average performance of all other segments, which needs to be realized separately for each segment. Change type *as-is average* performs well regarding the benefits, is easy enough to understand for business people and takes into account the cost needed to implement the change.

Table 7. Change types by requirements

Change type	Easy to understand	Big benefits	Small effort to achieve
ideal	$+++$	$+++$	-
other average	$+$	$++$	$++$
as-is average	$++$	$++$	$+++$

Based on Table 7 we propose to use the change type *as-is average* as the target level for operational business improvements. We thus select the corresponding interestingness measure from Table 6 as $P(AB) - P(A)P(B)$, which is also known as $Leverage(A \rightarrow B)$. Business meaning of this measure is that if the segment specified covered by the antecedent of a rule is improved so that it reaches average performance, then the change in the total density of problematic cases is reduced by $P(AB) - P(A)P(B)$. For the communication purposes we define the following measures.

Definition 1. *Let B be a set of problematic cases and A be a set of cases that will be improved in order to reach an as-is-average density of problematic cases. Then the Contribution$(A \rightarrow B)$ is $n(AB) - \frac{n(A)n(B)}{N}$, where $n(AB)$ is amount of problematic cases in segment A before improvement, $n(A)$ is amount of cases in segment A, $n(B)$ is original amount of problematic cases and N is total amount of cases. This measure tells how many cases will be improved when business improvement is focused on segment A.*

Definition 2. *Let B be a set of problematic cases and A be a set of cases that will be improved in order to reach an as-is-average density of problematic cases. Then the Contribution%$(A \rightarrow B)$ is Contribution$(A \rightarrow B)/n(B)$, where $n(B)$ is amount of problematic cases before business improvement. This measure tells how big share of the total business problem is improved when business improvement is focused on segment A.*

Definition 3. *Let B be a set of problematic cases and At be a case attribute for which all problematic segments will be improved in order to reach an as-is-average density of problematic cases. Then the AttributeContribution%$(At \rightarrow B)$ is $\frac{1}{2}\sum_{A_i \in AttributeValues(At)} Abs(Contribution\%(A_i \rightarrow B))$, where AttributeValues (At) is the set of all the sets of cases such that each individual set of cases contains all the cases having one specific attribute value for At. AttributeValues(At) has thus one set of cases for every separate value for At. This measure tells how potential the attribute is as a target for business process improvement, the higher the value is the better the potential. The division by 2 is used to ensure that AttributeContribution% is always between 0 and 100 %.*

Attribute contribution is used to quickly identify those case attributes that contribute most to the finding. If there are large differences in the distribution of problematic cases for the different values of At, then the attribute contribution for At is high. If attribute contribution is low for attribute At, then we know that At does not include relevant causes for the problematic cases.

3.6   Find the Best Categorization Rules and Attributes

Run a rule learning algorithm using the information defined in previous steps. Analysis is performed by identifying a set of rules $A \rightarrow B$ where B is the binary classification value. Analysis shows how much the overall density of problematic cases changes when a selected business change is targeted to the segment covered by the antecedent A of the rule.

According to the requirement *easy-to-understand by business people* we have received good results by limiting the antecedent A to contain only one conditional attribute (=dimension/column) and one category value for the column. The fact that simple rules perform very well on most business datasets has also been presented by Holte [6]. It is also possible to construct antecedents based on multiple conditional attributes and using data mining algorithms to find combinations that have high contribution. However, if antecedents contain multiple attributes then benchmarking all combinations results in a very long report.

3.7   Present the Results to Business People

A full influence analysis report shows all discovered rules sorted by the selected interestingness measure. Top of the list contains the problematic cases (=best improvement areas) and bottom of the list contains the best practice examples.

Curse of dimensionality is typically a big problem when finding causes from several thousand or more features. Our methodology solves this during the presentation step by only showing a fixed amount of top and bottom rules. For example an analysis may contain 1.000 dimensions with a total of 100 million distinct single dimension antecedents. Our suggestion is to only show for example the top 100 and bottom 100 antecedents. In this way the interesting dimensions are likely to have at least some values in the top or bottom ranges and user can continue checking that attribute in more detail.

Another possibility is to show the report first only for the dimensions. In the previous example where we have 1.000 dimensions we first show them ordered by the *AttributeContribution%* and user the selects one attribute for more details.

Influence analysis report for one attribute show the antecedents for one case attribute at a time. This view is specifically easy to understand for business people since the problematic and best practice areas are clearly shown in this benchmark report.

4   Example Analysis

In this chapter we will present an example analysis conducted according to the methodology steps described in Sect. 3.

Table 8. Case data

Case	Product
1	Hats
2	Hats
3	Jeans
4	Shirts
5	Hats
6	Shirts
7	Shirts
8	Jeans
9	Shirts
10	Hats

Table 9. Event log data

Case	Event log
1	{order(20150101), orderchange(20150107), production(20150115, Ger), delivery(20150119)}
2	{order(20150101), production(20150107, Ger), delivery(20150110)}
3	{order(20150101), orderchange(20150108), production(20150115, Swe), delivery(20150121)}
4	{order(20150101), production(20150112, Fin), delivery(20150113)}
5	{order(20150101), orderchange(20150110), production(20150120, Fin), delivery(20150127), delivery(20150206)}
6	{order(20150101), production(20150108, Ger), delivery(20150113)}
7	{order(20150101), production(20150106, Ger), delivery(20150112)}
8	{order(20150101), production(20150108, Fin), delivery(20150114), delivery(20150122)}
9	{order(20150101), production(20150112, Ger), delivery(20150117)}
10	{order(20150101), production(20150111, Ger), delivery(20150118)}

1. Let us analyse an order to delivery process where each case is an order.
2. Table 8 contains case attribute information containing the product and region for each case. Table 9 contains an event log for each case specifying the activity name and date of the activity occurrence in format *yyyymmdd*. Event *production* also includes the name of the country where production was conducted as event attribute.
3. Table 10 shows new categorization attributes that have been calculated based on the previous data. *Duration days* is based on total case duration. *#del* is the amount of events of type *delivery* occurring in the case. *Region* is the production country taken from the event *production*. *weekday* is the day of the week when the *production* event was conducted. *#order changes* is the amount of events of type *order change* occurring in the case. *trace* is the full event type sequence for the whole case.
4. Problematic cases are identified with a binary classification B such that $B = true$ if *durationdays* ≥ 20 else *false*. With this classification the cases 3, 5 and 8 have $B = true$ so the original density of problematic cases is $P(B) = 3/10 = 0.3$

Table 10. Example derived case data

Case	Dur. days	#del	Region	Weekday	#order changes	Trace
1	18	1	Ger	Fri	1	order-orderchange-production-delivery
2	9	1	Ger	Thu	0	order-production-delivery
3	20	1	Swe	Fri	1	order-orderchange-production-delivery
4	12	1	Fin	Tue	0	order-production-delivery
5	36	2	Fin	Wed	1	order-orderchange-production-delivery-delivery
6	12	1	Ger	Fri	0	order-production-delivery
7	11	1	Ger	Wed	0	order-production-delivery
8	21	2	Fin	Fri	0	order-production-delivery-delivery
9	16	1	Ger	Tue	0	order-production-delivery
10	17	1	Ger	Mon	0	order-production-delivery

Table 11. Contribution values for all rules $A \to B$ where B is $duration days \geq 20$

Antecedent	n(A)	n(AB)	ideal		average		as-is avg	
			$\Delta_1 n$	$\Delta P(B_1)$	$\Delta_2 n$	$\Delta P(B_2)$	$\Delta_3 n$	$\Delta P(B_3)$
$\#deliveries = 2$	2	2	-2	-0.2	-1.75	-0.18	-1.4	-0.14
$product = jeans$	2	2	-2	-0.2	-1.75	-0.18	-1.4	-0.14
$customer = female$	6	3	-3	-0.3	-3	-0.3	-1.2	-0.12
$\#orderchanges = 1$	3	2	-2	-0.2	-1.57	-0.16	-1.1	-0.11
$Region = Finland$	3	2	-2	-0.2	-1.57	-0.16	-1.1	-0.11
$ProductionWeekday = Fri$	4	2	-2	-0.2	-1.33	-0.13	-0.8	-0.08
$Region = Sweden$	1	1	-1	-0.1	-0.78	-0.08	-0.7	-0.07
$trace = order - orderchange - production - delivery - delivery$	1	1	-1	-0.1	-0.78	-0.08	-0.7	-0.07
$trace = order - production - delivery - delivery$	1	1	-1	-0.1	-0.78	-0.08	-0.7	-0.07
$ProductionWeekday = Wed$	2	1	-1	-0.1	-0.5	-0.05	-0.4	-0.04
$trace = order - orderchange - production - delivery$	2	1	-1	-0.1	-0.5	-0.05	-0.4	-0.04
$product = hats$	4	1	-1	-0.1	0.33	0.03	0.2	0.02
$ProductionWeekday = Mon$	1	0	0	0	0.33	0.03	0.3	0.03
$ProductionWeekday = Thu$	1	0	0	0	0.33	0.03	0.3	0.03
$ProductionWeekday = Tue$	2	0	0	0	0.75	0.08	0.6	0.06
$\#orderchanges = 0$	7	1	-1	-0.1	3.67	0.37	1.1	0.11
$customer = male$	4	0	0	0	2	0.2	1.2	0.12
$product = shirts$	4	0	0	0	2	0.2	1.2	0.12
$\#deliveries = 1$	8	1	-1	-0.1	7	0.7	1.4	0.14
$Region = Germany$	6	0	0	0	4.5	0.45	1.8	0.18
$trace = order - production - delivery$	6	0	0	0	4.5	0.45	1.8	0.18

5. Table 11 shows the influence analysis results for each of the presented three change types: *as-is average*, *other average* and *ideal*. Results are sorted by the change type *as-is average* effects. According to these results the business improvement efforts should focus in segments $\#deliveries = 2$ and $product = jeans$, since in both of these segments the amount of problematic cases will drop by 1.4 as shown in column $\Delta_3 n$.

5   Case Study: Rabobank Group ICT

We evaluated the influence analysis with a publicly available data from Rabobank Group ICT used in BPI Challenge 2014 [18]. The data contained 46.616 cases and a total of 466.737 events. After a process mining analysis we discovered that the average duration for cases is 5 days and median duration is 18 h. We decided to consider all cases that took more than one week to complete as problematic resulting in a total of 7.400 (15.9 %) problematic cases. Table 12 shows that the biggest contributor for this finding is $Impact = 5$. There is a total of 16.741 cases with $Impact = 5$, out of which 3.535 (21.1 %) are problematic. As a *contribution%* this corresponds to 11.9 % of the total amount of problematic cases. For process performance point of view this is intuitive since it is probably acceptable to have low (5 = lowest on scale 1..5) impact cases taking a long time compared to higher impact cases. Table 12 also shows that 28.5 % of cases having ServiceComp WBS (CBy) equal to WBS000091 are completed in more than one week, which makes WBS000091 a candidate for business process improvements. If WBS000091 would reach the average level of performance, then there would 4.2 % less problematic cases.

   Table 13 shows antecedents that have the biggest negative contribution. These can be regarded as the reasons why cases are completed within one week more often than average. If $\#Reassignments$ is zero, then only 5.9 % of cases will take more than one week. If these cases would take as long time as average

Table 12. Top positive contributors

Antecedent	n(A)	n(AB)	P(B|A)	Contribution	Contribution%
Impact = 5	16741	3535	21.1 %	877	11.9 %
Urgency = 5	16779	3538	21.1 %	874	11.8 %
Priority = 5	16486	3473	21.1 %	856	11.6 %
# Related Interactions = 2	2736	1108	40.5 %	674	9.1 %
#Update From Customer = 1	1692	793	46.9 %	524	7.1 %
Closure Code = Other	16470	3137	19.0 %	522	7.1 %
# Reassignments = 2	5378	1340	24.9 %	486	6.6 %
# Reassignments = 3	2191	814	37.2 %	466	6.3 %
# Reassignments = 4	1606	701	43.6 %	446	6.0 %
Category = request for information	8846	1810	20.5 %	406	5.5 %
CI Type (CBy) = computer	3404	865	25.4 %	325	4.4 %
ServiceComp WBS (CBy) = WBS000091	2453	700	28.5 %	311	4.2 %
CI Type (CBy) = application	29456	4979	16.9 %	303	4.1 %

Table 13. Top negative contributors

Antecedent	n(A)	n(AB)	P(B|A)	Contribution	Contribution%
# Reassignments = 0	27468	1628	5.9%	−2732	−36.9%
# Related Interactions = 1	43058	5907	13.7%	−928	−12.5%
Reopen Time = (blank)	44332	6285	14.2%	−752	−10.2%
ServiceComp WBS (CBy) = WBS000073	13173	1401	10.6%	−690	−9.3%
Service Component WBS (aff) = WBS000073	13342	1437	10.8%	−681	−9.2%
Impact = 3	6591	602	9.1%	−444	−6.0%
Priority = 3	6703	620	9.2%	−444	−6.0%
Urgency = 3	6536	607	9.3%	−431	−5.8%
CI Type (CBy) = subapplication	7711	800	10.4%	−424	−5.7%
Closure Code = User error	3554	152	4.3%	−412	−5.6%
Category = incident	37748	5582	14.8%	−410	−5.5%
CI Type (aff) = subapplication	7782	841	10.8%	−394	−5.3%
CI Name (aff) = SUB000456	3050	138	4.5%	−346	−4.7%

Table 14. Benchmark of distinct values of ServiceComp WBS (CBy)

ServiceComp WBS (CBy)	Contribution
WBS000091	4.2%
WBS000072	2.8%
WBS000088	2.4%
WBS000162	2.2%
WBS000263	1.4%
WBS000296	1.4%
WBS000271	1.1%
WBS000092	0.9%
...	
WBS000128	−0.6%
WBS000094	−0.6%
WBS000307	−0.7%
WBS000152	−0.7%
WBS000016	−0.8%
WBS000228	−1.0%
WBS000095	−1.7%
#N/B	−1.7%
WBS000073	−9.3%

Table 15. Analysis on case attribute level

Case attribute	Attribute contribution
Handle Time (Hours)	54%
KM number	38%
#Reassignments	37%
CI Name (CBy)	35%
CI Name (aff)	34%
Service Component WBS (aff)	27%
Related Interaction	26%
ServiceComp WBS (CBy)	24%
Closure Code	15%
#RelatedInteractions	13%
Impact	12%
Urgency	12%
Priority	12%
CI Type (CBy)	10%
CI Subtype (CBy)	10%
CI Subtype (aff)	8%
CI Type (aff)	6%
Category	6%
#RelatedIncidents	1%
Related Change	1%
#RelatedChanges	0%
Status	0%
Alert Status	0%

cases, then there would be 36.9% more problematic cases. Another observation from Table 13 is that only 10.6% of cases having ServiceComp WBS (CBy) equal to WBS000073 are completed late, which makes WBS000073 a positive benchmark.

ServiceComp WBS (CBy) was identified both as having a high positive and negative contribution. For business people it is often beneficial to show the contribution of all distinct values for this case attribute in one list order by contribution as shown in Table 14.

In Table 15 we see all case attributes listed by their attribute contribution. Obviously *HandleTime* in hours correlates strongly with case duration. Case attributes *CINames* and *ServiceComponents* have a strong correlation with cases taking a long time, which can be seen from their high attribute contribution. We also see that *#RelatedChanges* and *AlertStatus* have a very small effect to cases taking more than one week.

In this chapter we used influence analysis with real case data. We were able to identify causes for cases lasting more than one week. We also observed a benchmarking report for a particular case attribute *ServiceCompWBS(CBy)* that seems to contribute a lot to the finding. All the results have been shown in easy-to-understand lists ordered by the contribution metric. If these results would have been shown to the business people it is likely that they would have combined this information with their tacit knowledge and discovered even more underlying cause-effect relationships.

6   Summary

In this paper we have presented a methodology that makes operational development more effective. Our methodology is suitable for every business process that has large enough volume of cases. Using our influence analysis method a workshop group consisting of business people identifies problems and focuses business improvement resources for eliminating these problems.

We have first shown how to collect the required data and how to process the data by creating new dimensions and binary classification metric. We then present an interestingness measure that is easy to understand by business people and helps in selecting the focus area for business process improvement such that it maximizes improvement benefits and minimizes implementation costs. We propose using the change type *as-is average* with interestingness measure $P(AB) - P(A)P(B)$. We then defined three measures *Contribution*, *Contribution%* and *AttributeContribution%* to be used in influence analysis report. Finally we have applied our analysis to a real-life data.

We have used the influence analysis in more than 100 customer projects during the past 5 years. In practice the problem areas and best practice areas have been accurately discover by influence analysis. Influence analysis is implemented to a commercial product [12] showing both the change type *ideal* and change type *as-is average* results. Interactive usage in workshop meetings has proven to be very valuable and it motivates business people in same room to share their tacit knowledge to deepen the influence analysis findings. Typical scenario is that participants first try to guess the most influencing factors and when they then see the results their own hypotheses are strengthened or weakened. This process further facilitates participants' thinking and collaboration with each other. Based on the discussion the organization then selects the focus areas for business process improvements and starts monitoring the performance on monthly intervals using the same contribution measures.

This method applies to finding root causes for problems that occur very rarely as well as to maximizing objectives like delivery accuracy that should reach about

99 % performance. Also the method can be used to evaluate potential risks in any given segment by checking those areas that have low density of problematic cases in the as-is situation. Influence analysis also has an important application in deciding whether the organization should improve the whole process design or improve certain problem areas. If the contribution values for all rules are relatively low, then there is no clear problem that should be fixed. Thus if no focus area is found and business still needs to be improved, there is a need to improve the whole process design.

Acknowledgements. We thank QPR Software Plc for the practical experiences from a wide variety of customer cases and for funding our research.

References

1. Andersen, B., Fagerhaug, T.: Root Cause Analysis: Simplified Tools and Techniques. ASQ Quality Press, Milwaukee (2006)
2. Bay, S., Pazzani, M.: Detecting group differences: mining contrast sets. Data Min. Knowl. Disc. **5**(3), 213–246 (2001)
3. de Leoni, M., van der Aalst, W.M.P., Dees, M.: A general framework for correlating business process characteristics. In: Sadiq, S., Soffer, P., Völzer, H. (eds.) BPM 2014. LNCS, vol. 8659, pp. 250–266. Springer, Heidelberg (2014)
4. Geng, L., Hamilton, H.J.: Interestingness measures for data mining: a survey. ACM Comput. Surv. (CSUR) **38**(3), 9 (2006)
5. Goldratt, E.M.: Theory of Constraints. North River, Croton-on-Hudson (1990)
6. Holte, R.C.: Very simple classification rules perform well on most commonly used datasets. Mach. Learn. **11**(1), 63–90 (1993)
7. Inmon, W.H.: Building the Data Warehouse. Wiley, New York (2005)
8. Kakas, A.C., Kowalski, R.A., Toni, F.: Abductive logic programming. J. Logic Comput. **2**(6), 719–770 (1992)
9. Mayer-Schnberger, V., Cukier, K.: Big Data: A Revolution that Will Transform How We Live, Work, and Think. Houghton Mifflin Harcourt, Boston (2013)
10. Pearl, J.: Causality: Models, Reasoning and Inference, vol. 29. MIT Press, Cambridge (2000)
11. Piatetsky-Shapiro, G.: Discovery, analysis and presentation of strong rules. In: Knowledge Discovery in Databases, pp. 229–248 (1991)
12. QPR Software Plc.: QPR Software to Offer Business Process optimization with Automated Business Process Discovery Software QPR Process Analyzer, Press release 15 Feb 2011
13. Quinlan, J.R.: Induction of decision trees. Mach. Learn. **1**(1), 81–106 (1986)
14. Rozinat, A., van der Aalst, W.M.P.: Decision Mining in ProM. Springer, Heidelberg (2006)
15. Suriadi, S., Ouyang, C., van der Aalst, W.M.P., ter Hofstede, A.H.M.: Root cause analysis with enriched process logs. In: La Rosa, M., Soffer, P. (eds.) BPM Workshops 2012. LNBIP, vol. 132, pp. 174–186. Springer, Heidelberg (2013)
16. van der Aalst, W.M.P., et al.: Process mining manifesto. In: Daniel, F., Barkaoui, K., Dustdar, S. (eds.) BPM Workshops 2011, Part I. LNBIP, vol. 99, pp. 169–194. Springer, Heidelberg (2012)

17. van der Aalst, W.M.P., Adriansyah, A., van Dongen, B.: Causal nets: a modeling language tailored towards process discovery. In: Katoen, J.-P., König, B. (eds.) CONCUR 2011. LNCS, vol. 6901, pp. 28–42. Springer, Heidelberg (2011)
18. Van Dongen, B.F.: BPI Challenge 2014. Rabobank Nederland. Dataset (2014). http://dx.doi.org/10.4121/uuid:c3e5d162-0cfd-4bb0-bd82-af5268819c35
19. Webb, G.I., Butler, S., Newlands, D.: On detecting differences between groups. In: Proceedings of the Ninth ACM SIGKDD International Conference on Knowledge Discovery and Data Mining, KDD 2003 (2003)

Factors Affecting the Sustained Use of Process Models

Toomas Saarsen[(✉)] and Marlon Dumas

Institute of Computer Science, University of Tartu, Tartu, Estonia
{toomas.saarsen,marlon.dumas}@ut.ee

Abstract. The documentation of business processes via modelling notations is a well-accepted and widespread practice. While a given process model is created in a specific project and sometimes for a specific purpose, it is generally preserved so that it can be used subsequently, beyond the context where it was created. In this setting, the aim of the paper at hand is to uncover factors that affect the sustained use of process models in an organization. First, the paper outlines an a priori model of sustained process model use derived from existing factor models of business process modelling success and knowledge reuse. This a priori model is packaged as an assessment instrument and applied to four organizations from different domains. Based on these case studies, we identify a subset of factors and relationships that explain differences in the observed sustained use of process models across the organizations in question.

Keywords: Success factors · Process model use · Process modelling

1 Introduction

Business process management (BPM) is a central component of information and operations management practices in modern organizations. A common practice within BPM projects or programs is to capture the business processes of an organization in the form of business process models. Process models serve manifold purposes, including preserving and communicating knowledge as well as analyzing, redesigning and automating processes for the purpose of continuous business improvement [1].

Process models are generally created for a specific goal [2]. For example, a model of an order-to-cash process might be created in the context of the deployment of a new enterprise resource management system in an organization. However, said model can be subsequently re-used for other purposes such as training of new staff members or continuous process improvement. If process models are to serve as a unifying vehicle for managing business processes, it is desirable that they are reused over a sustained period of time, past the specific initiative or project where they were created.

Various studies have elucidated and analysed the determinants of knowledge sharing and reuse in organizations [3, 4]. In comparison, the reuse of process models – as an integral component of an organization's knowledge base – has received less attention. Some studies have considered the question of process model use and reuse, but only in the context of specific projects, rather than sustained use over time.

© Springer International Publishing Switzerland 2016
M. La Rosa et al. (Eds.): BPM Forum 2016, LNBIP 260, pp. 193–209, 2016.
DOI: 10.1007/978-3-319-45468-9_12

In this setting, this paper studies the question of *what factors determine whether process models are used in a sustained manner or only for the purposes they were initially created?* To address this question, we follow a two-phase research approach. In the first phase, we analyze the literature on success, impact and reuse factors of process models and more broadly knowledge reuse. Drawing upon previous studies, we build an a priori factor model of sustained process model use. In the second phase, we conduct case studies in four organizations. In these case studies, we assess the current state of each organization with respect to the identified factors on the one hand, and their level of sustained process model use on the other hand. Based on data collected during the case studies, we establish possible relations between the identified factors and the observed process model use in the organizations under scrutiny.

The rest of the paper is structured as follows: Sect. 2 provides an overview of related literature, putting forward existing models that may be used to explain process model use or reuse. Section 3 presents the a priori model of sustained process model use. Section 4 discusses the case studies and associated findings. Finally, Sect. 5 concludes and sketches directions for future work.

2 Theoretical Background

Process models are generally created and initially used in the context of specific BPM initiatives or projects with certain purposes in mind. Process models can be created, for example, in the context of a process improvement project [5] or within the scope of a software integration project [6], and used for the purposes of the project where they are created. Once created, a process model or collection thereof can be reused for different purposes outside the scope and timeframe of the project. For example, a process model created in the context of a software integration project could be used later in the context of a process analysis and improvement project or vice versa. Such repeated use is called 'reuse' – a repeated use of the process model for different purposes or tasks than initially envisaged [7]. Process model reuse can occur in a one-off manner, or can recur over time.

Sustained use – called 'continued use' by some authors [8] – occurs when a process model or collection thereof is reused on a regular basis over and over again past the project in which they were initially created and for different purposes or tasks. This regularity makes that the model becomes part of the general knowledge of the organization, or of a subset thereof. Thus, the question of what are the factors that determine sustained process model use is intertwined with two other questions, namely: (i) what determines the success of projects or initiatives where a collection of process models is created and initially used; and (ii) what determines the fact that a given process model or a collection of process models is re-used in a sustained manner past the project or the initiative where they were initially created.

In literature review, we focused on papers on knowledge and more specifically, process model reuse in organizations. Additionally, papers on process modelling as an essential presumption of process model reuse were linked into our review.

2.1 Process Modelling Project Assessment

Process modelling project success factors have been studied by Bandara et al. [9] who propose a model of critical success factors of individual process modelling projects. The focus is on project success and the initial use of the process model during the project. This model is composed of eight success factors and five success measures. The success factors include project-specific factors and modelling-related factors. Examples of success factors are 'Modelling Expertise' and 'Modelling Tool'. The purpose of success measures, on the other hand, is to assess the initial use of process models and the impact that such initial use creates in an organization. Success measures in Bandara et al.'s model include, for example, 'Model Quality' and 'Process Impact'. The proposed model summarizes previous studies on process modelling success factors and has been tested in practice.

At a more upstream level, Eikebrokk et al. [10] have proposed a theoretical model of determinants of business process modelling in organizations. In other words, they study the question of why certain organizations have practiced modelling over long periods of time, whereas others have not. In our study, however, we focus on a complementary question, namely: given an organization where process modelling has been practiced, what determines the fact that some process models get to be used on a sustained basis while others are only used in projects where the models are created.

Another related study is the process modelling impact framework of Bernhard and Recker [11]. This study synthesizes different studies on process model use and proposes a model to explain a perceived or actual impact of process modelling along an organization's objectives. This model highlights seven factors related to process modelling initiatives and process model use. However, the model in question is not intended to assess process model use per se, but rather the organizational impact that process model use creates.

2.2 Knowledge and Process Model Reuse

Determinants of knowledge reuse in organizations have been studied by Watson and Hewett [12], who proposed a success factors model (eight factors) influencing knowledge reuse and user contribution in an organization. Examples of success factors in their model are 'Training in Knowledge Reuse' and 'Value of Knowledge'.

Many researchers have tested different factors based on DeLone and McLean success model [13]. This model focuses on the information system and knowledge usage in an organization and on influences between different factor groups. Success related to different quality dimensions (information, system, service) has been studied by Jennex and Olfman [8]. Success factors tested in their model (nine factors) are, for example, 'Linkage (of the information)' and 'Management Support'. Jennex and Olfman [14] provide a comparative review and synthesis of determinants of knowledge management success, as well as a detailed comparative analysis of four success factor models in this area. Their synthesis puts forward a number of organizational, tool and user-related factors that we take as input for constructing our a priori model.

Success factors related to process model reuse have been studied by Nolte et al. [7] who propose a set of factors that determine process model reuse after the process modelling project. Their model consists of 16 factors (arranged into five categories) including 'Software Ease of Use' and 'Modelling Expertise'.

From the angle of information system use, factors that influence sustained use have been researched by Recker [15] in his study where factors influencing the use of software are under scrutiny. In the study, important factors influencing the use of software are, for example, 'Perceived Ease of Use' and 'Perceived Usefulness'.

An important component highlighted in aforementioned articles is the quality of information base, first and foremost in the context of a process model [7] or of a knowledge base [12], but also more widely on various aspects of tools and organization [14]. The issue of quality has been separately addressed in article [16], where specific reference is made to quality parameters in the context of different important objects (such as the modeller, tool, aim of modelling); it is also analysed how different aspects of quality are interrelated.

Quality of process models [17] is more narrowly treated in articles [18, 19] where the reuse of process models from the angle of the end user is analysed – which parameters of process diagrams facilitate better understanding of information by the reader of the process model and reduce the number of mistakes in the creation of models. Here, the parameters of model quality metrics are, for example, 'Complexity' and 'Size'. We did not involve more detailed quality metrics (variables) associated with the process model. Rather, the focus was on more gen-eral factors that the organization can support and influence through different activities. Thus, these topics have been incorporated into our model through more general factors such as 'Ease of Interpretation' (clarity and ease of the model for the end user) and 'Structure' (presentation of complex and extensive information through easily understandable structure) [20].

Process model reuse may occur at different levels of granularity as analysed by Holschke et al. [21]. This latter paper focuses on process model reuse in the context of modelling rather than on the question of continued use of a process model over time.

The reuse of models is an important issue in the context of reference models [22] that bring together important knowledge from a given field and presents it as a complete model. Important aspects in the use of reference models have been examined by Frank [23] who brings out 'Understandability', 'Tools', 'Skills' as significant topics. Reference models are intended for repeated use rather from the angle of development for managers and analysts in shaping the organization or in the creation of new systems. The focus of our study is rather on the wider internal use of process models.

The next section introduces the a priori model of sustained process model use that we will base on models of success factors focused on different phases of BPM.

3   Assessment Framework for Process Model Use

This section introduces the proposed assessment framework for process model use. First, we will provide an overview of the framework and its rationale. Next, we will introduce the success factors. Finally, we are going to introduce an assessment instrument for applying the framework to a specific organization. Definitions of different factors have been provided in the Appendix.

3.1   Overall Structure

The proposed assessment framework is grounded on a life cycle model of a BPM programme [24]. In this model, a BPM programme consists of a number of BPM projects that evolve concurrently (or sequentially), each one following a four phase life cycle: (1) project preparation; (2) project implementation; (3) deployment and initial use of the produced models; (4) post-deployment and sustained use of the models. Moving along the phases of a BPM life cycle, we highlighted the topics and categories in the context of which the factors could be observed.

The project preparation phase is concerned with the identification and scoping of business needs and goals, resource planning, risk analysis, and other project preparation activities [25]. This phase brings the category 'Organization' into our framework.

The project implementation phase includes activities where the modelling team investigates which processes are involved, collects relevant data about these processes, produces the process models, performs corresponding quality checks and discusses the models to relevant stakeholders [26]. Within the modelling phase, focus is on modelling (category 'Modelling') and on the model that is created as a result (category 'Process Model').

The project deployment phase includes the publication of models (category 'Tool') to their intended audience and other activities related to the initial use of the model within the scope of the project. For example, individual models can be used for process analysis, re-design and IT system implementation [6].

The post-deployment phase encompasses activities where the models are used for purposes beyond the scope of the project in which they were produced. This phase includes model maintenance (e.g. corrective or perfective updates from outside the scope of the project), reuse of parts of the model in other process models, and perusal of the model [27]. The post-deployment phase brings into our model the category 'User' – which draws together factors pertaining to the (long-term) users of the model. Activities implemented in previous phases influence the context where the process model is used; the main difference with the previous phases is the shift in emphasis which moves from modelling to everyday use. We define sustained process model use as regular, post-deployment use by multiple stakeholders for different purposes.

3.2   Categorization of Factors

Moving along the life-cycle model, we concentrated different factors from multiple success factor models under the categories given in Sect. 3.1 (the focus of most articles is on the phase of 1-2 BPM life cycle). In order to avoid overlapping between factors under a category, we followed the orthogonality rule between factors. We kept those factors in the table, which had been brought out in at least two different success factor models. The resulting set of factors is summarized in Table 1.

Table 1. Success factors under different categories.

	Organization			Modelling							Model					Tool	User			
	Management Support	Clear Goals and Purposes	Subjective Norms	Modelling Expertise	Stakeholders Participation	Information Resources	Project Management	Modelling Methodology	Modelling Language	Modelling Tool	Richness	Knowledge Quality	Value of Knowledge	Structure	Ease of Interpretation	Ease of Use	Usefulness	Competence	Motivation	Knowledge Networking
Process Modelling																				
Bandara et al. 2005 [9]	x			x	x	x	x	x	x	x										
Raduescu et al. 2006 [29]	x	x	x	x	x	x	x	x	x	x										
Rittgen 2010 [30]			x		x	x														
Lu and Sadiq 2007 [31]								x	x	x										
Process Model use																				
Nolte et al. 2013 [7]			x										x	x	x	x	x	x	x	x
Rosemann 2006 [28]		x	x	x	x		x	x	x	x	x	x	x	x	x	x	x	x		x
Recker 2006 [15]																x	x			
Mendling et al. 2010 [20]													x	x						
Knowledge Management																				
Jennex and Olfman 2005 [14]	x	x	x	x												x	x		x	x
Jennex and Olfman 2006 [8]	x											x	x			x				
Watson and Hewett 2006 [12]													x	x		x		x		
Yew Wong 2005 [32]	x	x	x													x	x	x	x	x

Next, we will present a summary explanation by categories of factors, following the BPM lifecycle.

To start with, a process model has to be created. Process modelling projects are usually complex and voluminous, thus different authors have highlighted different critical aspects/factors to be emphasized ('Stakeholders Participation', 'Management Support', Information Resources', 'Project Management', 'Modelling Expertise'). Furthermore, technical choices regarding methodology and tools that influence wider use of the model also after the end of the process modelling project, are important as well ('Modelling Methodology', 'Modelling Language', 'Modelling Tool').

While creating a process model, it is important to establish a sound information base for analysis and planning. There are two criteria for the user who will be using the model in a sustained manner after the project: usefulness and ease of use.

Usefulness is related, first of all, to the existence of necessary data ('Richness'). Second, data has to reflect real processes ('Knowledge Quality'): (1) during the process modelling project, different facts and relations in the model must reflect real processes; (2) changes in the process have to be reflected in the model after the project (the model has to be updated). Finally, all this information should be valuable to the user ('Value of Knowledge').

The basis for ease of use is, above all, clear and comprehensive structure of the process model. Process models are complicated and thus, a flexible structure (process hierarchy) is extremely important to decompose facts first and find out needed information later ('Structure'). In addition to the general structure, smaller groups and views of information (diagrams, lists of facts) must be well presented to the reader ('Ease of Interpretation').

Proper software tools have to be used to gather information from the process model. First, we summarize technical issues (accessibility, system quality, service quality) into the factor 'Ease of Use' – there should not be any technical obstacles in using software. Functional aspects of the software have been collected under the factor 'Usefulness' – a functionality necessary for browsing process models is provided.

A model of good content and technical quality together with comfortable software create the necessary prerequisites for the user of the process model user – an experienced and motivated employee, interested in gathering information from the process model and ready to contribute feedback for model update. First, competence concerning the process model and tool use is needed ('Competence') - many authors emphasize training and learning under this factor. The user has to be motivated to use knowledge for different purposes (getting new information, verifying facts and relations) in daily operation ('Motivation'). Finally, (positive) experience about sharing information in the organization is necessary ('Knowledge Networking') – first in finding the necessary information, then using it and finally sharing it with colleagues.

Everything described above will be carried out in a specific organization with technical and cultural environment that has developed over the years. Success factors that characterize general attitudes in the organization toward BPM initiatives are under category 'Organization'. The first question in the context of organizations and projects is – why BPM? The answer should be clear and communicated in the organization ('Clear Goals and Purposes'). In parallel, attitudes of different employees toward BPM initiatives and the process model have been reflected ('Subjective Norms'). Success factor 'Management Support' was already mentioned in the context of process modelling project. Management support is the key to success during all phases of a BPM life cycle. For this reason, we have moved the success factor 'Management Support' from the category 'Process Modelling' to the category 'Organization' in the context of our framework.

3.3   Assessment Instrument

Our assessment framework consists of a number of factors, which affect different types of process model usage in different phases of a BPM programme. The proposed factors were derived from different studies highlighted in Sect. 2 and analysed via the categorization given in Sect. 3.2.

Each factor is rated with reference to *activities* performed as part of the BPM project and considered by the organization's assessors as supportive of the factor in question. As a result, we cannot get a direct assessment (result) for the factor; rather, we can see which factors have been emphasized in the organization and which have been influenced. The choice of activities associated to a given factor is left open for assessors. For example, in assessing the factor 'Modelling Expertise', possible activities may include 'in-house development of modeller expertise', 'training of employees in process modelling' or 'outsourcing of modelling expertise'. The factor 'Management Support' could be assessed through activities that reflect positive (or negative) attitudes of management towards a BPM project or programme – for example, 'management participation in the BPM project' and 'mentions and recognition of BPM projects at board meeting(s)'.

Factors could be described (assessed) either through planning or already accomplished activities. If a project has already been implemented, then the real activities that constitute a factor (for example, modelling activities which reflect the 'Modelling Expertise') should be highlighted.

With reference to activities, each factor is rated via five-point Likert scale [33] with following labels:

- -2 – no activity has been undertaken or is planned regarding a factor;
- -1 – activities are planned, but not yet realized regarding a factor;
- 0 – there are activities partially (or fully) realized regarding a factor, but without real influence;
- 1 – activities have been realized regarding a factor with some positive results;
- 2 – activities have been completed regarding a factor and have led to observable results.

Based on the rates of factors, an average for every category (fourth column in Table 2) was calculated. In addition to the assessment concerning the influence of different factors in various BPM phases, we asked the interviewees for their assessments on the importance of factors with the view of positively influencing the continued use of the process model in the organization – participants in interviews ranked the factors under every category (the most important rank = 1).

Table 2. Example of an assessment table filled in during interviews.

Factor	Activities	Results	Grade	Comment	Rank
Modelling Expertise	An outside consultant was used for process modelling. Our people (development department) attended modelling activities and obtained experience concerning process modelling. After the project in-house training was organized	Excellent expertise in the context of the project. Modelling experience for our modellers	1	BPM knowledge is sufficient for process model update today, but backup is needed	1
Stakeholder Participation	Employees did not attend the project. Department managers attended the BPM training organized after the project	BPM (basic) knowledge for our department managers	0	More users should be involved in the BPM project in the future	3
...					

In order to assess whether process models are used continually, we checked technical user logs. Process model was considered as used in a sustained manner when:

- process model use had continued after the process modelling project (1 + years);
- users group expanded after the project;
- users were using the process model on a regular basis (at least few cases in a month per every user).

Our focus was on the process models with active use over a long period: first initial use during the process modelling project followed by active use over a period of more than one year after the initial production of the model.

Moving along the time axis (BPM phases), we will concentrate on how different factors have been influenced in the organization (as a result, different categories as a whole) and what is the actual final result in view of everyday use. We will collect expert assessments of process managers regarding the influence of each factor from the angle of sustained use on the basis of classifications.

4   Case Studies

We can recall from Sect. 1 that the overarching question of the study is the following: what are the factors that determine whether process models are used in a sustained manner, or only for the purposes they are initially created? Having proposed a framework for assessing process modelling factors, we have decomposed the research question into following sub-questions:

- which factors of the a priori model are highlighted by organizations as most relevant for sustained use?
- are the grades assigned by process modelling stakeholders in an organization to the different factors in the a priori model in accordance with the actual use of process models after the process modelling project has been finished?

To address these questions, we followed a multi-case-study approach [34]. We determined that the case study method was suitable in our context as it allowed us to collect qualitative insights from practicing experts embedded in organizations where process models have been produced and used. The possibility of gathering such qualitative insights was considered to be important, given that the proposed a priori model – though derived from a synthesis of previous models – is new and not previously validated in practice. For this reason, an exploratory approach was selected to validate our a priori model and investigate raised questions in parallel [35].

Multiple organizations were involved in the study in order to increase reliability and generalizability of the findings. The data collection was based on focused interviews designed to put into evidence concrete activities performed by the organization in support of each factor, as well as influences between factors and sustained model use (or lack thereof).

Below, we will discuss the organizational setting of case studies, the case study protocol employed (including data collection steps) and the findings.

4.1 Case Study Setting

We selected four organizations as case studies from different points along two spectra: public-private; medium-large [36]. The four organizations are:

- Bank of Estonia – a large constitutional public institution that operates under its own statutes and under the law, with a long history and experience with BPM.
- Estonian Telecom – a large private company formed via the merger of two previous telecommunication companies, both with long experience in BPM.
- Estonian Agricultural Registers and Information Board (ARIB) – a medium-size public organization implementing a range of business process-related projects.
- Elisa Estonia – a medium-size branch of a private international telecom service provider with many years of experience with BPM.

The case studies were conducted during 2014-2015. Below, we will present the case study protocol and summarize the findings.

4.2 Case Study Protocol

First, an initial contact was established with a member of the organization in order to present our broad vision of BPM success factor analysis.

Second, an assessment was organized in cooperation with the BPM team of each organization, including the BPM project and process managers. The assessment framework for process model success factors was introduced to the BPM team ($\sim$ 15 min) before the assessment. Next, we covered the success factors following the BPM life cycle, e.g. time line. The data collection was based on the structure of a priori model described in Sect. 3.2. For each success factor, we drew up a list of activities which had either been carried out or were planned to be carried out, and which characterise or support the given factor. The BPM team was asked to explain the results of these activities and the influence achieved in their organization. Information was recorded in a structured table composed of the following columns: factor; activities related to the factor; results of activities, grade for the factor; comments and ideas. An example of a part of a completed assessment table is presented in Table 2. Columns 'Activities', 'Results' and 'Comment' were filled in during the interview. The interview lasted for about two to three hours. Data collections were conducted in the context of recently implemented BPM projects and in terms of complete BPM programmes with the focus on process models used afterwards. The table filled in during the interview was the basis for the factor assessment after the meeting. We applied the assessment instrument described in Sect. 3.3. Grades were stored in the fourth column in the table - 'Grade'.

Third, separate meeting for the table and assessment results review were organized with BPM teams of each organization. During the meeting (about one hour) important improvements and details were collected and added into the table (columns 'Activities' and 'Comments'), if needed, the grades of assessment were justified (column 'Grade'). BPM team members ranked the assessed factors by importance in the context of categories, thus giving their evaluation to the importance of factors to influence the reuse of a process model. The first had to be a factor that, in assessor's opinion, has the most significant impact on the reuse of a process model (number 1), and the last had to be a factor with the lowest impact on the reuse of a process model in assessor's opinion.

The fourth meeting (about one or two hours) was aimed at reviewing the actual usage of process models in the organization. For each model referenced in previous meetings, the number of users and frequency of usage of the process model during the process modelling project and after the project was determined. Information was provided by the project manager of the BPM programme, the administrator(s) of the intranet and process modelling repository where models were maintained and published. Based on these data, we classified the process models into those that had undergone sustained use and those that were not used in a sustained manner according to the definition of sustained use previously introduced. Three to seven people participated in the study from each organization (21 in total).

4.3   Findings

Every organization had a diverse know-how of BPM projects and a different perspective of process model usage. Our findings during the interviews and analyses of the BPM programmes of these organizations highlighted factors that affected process model usage in a sustained manner after having completed several BPM projects.

There were diverse experiences concerning process modelling (projects) in every organization that participated in the case study (average of category 'Process Modelling' 0.9). Organizations highlighted mainly the influence of *project modelling activities on process model quality*: "The initial models were too technical and of poor quality, keeping in mind the wider audience." It was underlined in the interviews that quality depends directly on modeller's experience and skills.

Process model quality was the central topic in the context of models used in a sustained manner in organizations (average of category 'Process Model' in the organization higher than 0.5). The structure of the model (factor 'Structure') was highlighted as a key in making technically complicated models suitable for regular users and reaching sustained use after the modelling project: "The only thing we elaborated after the project was the general structure of the model". Every other factor under the category 'Process Model' was already supported and had achieved the necessary level during the process modelling project.

The average grade along the "process modelling tool" was relatively high (category 'Tool' above 1.0). In process modelling phase, software functionality was emphasized as an attribute that fully supports the modeller upon entry and analysis of information; from the perspective of process model users, simplicity both regarding the uses as well as the user interface was underlined first and foremost. Modern BPM tools provide versatile functionality for process modellers and *different types of reports and views extracted from the process model for consumption by a wide range of users*. In all organizations, software used in the project or its outputs were integrated into other systems of the enterprise "after the project, the model was integrated into our knowledge management system".

In our assessment, we gave a high grade to factors under the category 'User' (average 0.4). *Practical experience was especially highlighted*, different trainings and courses were of secondary importance in our interviews: "Our users grow along with BPM projects". Factor 'Competence' was always higher than factor 'Motivation'. Sustained use was achieved with models where the grade of factor 'Motivation' was closer to the grade of factor 'Competence'.

Success factors related to organizations were variable (averages of category 'Organization' between -0.4 and 1.1) – even low grades for factors in the category 'Organization' were not an obstacle for starting to use the process model in a sustained manner in the organization. Success factors (especially 'Top Management Support ') under category 'Organization' were more likely *related to process modelling project*: "Our management decided to start BPM activities in our organization five years ago". Sustained use of process models was rather a bottom-up initiative (especially in organizations where the grade for category 'Organization' was lower) related to BPM team or a small group of people: "Business people participating in the project started to use the model on a regular basis after the project was finished". Organizations where the grade for category 'Organization' was higher emphasized *positive influence on the users* (employees): "The active use of the model by the management set an example to the rest of the members of the organization".

4.4   Limitations and Threats to Validity

The findings of this research should be construed in the light of typical limitations and threats to validity of a case study research, particularly with regard to low generaliz-ability. To mitigate this threat to validity, we conducted multiple case studies (multi-case-study approach) and supported the findings with observations across the case studies. We also selected case studies from different types of organizations in different domains (public vs. private large vs. small). However, all four case studies were conducted in the same geographical region (Estonia). Also, the findings are based on a relatively small number of business process modelling projects and process models (8 projects in total). The involvement of more organizations, projects and process models into the research would increase the validity of results.

Another threat to validity comes from the adoption of an a priori model that scoped the set of factors considered in the case studies. This threat is mitigated however by the fact that the a priori model has been built on the basis of success factor models created and validated by different researchers in previous work.

The data collected during the case studies was mainly qualitative. The only quantitative data was related to use of process models (number of "model use" events and their time). These quantitative data were gathered to the extent required to deter-mine if a given process model was used in a sustained manner or not. A more in-depth quantitative analysis of actual use of process models could increase the reliability of the results and reveal more details about sustained use of process models.

5 Conclusion

We have proposed a model to explain the sustained use of process models and validated it on four case studies. The findings of the study are summarized in Fig. 1. The boxes correspond to the categories of factors presented in Table 1, while arrows indicate the identified influences between factors in a category and sustained use of process models. The statements in case studies supporting each influence arrow can be found in Sect. 4.3 (cf. statements highlighted in italics). Factors have been ranked under each group based on the participants' assessment collected in the third meeting (cf. last column of Table 2: "Rank").

A notable observation highlighted by case studies is that the characteristics of process models influence their sustained use. One factor in particular that was highlighted as contributing to sustained use was the 'Structure' of the process model. The importance of structure is also confirmed by study [37, 38], where the topic of process hierarchy came up through studying the quality of a process model and the influence it exerted on process management in an organization. Also, structure is an essential component of the quality of the model and comprehensibility to the user [20].

In the 'User' category, 'Motivation' appears to be a key factor in the context of our study. Significance of motivation is also outlined in the study by Bhatt [39], where the topic was approached more widely from the angle of organizational behaviour.

Indication of support from the management was not surprising, as the launch of large projects needs such support [14]. In the context of our study, indication of the impact of management on users through positive example was found to be important.

In our future work, we plan to conduct more detailed studies within mature organizations with a longer history of process modelling and more detailed (quantitative) data of process model use over time. This would enable us to study the sustained

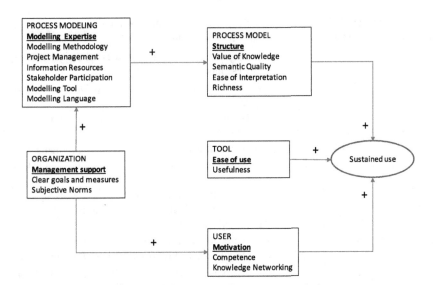

Fig. 1. Direct influences between different factor groups

use of process models longitudinally as well as cross-sectionally across different areas of an organization. We also plan to expand the scope of organizations covered by the study to cover a wider geographical context.

Acknowledgments. This research is supported by the Estonian Research Council.

Appendix

Group	Factors	Definition
Organization	Management Support	The level of commitment by senior management in the organization to the BPM activities in terms of their own involvement and the willingness to allocate valuable organizational resources
	Clear Goals & Purposes	The clarity of goals and purposes of the BPM initiatives in the organization
	Subjective Norms	The perceived opinions of a person or group whose beliefs may be important to the individual about process model re-use
Process Modelling	Modelling Expertise	The experiences of process modellers in terms of conceptual modelling in general and process modelling in particular
	Stakeholders Participation	The degree of input from users in the design, approval and maintenance of the models
	Information Resources	Availability of information during the project
	Project Management	The management of the process modelling project, including defining the project scope, aims, milestones, and plans
	Modelling Methodology	A detailed set of instructions that describes and guides the process of modelling
	Modelling Language	The grammar or the 'syntactic rules' of the selected process modelling technique
	Modelling Tool	The software that facilitates the design, maintenance and distribution of process models
Process Model	Richness	Availability of necessary information in the process model
	Sematic Quality	The degree of correspondence between information conveyed by a process model and the domain that is modelled
	Value of Knowledge	The degree to which a person believes (re-)using a particular process model will help to achieve the intended goal
	Structure	The degree to which a person believes that finding necessary information from the model is simple
	Ease of Interpretation	The degree to which a person believes that interpreting a process model would be effortless

(Continued)

(Continued)

Group	Factors	Definition
Tool	Ease of Use	The degree to which a person believes that the use of modelling software for using a process model would be easy
	Usefulness	The degree to which a person believes that using a modelling software will be effective in using a process model
User	Competence	The amount of knowledge the users have of the modelled domain and the use of the process models
	Motivation	Using a process model for no apparent reason other than the task of using it, e.g. to gain knowledge of a process
	Knowledge Networking	Users knowledge about the organization (processes) and willingness to share it

References

1. Davies, I., Green, P., Rosemann, M., Indulska, M., Gallo, S.: How do practitioners use conceptual modeling in practice? Data Knowl. Eng. **58**, 358–380 (2006)
2. Indulska, M., Green, P., Recker, J., Rosemann, M.: Business process modeling: perceived benefits. In: Castano, S., Dayal, U., Casati, F., Oliveira, J.P.M., Laender, A.H. (eds.) ER 2009. LNCS, vol. 5829, pp. 458–471. Springer, Heidelberg (2009)
3. Dalkir, K.: Knowledge management in theory and practice. Routledge, London (2013)
4. Markovic, I., Pereira, A.C.: Towards a formal framework for reuse in business process modeling. In: Hofstede, A.H., Benatallah, B., Paik, H.-Y. (eds.) BPM Workshops 2007. LNCS, vol. 4928, pp. 484–495. Springer, Heidelberg (2008)
5. Jeston, J., Nelis, J.: Business process management. Routledge, London (2014)
6. Rosemann, M., vom Brocke, J.: The six core elements of business process management. In: Handbook on Business Process Management 1, pp. 105–122. Springer, Heidelberg (2015)
7. Nolte, A., Bernhard, E., Recker, J.: " You've modelled and now what?"-exploring determinants of process model re-use. In: 24th Australasian Conference on Information Systems 2013, pp. 1–11. RMIT University (2013)
8. Jennex, M.E., Olfman, L.: A model of knowledge management success. Int. J. Knowl. Manage. **2**, 51–68 (2006)
9. Bandara, W., Gable, G.G., Rosemann, M.: Factors and measures of business process modelling: model building through a multiple case study. Eur. J. Inf. Syst. **14**, 347–360 (2005)
10. Eikebrokk, T.R., Iden, J., Olsen, D.H., Opdahl, A.L.: Understanding the determinants of business process modelling in organisations. Bus. Process Manage. J. **17**, 639–662 (2011)
11. Bernhard, E., Recker, J.C.: Preliminary insights from a multiple case study on process modelling impact. In: Australasian Conference on Information Systems 2012, pp. 1–11 (2012)
12. Watson, S., Hewett, K.: A multi-theoretical model of knowledge transfer in organizations: determinants of knowledge contribution and knowledge reuse. J. Manage. Stud. **43**, 141–173 (2006)

13. Delone, W.H., McLean, E.R.: The DeLone and McLean model of information systems success: a ten-year update. J. Manage. Inf. Syst. **19**, 9–30 (2003)
14. Jennex, M.E., Olfman, L.: Assessing knowledge management systems. Int. J. Knowl. Manage. **1**, 33–49 (2005)
15. Recker, J.C.: Reasoning about discontinuance of information system use. J. Inf. Technol. Theor. Appl. **17**(1), 41–66 (2016)
16. Krogstie, J., Sindre, G., Jørgensen, H.: Process models representing knowledge for action: a revised quality framework. Eur. J. Inf. Syst. **15**, 91–102 (2006)
17. Vanderfeesten, I., Cardoso, J., Mendling, J., Reijers, H.A., van der Aalst, W.M.: Quality metrics for business process models. In: BPM and Workflow Handbook, pp. 179–190 (2007)
18. Sánchez-González, L., García, F., Mendling, J., Ruiz, F., Piattini, M.: Prediction of business process model quality based on structural metrics. In: Parsons, J., Saeki, M., Shoval, P., Woo, C., Wand, Y. (eds.) ER 2010. LNCS, vol. 6412, pp. 458–463. Springer, Heidelberg (2010)
19. Mendling, J., Neumann, G., van der Aalst, W.: On the correlation between process model metrics and errors. In: 26th International Conference on Conceptual Modeling 2007, vol. 83, pp. 173–178. Australian Computer Society, Inc. (2007)
20. Mendling, J., Reijers, H.A., van der Aalst, W.M.: Seven process modeling guidelines (7PMG). Inf. Softw. Technol. **52**(2), 127–136 (2010)
21. Holschke, O., Rake, J., Levina, O.: Granularity as a cognitive factor in the effectiveness of business process model reuse. In: Dayal, U., Eder, J., Koehler, J., Reijers, H.A. (eds.) BPM 2009. LNCS, vol. 5701, pp. 245–260. Springer, Heidelberg (2009)
22. Fettke, P., Loos, P.: Classification of reference models - a methodology and its application. Inf. Syst. e-Bus. Manage. **1**, 35–53 (2003)
23. Frank, U.: Evaluation of reference models. Reference modeling for business systems analysis, pp. 118–40 (2007)
24. Vom Brocke, J., Rosemann, M.: Handbook on business process management. Springer, Heidelberg (2010)
25. Westland, J.: The Project Management Life Cycle: A Complete Step-By-Step Methodology for Initiating, Planning, Executing & Closing a Project Success. Kogan Page Publishers (2007)
26. Harmon, P.: Business process change. Morgan Kaufmann, San Francisco (2014)
27. Brocke, J.V., Rosemann, M.: Handbook on Business Process Management 2: Strategic Alignment, Governance, People and Culture. Springer Publishing Company, Inc, Cambridge (2014)
28. Rosemann, M.: Potential pitfalls of process modeling: part A. Bus. Process Manage. J. **12**, 249–254 (2006)
29. Raduescu, C., Tan, H.M., Jayaganesh, M., Bandara, W., zur Muehlen, M., Lippe, S.: A framework of issues in large process modeling projects. In: European Conference on Information Systems 2006, pp. 1594–1605 (2006)
30. Rittgen, P.: Success factors of e-collaboration in business process modeling. In: Pernici, B. (ed.) CAiSE 2010. LNCS, vol. 6051, pp. 24–37. Springer, Heidelberg (2010)
31. Lu, R., Sadiq, S.: A survey of comparative business process modeling approaches. In: Business information Systems 2007, pp. 82–94. Springer, Berlin Heidelberg (2007)
32. Yew, W.K.: Critical success factors for implementing knowledge management in small and medium enterprises. Ind. Manage. Data Syst. **105**, 261–279 (2005)
33. Lantz, B.: Equidistance of likert-type scales and validation of inferential methods using experiments and simulations. Electron. J. Bus. Res. Methods **11**, 16–28 (2013)

34. Yin, R.K.: Case study research: Design and methods. Sage publications, Newbury Park (2013)
35. Kitchenham, B., Pickard, L., Pfleeger, S.L.: Case studies for method and tool evaluation. IEEE Softw. **12**, 52–62 (1995)
36. Cronje, G.J.D, Toit, G.S.D., Motlatla, M.D.C., Marais, A.D.: Introduction to business management. Oxford University Press (2003)
37. Ljung, L.: System identification. Birkhäuser, Boston (1998)
38. Malinova, M., Mendling, J.: The effect of process map design quality on process management success. In: European Conference on Information Systems 2013, paper 160 (2013)
39. Bhatt, G.D.: Knowledge management in organizations: examining the interaction between technologies, techniques, and people. J. Knowl. Manage. **5**, 68–75 (2001)

Business Matter Experts do Matter:
A Model-Driven Approach for Domain Specific
Process Design and Monitoring

Adrian Mos$^{(\boxtimes)}$ and Mario Cortes-Cornax

Xerox Research Center, 6 Chemin de Maupertuis, Meylan, France
{adrian.mos,mario.cortes}@xrce.xerox.com

Abstract. Business process design and monitoring are essential elements of Business Process Management (BPM), often relying on Service Oriented Architectures (SOA). However the current BPM approaches and standards have not sufficiently reduced the Business-IT gap. Today's solutions are mostly domain-independent and platform-dependent, which limits the ability of business matter experts to express business intent and enact process change. In contrast, the approach presented in this paper focuses on BPM and SOA environments in a domain-dependent and platform-independent way. We propose to add a domain specific-layer on top of current solutions so business stakeholders can design and understand their processes in a more intuitive way. We rely on previously proposed technical solutions and integrate them in an end-to-end methodology (from design to monitoring and back). The appropriateness and the feasibility of the approach is justified through a use case and a complete prototype implementation.

Keywords: Model-driven methodology · Process monitoring · DSL · BPM · SOA

1 Introduction

Business process design connected to execution and monitoring are critical for successful Business Process Management (BPM) [21]. Today, the Business Process Model and Notation [16] (BPMN 2.0) has become the de-facto standard for business process modelling. With the aim at filling the Business-IT gap, significant effort has been put into bringing BPMN executable and closer to Service Oriented Architectures (SOA). A BPM Suite (BPMS) manages the process execution directing SOA calls to the appropriate services and generally provides monitoring infrastructure. While these components help alleviate agility problems that business stakeholders encounter, there are important limitations to the current approaches. We observed that most of the existing solutions are domain-independent and platform-dependent, which limit the power of business matter experts at the design and monitoring stages.

© Springer International Publishing Switzerland 2016
M. La Rosa et al. (Eds.): BPM Forum 2016, LNBIP 260, pp. 210–226, 2016.
DOI: 10.1007/978-3-319-45468-9_13

Concerning **process design limitations**, the BPMN standard lacks guidance to reach executable processes from high-level process models. Silver [24] highlights this problem, and proposes a level-based top-down approach to design business processes (*Descriptive level, Analytical level* and *Execution level*). However, the generality of the most common BPMN 2.0 graphical elements, in particular the Task element, reduces semantic expressiveness [12]. Business analysts require dedicated means (e.g., specific type of task with implicit domain knowledge) to effectively model their business domain (ex. logistics, healthcare, transportation, etc.) [18]. Domain Specific Languages (DSLs) are an effective means to deal with these problems, providing improvements in expressiveness and ease of use [11]. More specifically, Domain Specific Process Modelling Languages (DSPMLs) [6] permits business stakeholders to design their processes in a much more intuitive way than BPMN.

Regarding **monitoring limitations**, BPMS solutions collect and present data at the level of the process description, which is generic. This fact results in monitoring information that is collected in a generic way with respect to the business domain (ex., "activity", "gateway" or "event") with no correlation with the business concepts (ex. "order handling" or "shipping") apart from the simple matching "label - BPMN element". This causes a number of problems: (1) it is hard to make use of the monitoring data in order to present meaningful metrics for business users, without significant configuration efforts for each BP; (2) it is difficult to correlate the business concepts to the execution of services in the SOA layer; (3) it is difficult to set wide-ranging SLAs that affect all BPs in the organization equally. For instance, it may be necessary to specify that all the "shipping" operations, regardless the BP in which they occur, must execute in less than 2 days.

In this paper, we present an approach that focuses on BPM and SOA environments in a domain-dependent and platform-independent way. Previous technical solutions [13–15] are combined to present a methodological, model-driven approach that integrates domain specific modelling with domain specific monitoring in an end-to-end solution. The appropriateness and the feasibility of our approach is shown through a use case and a complete prototype implementation. The rest of the paper is structured as follows. Section 2 describes a general overview of our method, based on a running example. Section 3 details the steps of the approach. Section 4 focuses on the prototype implementation. Section 5 presents related work and finally, Sect. 6 concludes and discusses future work.

2   Overview of the Approach

Figure 1 gives an overview of the approach from a modeller (business analyst and architect) point of view. Each number corresponds to one key step that will be further described in the following sections. The figure contains a simplified order handling process. The orders are received either by a submission web form or by standard mail. In the latter case, some document pre-processing is necessary in order to handle the order (i.e., scanning, Optical Character Recognition (OCR), and segmentation to extract the different sections). The order's comments, which could be in different languages, need to be handled before the approval. Afterwards, some classical processing steps such as payment, packaging, preparation of the documents (i.e., tracking number, bill), as well as the actual shipping and the confirmation are defined. In dotted lines, the business stakeholder indicates the exceptional paths. Each symbol represents a *Domain Concept*, which makes reference to an enterprise well defined know-how element.

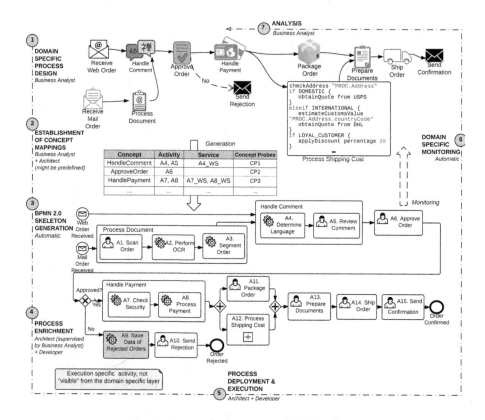

Fig. 1. Approach Overview with Main Steps

The first step corresponds to the **domain specific design**, using a DSPML (*Step 1* in Fig. 1). The domain specific language must have been previously designed based on the generic domain meta-model that we propose. Potentially, several DSPMLs can be combined, as the example shows. For instance, in order to define the process of calculating the shipping cost, a textual description may be more appropriate. In the graphical part, we advocate taking into account the principles of notations defined by Moody [12]. More details about a particular language are out of the scope of this paper. However, rich language definitions are possible for various domains, as we show also in [14].

The analyst can then **establish the concept mappings** (*Step 2* in Fig. 1). While business concepts are already connected by default to the abstract services from the enterprise repository, the links can still be modified at this stage. This is essential in grounding the domain knowledge in technical realities. For instance, "Handle Payment" corresponds to two technical services. It will imply the creation of the corresponding service tasks in BPMN. The mapping between domain concepts with the process activities relies on a pivot meta-model and unique ID (UID) attributes. The so-called Common meta-model (CommonMM) is a central, simplified representation of the main generic process concepts common to business process descriptions, such as activity, flow and gateway. It is significantly simpler than fully-fledged BPMN because its objective is simply to extract the essence of the structure of various business processes. Our hypothesis is that a descriptive level [24] (reduced amount of symbols but semantically enriched) is enough to define high-level domain-specific process models.

The **BPMN 2.0 skeleton is generated** relying on the aforementioned CommonMM (*Step 3* in Fig. 1) and the concept mappings (see table with concepts mapped to activities). Note that the concept-to-activity mappings are generated or validated at this stage. Also note that the transformations are transparent to the business analyst. At most, the latter will have to agree with the business architect on the correspondence between the domain concepts and the to-be activities supported by generation templates. Once transformed into an instance of the CommonMM, the processes can be converted to the process modelling language of choice.

Generated BPMN models are typically enriched and refined (*Step 4* in Fig. 1). Extra activities, a complete data model or a resource model may be necessary in order to enable executability.

Deployment and execution follow (*Step 5* in Fig. 1). The only constraint that we impose here is the preservation of the concept mappings (i.e., not manually deleting the generated UIDs). Extra activities that may be added in the BPMN are considered as technical additions and of reduced interest from a business point of view (ex. activity A9). These activities will not be represented at the DSPML level when showing information coming from the domain specific monitoring infrastructure. The deployment phase is necessary to install the process artefacts and bind the generated abstract services with actual services, which will be running for instance in an enterprise service bus.

Monitoring (*Step 6* in Fig. 1) aims at aggregating and displaying data in the domain specific environment relying on information from the concept mappings. Our proposition aims to address the aforementioned shortcomings of today's monitoring capabilities for BPMS/SOA applications. A layer of abstraction is added on top of the existing capabilities rather than replacing them. The platform-independence ensures compatibility with a wide range of existing systems and platforms.

Finally, in an **Analysis** stage (*Step 7* in Fig. 1) the monitored data is studied to iteratively improve the process. Iteration may also imply the enrichment of the enterprise know-how, which is capitalised through the domain concepts.

To summarise, the interest of the contribution is twofold: (1) the approach takes into account in a very specific way the business stakeholders, enabling domain specific modelling and monitoring; and (2) the entire cycle is integrated in a continuous improvement approach, supported by tools through model-driven transformations.

3   A Model-Driven Approach for Domain Specific Process Design and Monitoring

This section details the main ideas of our model-driven approach for domain specific process design and monitoring, which considers business stakeholders as first class-citizens for BPM. The section mainly focuses on *domain-specific design*, *establishment of concept mappings* and *domain-specific monitoring* which are the most relevant part of the work. The *BPMN generation*, the *process enrichment*, the *deployment and execution* and the *analysis*, while implemented and integrated, are not described in much detail, as they are relatively common BPM activities.

3.1   Domain-Specific Design Through Domain Concepts

The interest and the limits of DSPMLs have already been presented in previous work [13]. Naturally, our goal is not to propose a particular DSPML as their aim is to be adapted to particular business needs. Instead, we propose a generic domain description meta-model (MM), which provides a structural view of the domain. We then illustrate it with examples corresponding to the use-case described in the previous section.

The upper part of Fig. 2 provides in a simplified way, the meta-models used to define the key points of the business domain in a generic way. They represent business domain information for an enterprise, with regard to the specification of concepts that are going to be reused in the business processes. The domain meta-model is useful for several proposes: (1) to store the domain information in a central repository on a collaboration and distribution server. This allows common access to the defined concepts to all the business users; (2) to generate a domain editor (textual) that can be used stand-alone or embedded in a graphical editor as part of a diagram designer; (3) to make the connection with the pivot meta-model specifying how process steps are going to be represented. This point is important when in a diagram, the user specifies that a process step is going to perform a business function corresponding to a business concept; (4) to inform and update SLA for business concepts. An enterprise-wide SLA management ensures that all activities and all processes that refer to a particular business concept would be marked with appropriate SLA constraints. This can bring important advantages when changes to company policies have sweeping implications on many SLAs, as they can be automatically propagated to all the relevant activities and processes.

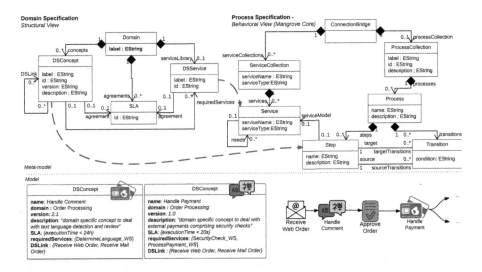

Fig. 2. Domain Specific Concepts Design Relies on a Generic Domain Meta-model

The meta-model in Fig. 2 defines a *Domain*, which contains a set of domain specific concepts (*DSConcept*). A *Domain* also contains *SLA* elements, describing the agreement details. A *DSConcept* relates to *DSService* elements describing the actual SOA services required in the domain. Note that services can be abstract entities bound later in the deployment phase [7].

Illustration Based on the Use Case. A Domain Concept supports the representation of business domain knowledge in an enterprise. Figure 2 illustrates in the bottom part how knowledge common to the enterprise is stored in two example domain concepts (in contrast to a pure BPMN approach where such information would be implicit in the minds of the designers). These concepts would typically be stored in shared repositories. The information comprises for instance a name (verb+object) a version number and the SLA. Links between domains concepts are defined in order to define dependencies. For example, the concepts: "Handle Payment" and "Handle Comment" are related to the "Receive Mail Order" and the "Receive Web Order" business activities. This means that a common DataObject will be shared between the BPMN activities that are generated. Note that the data-model generation is currently not supported by our solution, although it is being investigated. However, these links provide necessary hints to the architects and analysts that enrich the generated BPMN skeleton.

3.2   Establishment of Concept Mappings

In their simplest form, concept mappings are connections between business concepts and the SOA services that are used by them. This relation, could be defined by means of process activities. A simple example of the concept mappings is presented in Fig. 2. Concept mappings are defined as following:

- Set of services $S = \{s_1, s_2, ..., s_q\}$
- Set of processes $P = \{p_1, p_2, ..., p_m\}$
- For each process p_k, a set of activities $Ak = \{a_{k1}, a_{k2}, ..., a_{kt(k)}\}$ where the number of the activities in the set t(k) depends on the complexity of p_k
- The set of all activities in all processes $A = A_1 \bigcup A_2 \bigcup ... \bigcup A_{|P|}$

The goal of concept mappings is to determine the following sets:

- Set of concepts $C = \{c_1, c_2, ..., c_n\}$
- $ConceptMappings(CM) = \{c_j, s_j : \forall c_j \in C; S_j \subseteq S\}$ which contains for each concept its list of services, e.g., $HandlePayment, (s_1, s_2)$.
- $ActivityMappings(AM_k) = \{a_k, c_j : \forall a_{ki} \in A_k; c_j \in C\}$ which contains for process p_k its activities and the concepts they map to.
- $AM = AM_1 \bigcup AM_2 \bigcup ... \bigcup AM_{|P|}$ which contains for each activity all processes the concept it maps to.

Obtaining the sets C and CM requires that the business concepts used in the processes be clearly identified together with their required SOA services. Concepts are defined by business experts, connected to abstract services initially and eventually bound to real SOA services in the deployment stage as discussed in Sect. 3.5. The modelling environment needs to propose to the business expert a set of relevant SOA services. Other approaches, more or less automatic, for concept mapping could be applied [13]. Once the concepts have been identified, it is necessary to obtain the AM set by mapping the BP's activities to the concepts (typically done automatically at the BPMN generation phase).

Illustration Based on the Use Case. A concept can have an immediate correspondence with a process activity (ex. "Approve Order") or several activities (ex. "Handle Comment", which refers to *Determine Language* and *Review Comment* in Fig. 1). A domain concept which is described with a textual DSL as for example the "Process Shipping Cost", corresponds to a sub-process that will generate several BPMN activities. The sub-process itself contains a number of domain concepts that correspond to the knowledge about price management. These correspondences will vary depending on the enterprise domain concepts. In fact, the freedom to define such mappings brings an important level of flexibility in how business knowledge gets transferred into processes that are governed in a uniform way at the business level.

3.3   BPMN Skeleton Generation

The BPMN generation relies on a Common Meta-model (CommonMM), which is a simplified representation of the main generic process concepts. The reason why the DSPML-based processes are not directly transformed into the generic language is to introduce flexibility in the approach. As the generic language (usually BPMN) evolves, only the transformation between the CommonMM and the target MM needs to be updated. It could be argued that the use of a simplified version of the BPMN meta-model, where only the descriptive objects are included, could facilitate the transformation process. However, if we aim to strictly follow the BPMN 2.0 meta-model, a complex class hierarchy should be respected. This particularity may not be shared with other process languages and would complicate transformations (ex. a *Task* element subsequently inherits from *Activity, Flow Node, Flow Element,* and *Base Element*). For our prototype, we use Mangrove Core[1] as our CommonMM (a simplified version is depicted in the upper right side in Fig. 2). Mangrove Core is a meta-model that unifies business processes and SOA elements. It provides behavioural support to the domain definition in order to define the necessary steps in a process. This framework, does not aim to manage a large collection of processes, such as APROMORE [20]. Instead, it focuses on preserving the sync between the common elements of business processes and architectural constructs from the various related diagrams.

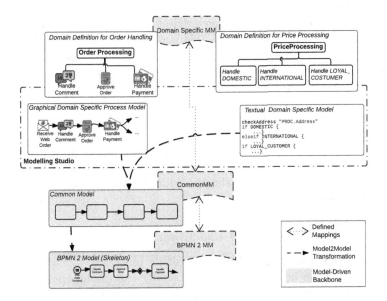

Fig. 3. Model Transformation from Domain Specific Models to BPMN 2.0 Model

In our approach, several target languages can be supported incrementally over time. When a new target is added, new transformations need of course to be added between the CommonMM and the new MM. We do not go into the details about the transformation process as the paper focuses on this general methodology. More details about the two-way synchronization between domain specific models and BPMN are presented in [14].

Figure 3 depicts how the BPMN generation is performed through model transformations. In our running example, two domain specific models are merged in a unified BPMN model. This shows the capacity of adaptation of the approach

---

[1] http://www.eclipse.org/proposals/mangrove/.

to different business expressibility needs. Both domain specific models leverage the DomainMM, which is mapped (i.e., MM concepts are linked) to the CommonMM. The latter is mapped to the target meta-model (in this case BPMN). The depicted meta-models provide a model driven backbone, where different domain specific models can be plugged in. The modelling studio (see Fig. 3) is the tool that permits the business analysts to build specific process models connecting the predefined domain concepts using various process representations, based on their specific business domain.

3.4 Process Enrichment

This stage relates to the need of the generated BPMN skeleton to be enriched if execution is targeted. New activities (ex. A9 in our running example), specific gateways and events, as well as several details may need to be added to the process model. We do not go into much details here as our approach does not impose any significant restrictions to this stage. The only constraint that the approach brings is to preserve the generated activities (tasks or sub-processes), so the link between the domain concepts and the process activities be maintained. Indeed, we did not force a perfect vertical alignment that could be very costly and unrealistic as described in [25]. The double synchronization mechanism explained in previous work [14] permits to make (and propagate) changes in the domain model as well as in the generated BPMN model. The tracking of generated elements can be based on several identity-preserving mechanisms, of which a simple example is the usage of unique IDs injected in hidden properties of BPMN elements. This mechanism enables the possibility to make changes in the domain model as well as in the generated model.

3.5 Process Deployment and Execution

Concerning deployment, when defining business processes, individual business process activities can be connected to the service-execution capabilities of the enterprise, thus allowing any business process to be easily translated into an executable workflow on the platform of choice. This capability is enabled in our approach by providing mappings for each domain concept in order to specify how it should be grounded in the SOA. These mappings are done with idealized or abstract services in a two-step mechanism, in order to ensure better portability (and reusability) across the enterprise, as well as encourage proper adoption of good SOA-practices in future evolutions of the enterprise SOA. These abstract services (AS) would then be further connected to the real services in the repositories. The creation of these mappings would typically be performed by IT experts that have a good understanding of the domain and who envisage an ideal connection to a SOA. These abstract, idealised services, would not necessarily correspond on a 1 to 1 basis with business concepts as we show in the example. That is because there are important differences in concerns when defining business elements and when defining the service infrastructure, due to varying needs for reusability, performance and evolution of these two layers.

In our approach, this two-step binding mechanism explained in [15] is applied to link domain concepts to any number of AS first and then each AS to real SOA services.

In order to execute the process, BPMS usually need at least a data-model defining the artefacts that flow in the process, a resource-model establishing the links between the roles defined in the process and actual users and the implementation of gateway conditions (usually based on data). These artefacts can be partly generated by the presented approach, but they may need to be enhanced by technical architects.

3.6   Domain-Specific Monitoring

The main elements involved in domain specific monitoring are the Concept Probes (CPs) and the Business Process Probes (BPPs). There is a one-to-one correspondence between CPs and domain concepts. CPs collect an arbitrary number of metrics, such as execution time or execution status from the activities that are mapped to a domain concept. Once the CPs are created, they need to be bound to the monitoring capabilities of the existing infrastructure, effectively acting as an extra monitoring layer on top of the actual BPMS and SOA platforms. BPPs aggregate data from the BPMS and the various CPs. In order to enable them, they have to be linked to the domain concepts at design time (which is performed automatically). When all the required mappings are available, the probes are created, instantiated and deployed automatically respecting a predefined template. More technical details about concept probes can be found in [13]. Here, we summarise their main functionality. Both CPs and BPPs are divided in three main components with particular concerns: the *Raw Data Collection Component*, mainly collects data from the activities corresponding to each concept and the related technical services. The *Analysis Component* is in charge of the aggregation of a raw data into composite metrics. These composite metrics are data structures that present the aggregate monitoring information combining the individual metric data for BPMS, SOA and other collection points such as Network Monitoring, App Server Monitoring and Operating System Monitoring. Finally, the *Alerts Reporting Component* allows the registration of SLA requests through a configurable alert port. It uses the analysis component to constantly compare the aggregated metric values with the required thresholds.

The approach provides the business stakeholders with means to govern their processes at a high level, with impact to the entire collection of business processes in a domain, if required. Relying on domain concepts, they are able to consistently manage the execution parameters of a large collection of process descriptions and their instances. For example, if the Shipping concept is already defined, it is automatically reused in any process description detailing shipping operations, carrying over the reuse of the generation and the monitoring infrastructure. The definition of corporate-level SLA is easily implemented and maintained. Relying on the generative approach, changes are spread through the different layers. In the long run, the monitoring mechanisms enable better decision making, based on domain specific information, by putting the appropriate level of information in the tools used by the business-matter experts. Section 4 discusses the prototype implementation and provides more details on the actual set up of the monitoring probes.

3.7   Analysis

In order to close the iterative lifecycle loop depicted in Fig. 1, an analysis step is necessary (*Step 7* in the figure), where the analysts study the monitored data in order to improve the process. The novelty in our approach is that the new know-how acquired in the enactment of the process may imply the update or creation of domain concepts. One of the biggest advantages of the approach is that if an updated concept is being used in a collection of processes, the changes will more easily propagated through the complete stack.

4   Prototype Implementation and First Validation Steps

Figure 4 depicts the architecture of the prototype illustrated for our use case. The picture shows the domain specific layer as an additional layer to the BPM and SOA stack. A domain specific editor would be the entry-point for a business stakeholder, providing domain specific process design (based on domain concepts), BPMN generation (which is transparent to business stakeholders) and display of monitoring result (outcome of the concept and process probes). We present some key points of the prototype implementation supporting the process life-cycle. This prototype is mostly based on Eclipse technologies, which are highly relevant in the BPM landscape as many BPM suites are actually built using the Eclipse platform. The discussion relies on the seven steps of our model-driven methodology.

Process Design and Concept Mappings. The Eclipse Modelling Framework[2] is used for the definition of the domain-specific meta-models. Ecore metamodels are the inputs for the Sirius toolkit[3], which allows rapid creation of graphical domain-specific modelling studios. Figure 5 shows a screenshot of the graphical studio. It depicts how concepts from the domain palettes can be used to compose processes that have predefined SOA connections to domain services. Monitoring information can be shown in various ways, in this particular example, execution times in the process elements indicate the BPMN activities' contribution to the overall execution time. The service contribution time is indicated in the DSConcept-Service links (dotted lines). Today, the creation of the domainspecific editor has to be supported by technical architects and developers. However, we are working on a generative approach that permits to dynamically create these modelling editors from the definition of the domain concepts.

BPMN 2.0 Generation. In addition to the Mangrove Core meta-model that we use, the Mangrove project provides a variety of plugins for model transformations as well as some editor extensions. The model-transformation plug-ins

---

[2] http://www.eclipse.org/modeling/emf/.

[3] https://eclipse.org/sirius/.

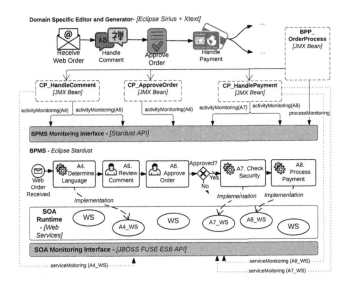

Fig. 4. Prototype Architecture

contain code that convert supported meta-models to Mangrove Core and vice-versa. They are invoked from editor plug-ins that are connected to the supported editors through standard extension points. Note that the generator only outputs the model definition and not the visual layout of the model. The BPMN 2 Modeller[4] is used to initialise the graphical representation from the generated model with a built-in Mangrove support wizard.

Enrichment of BPMN Models, Deployment and Execution. In our scenario, the generated BPMN skeleton is further enriched with a simple data-model, the implementation of the gateway conditions and a resource-model in order to enable execution. As Fig. 4 indicates, we use the Eclipse Stardust[5] BPMS to execute our process. The choice of this BPMS was made because of the maturity of the tool and openness of its process monitoring API, which easily allows access to detailed process monitoring information from external components (our concept probes).

Monitoring. The generation of the concept probes is done through template instantiation. Once they are generated they need to be managed as components managed by the monitoring framework. We use the Java Management Extensions (JMX)[6] for our distributed monitoring infrastructure managing the probes as well as for integrating with existing monitoring frameworks. JMX is supported by a large variety of infrastructures, both commercial and open-source.

---

[4] https://www.eclipse.org/bpmn2-modeler/.
[5] https://www.eclipse.org/stardust/.
[6] https://docs.oracle.com/javase/tutorial/jmx/.

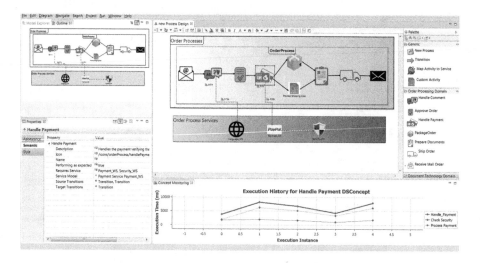

Fig. 5. Screenshot of the Eclipse-based graphical studio

As an initial validation step, we rely on the SEQUAL (SEmiotic QUALity Framework) [8], which is widely used and goes beyond the modelling language to characterise its quality. We conclude that the proposed approach can significantly complement other BPMN approaches regarding the SEQUAL framework: the *domain, comprehensibility,* and *organisational* appropriateness are improved by the fact that the actual focus is specific to the domain. Indeed, the framework advocates that a language must be powerful enough to express anything in the domain but no more. Also, a language should be easily extensible in order to adapt to changing business needs. These points clearly justify the interest of a DSPML on top of a BPMN model. The *modeller* appropriateness and the *participant* appropriateness will not change significantly as we propose to ultimately rely on BPMN. In fact, the framework recommends the use of well-known modelling languages and our approach targets basic BPMN generation. Finally, the use of proven model-driven technologies such as Sirius permit a good *tool* appropriateness. Obviously, these improvements will highly depend on the proposed DSPML, but the approach provides the means to achieve them. Qualitative evaluations with final users are envisaged in order to complete the validation. Practical experiments may result in changes or refinements of the approach. The method could be extended to incorporate an user-centred approach to build the DSPML as discussed in [19].

5   Related Work

Related work can be analysed from two main aspects: the model driven approach and the monitoring capability. Related to the **model-driven** part, Heitkotter [4] proposes DSLs4BPM, an approach for creating domain-specific process modelling languages. On the same line, Grundy et al. [3] rely on Eclipse tooling to

propose domain specific visual language editors. The difference with our approach is that these works do not provide a structured methodology to design
and analyse the processes as we do. More important, the monitoring part, which
is essential for business experts, is not considered. Becker et al. [2] propose the
modelling method called PICTURE, which specially focuses on public admin-
istration processes. The so-called "process building blocks" could be compared
with our domain concepts, as they are high-level domain-specific artefacts that
help build the actual process. Kumaran et al. [9] follow the same line, proposing
to automate complex and variable workflows in a service delivery management
architecture. The main difference is that our approach can leverage BPMN solutions (the de-facto standard) in order to reach execution and monitoring. Other
works propose extensions to BPMN 2.0 in order to be domain-specific [22]. These
approaches are limited by their focus on a very concrete problem space while
still having to deal with the aforementioned complexity and generality of BPMN
2.0. Goal-oriented approaches [10,23] use goal models as a preliminary step for
process modelling. However, the graphical notations of the more popular goal oriented languages (i*, KAOS and MAP) still lack of *Semantic Transparency* [12].
There is also limited tool support for goal modelling. In addition, the goal-driven
generation approaches tend to propose goal models closely tied to the business
process.

Considering the **monitoring** part, there are approaches that recur to aggregation mainly to compose events from a low-level monitoring source (using Complex Event Processing queries) in order to extract more meaningful data out of
raw events [5,17]. Such approaches use a variety of techniques to derive better understanding of raw events, but they fundamentally still stay at a generic
level with regard to the business domain. There are also approaches that try
to correlate execution events to the originating processes using some forms of
traceability between model elements and execution events. For instance, in [1],
the authors argue for the existence of domain-specific patterns for interpreting
events, without giving a complete solution. Their suggestion is in line with our
proposition in the idea of presenting information corresponding to domain elements, but they mostly focus on interpreting CEP events, while our approach
targets structured probes that connect directly with monitoring APIs. In summary, the studied approaches recur to generic event analysis and do not provide
a "native" monitoring probe layer that directly correspond to the business concepts. To the best of our knowledge, there is no work providing an end-to-end
solution for domain specific process design and monitoring.

6   Conclusion and Future Work

Existing design and monitoring approaches are typically technology-specific and
generic with respect to the business domain. This limits the ability of business
matter experts to express their intent and enact process change. This paper lever-
ages current BPM and SOA solutions adding a layer that is domain-dependent
and platform-independent in order to facilitate process design by business matter

experts. The approach presented in this paper also simplifies the management of complex business processes that span multiple domains of expertise through the support of several domain definitions during process design.

We have presented a methodological and iterative approach that relies on seven main steps : (1) *domain specific design* using the so-called domain concepts, which comprise the explicit representations of enterprise domain know-how; (2) *the establishment of concept mappings* between domain concepts and process activities and technical services; (3) *BPMN generation* relying on a pivot meta-model that enables flexibility and facilitates model transformations; (4) *process enrichment*, which does not seek perfect vertical alignment between high-level models and executable ones but keeps artefacts in sync relying on concept-mappings; (5) *deployment and execution*, which defines a two-step binding mechanism between domain-concepts and technical services; (6) *domain specific monitoring*, based on Concept Probes and Business Process Probes that map service and process monitoring metrics to the domain concepts and (7) the *analysis* of the monitored data, which may imply the enrichment of the domain concept repository. The presented methodology is supported by tools that automate the generation and synchronisation activities. We used a mature set of open-source tools from the Eclipse Ecosystem to implement a fully functional prototype and used a running example throughout the paper to illustrate the interest and applicability of our proposition.

We are focusing our next explorations on the following three main points. Firstly, the automatic generation of graphical process model editors from domain specifications mapped to the definition of the abstract syntax of the language and additional functional templates. Secondly, the integration of collaborative modelling in the aforementioned editors, which is critical in business process design. Thirdly, the automatic generation of various artefacts for the process data-model that could be used in the actual process implementation. We also aim to connect the data-model to the monitoring probes in order to correlate execution information to process data flow. These points are all under advanced stages of exploration, with a prototype being developed using Eclipse-based open-source technologies.

References

1. Ammon, R.V., Silberbauer, C., Wolff, C.: Domain specific reference models for event patterns-for faster developing of business activity monitoring applications. In: VIP Symposia on Internet Related Research with Elements of M+ I+ T+. vol. 16 (2007)
2. Becker, J., Pfeiffer, D., Räckers, M.: PICTURE-a new approach for domain-specific process modelling. In: CAiSE Forum, pp. 11–15 (2007)
3. Grundy, J., Hosking, J., Zhu, N., Liu, N.: Generating domain-specific visual language editors from high-level tool specifications. In: 21st IEEE/ACM International Conference on Automated Software Engineering (ASE), pp. 25–36. IEEE (2006)
4. Heitkötter, H.: A framework for creating domain-specific process modeling languages. In: 4th International Conference on Software and Data Technologies (ICSOFT), pp. 127–136 (2012)

5. Hummer, W., Inzinger, C., Leitner, P., Satzger, B., Dustdar, S.: Deriving a unified fault taxonomy for event-based systems. In: Proceedings of the 6th ACM International Conference on Distributed Event-Based Systems, pp. 167–178. ACM (2012)
6. Jablonski, S., Volz, B., Dornstauder, S.: Evolution of business process models and languages. In: 2nd International Conference on Business Process and Services Computing (BPSC), pp. 46–59. Citeseer (2009)
7. Jacquin, T., Mos, A.: Deployment of business processes in service-oriented architecture environments (Apr 28 2015), US Patent 9,021,420
8. Krogstie, J., Sindre, G., Jørgensen, H.: Process models representing knowledge for action: a revised quality framework. Europ. J. Inf. Syst. **15**(1), 91–102 (2006)
9. Kumaran, S., Bishop, P., Chao, T., Dhoolia, P., Jain, P., Jaluka, R., Ludwig, H., Moyer, A., Nigam, A.: Using a model-driven transformational approach and service-oriented architecture for service delivery management. IBM Syst. J. **46**(3), 513–529 (2007)
10. Lapouchnian, A., Yu, Y., Mylopoulos, J.: Requirements-driven design and configuration management of business processes. In: Alonso, G., Dadam, P., Rosemann, M. (eds.) BPM 2007. LNCS, vol. 4714, pp. 246–261. Springer, Heidelberg (2007)
11. Mernik, M., Heering, J., Sloane, A.M.: When and how to develop domain-specific languages. ACM Comput. Surv. (CSUR) **37**(4), 316–344 (2005)
12. Moody, D.L.: The "physics" of notations: toward a scientific basis for constructing visual notations in software engineering. IEEE Trans. Softw. Eng. **35**(6), 756–779 (2009)
13. Mos, A.: Domain specific monitoring of business processes using concept probes. In: Service-Oriented Computing - ICSOC Workshops, pp. 213–224. Springer (2015)
14. Mos, A., Jacquin, T.: Improving process robustness through domain-specific model transformations. In: 17th International Enterprise Distributed Object Computing Conference Workshops (EDOCW), pp. 188–193. IEEE (2013)
15. Mos, A., Jacquin, T.: A platform-independent mechanism for deployment of business processes using abstract services. In: 17th IEEE International Enterprise Distributed Object Computing Conference Workshops (EDOCW), pp. 71–78. IEEE (2013)
16. OMG: Business process model and notation (BPMN) version 2.0 (2011). http://www.omg.org/spec/BPMN/2.0
17. Pedrinaci, C., Lambert, D., Wetzstein, B., Van Lessen, T., Cekov, L., Dimitrov, M.: Sentinel: a semantic business process monitoring tool. In: Proceedings of the First International Workshop on Ontology-Supported Business Intelligence, p. 1. ACM (2008)
18. Pinggera, J., Zugal, S., Weber, B., Fahland, D., Weidlich, M., Mendling, J., Reijers, H.A.: How the structuring of domain knowledge helps casual process modelers. In: Parsons, J., Saeki, M., Shoval, P., Woo, C., Wand, Y. (eds.) ER 2010. LNCS, vol. 6412, pp. 445–451. Springer, Heidelberg (2010)
19. Rieu, D., Santorum, M., Movahedian, F., et al.: A participative end-user method for multi-perspective business process elicitation and improvement. Softw. Syst. Model., 1–24 (2015)
20. de la Rosa, M., Reijers, H.A., Van Der Aalst, W.M., Dijkman, R.M., Mendling, J., Dumas, M., García-Bañuelos, L.: Apromore: An advanced process model repository. Expert Syst. Appl. **38**(6), 7029–7040 (2011)
21. Rosemann, M., vom Brocke, J.: The six core elements of business process management. In: vom Brocke, J., Rosemann, M. (eds.) Handbook on Business Process Management 1. LHLS, pp. 105–122. Springer, Heidelberg (2015)

22. Saeedi, K., Zhao, L., Sampaio, P.R.F.: Extending BPMN for supporting customer-facing service quality requirements. In: 17th IEEE International Conference on Web Services (ICWS), pp. 616–623. IEEE (2010)

23. Santos, E., Castro, J., Sanchez, J., Pastor, O.: A goal-oriented approach for variability in BPMN. In: Workshop em Engenharia de Requisitos (WER) (2010)

24. Silver, B.: BPMN Method and Style: A levels-based methodology for BPM process modeling and improvement using BPMN 2.0. Cody-Cassidy Press, US (2009)

25. Weidlich, M., Barros, A., Mendling, J., Weske, M.: Vertical alignment of process models – how can we get there? In: Halpin, T., Krogstie, J., Nurcan, S., Proper, E., Schmidt, R., Soffer, P., Ukor, R. (eds.) Enterprise, Business-Process and Information Systems Modeling. LNBIP, vol. 29, pp. 71–84. Springer, Heidelberg (2009)

Author Index

Printed in the United States
By Bookmasters